Bluescreen Compositing

A Practical Guide for Video & Moviemaking

Bluescreen Compositing

A Practical Guide for Video & Moviemaking

John Jackman

Routledge
Taylor & Francis Group
LONDON AND NEW YORK

First published 2007
by Focal Press

Published in the UK
By Routledge
2 Park Square, Milton Park, Abingdon, Oxfordshire OX14 4RN
711 Third Avenue, New York, NY 10017, USA

Routledge is an imprint of the Taylor & Francis Group, an informa business

Library of Congress Cataloging-in-Publication Data
Application submitted

British Library Cataloguing in Publication Data
A catalogue record for this book is available from the British Library

ISBN 13: 978-1-578-20283-6 (pbk)
ISBN 13: 978-1-138-45981-6 (hbk)

Cover Design: Eric DeCicco
Interior Design: Gail Saari

Contents

Foreword ix

1 Introduction 1

2 The Basics of How Compositing Works 5

Terminology 9
Creating the Matte 12

3 Types of Keying Processes 15

Under the Hood 18
Blending Modes 18

4 Simple Non-Action Compositing Solutions 25

Fixing Flaws 25
Motion Tracking a Matted Overlay Fix 30
Manual Tracking 33
Digital "Glass Paintings" 35
So What's the Big Deal? 40

5 Setting Up a Chroma Key Studio 41

Planning Your Studio 42
Chroma Key Paint 47
Fabric 49
Paint, Tape, and Fabric 50
Background Lighting 51
Temporary/Portable Solutions 54
High-Tech Alternatives 56

6 **Lighting for Chroma Key** 59

Basics of Lighting 59
Lighting the Background 63
Checking the Evenness of the Lighting 71
Lighting for Luma Keying 78
A Final Word About Lighting 81

7 **Costuming and Art Design for Color-Based Compositing** 83

Blue or Green—or Red? 86
Selecting Foreground Colors 88
Non-color Factors 90

8 **Video Format Problems** 93

And Now...HDCAM! 99
See for Yourself! 99

9 **Creating the Plates** 101

Previsualization 101
Creating the Foreground Plates 104
Real-World Background Plates 105
Working in 3D Programs 110
Lighting 111
Chroma Content and Color Balance 111
Resolution 112
Aspect Ratio 114

10 **Problems in Post** 115

Cleaning Up Those Edges 117
Eliminating Jaggies 118
Removing Spill 120
Fixing Problem Mattes .121

11 **Live Keying** 127

Switchers, Special Effects, and Keying 128
The Production Switcher 128
Digital Video Mixers 131
Toasters and 'Casters 132

Dedicated Keyers 134
Weathercasting 136
Virtual Studio 137

12 Tutorials **143**

Tutorial A: Nonlinear Editors 144
Tutorial B: After Effects .151
Tutorial C: Keylight 158
Tutorial D: Primatte and Walker Effects Light Wrap 162
Tutorial E: zMatte 167
Tutorial F: Boris Red 171
Tutorial G: Ultimatte AdvantEdge. 175
Tutorial H: Serious Magic ULTRA 2 183
Tutorial I: Apple Shake .188

13 Creating New Visions with Changing Technology **193**

So What Works?. 194
Upping the Ante: HD and the Big Screen 196
New Opportunities, New Challenges 197

Appendix A: Glossary **203**

Appendix B: Building a Permanent Cyclorama **219**

Appendix C: Calibrating Your Monitor **221**

Calibrating an NTSC SMPTE-C Phosphor
CRT Video Monitor .221
Calibrating Other Types of Monitors 222

Appendix D: Manufacturers **224**

Index **226**

DVD Credits **233**

Supplementary Resources Disclaimer

Additional resources were previously made available for this title on DVD. However, as DVD has become a less accessible format, all resources have been moved to a more convenient online download option.

You can find these resources available here: www.routledge.com/9781138459816

Please note: Where this title mentions the associated disc, please use the downloadable resources instead.

Foreword

Compositing is the art of creating separate picture elements and then combining them in a seamless manner that creates a new image. Usually, that image is one that would not be possible in any other way. This book is sort of like that in that the talents, special gifts, and "push" of several people made it happen; and it certainly wouldn't have been possible without them.

Special thanks first to Paul Temme, now Acquisitions Editor for Focal Press, who talked me into doing this book; a special tip of the virtual hat to my friend and technical editor, Richard Clabaugh, who helped immensely in making sure that the text was both clear and accurate; and above all thanks to my wife Debbie, who puts up with all this crazy stuff.

Happy compositing!

John Jackman
Lewisville, NC
October 2006

Introduction

1

I was seven years old when Dick Van Dyke and Julie Andrews danced with animated penguins in *Mary Poppins*, and I remember being obsessed with how the movie magic of combining live characters with animation had been accomplished. My father came up with some oversimplified explanation of the movie magic—one that kept me happy for the moment. A few years later, I was fascinated with the special effects in the *Star Trek* television series, effects that now seem so hokey and even quaint, but which at the time seemed quite amazing. But it was a movie thirteen years later and set in another galaxy that really set my head spinning about special effects. That movie, of course, was *Star Wars*, and unless you lived through the dismal cinema fare of the 70s you can hardly imagine what an impact that movie had on us all. Actual storytelling! Mythic themes! Spaceship fights! Corny dialogue! And best of all, the most astounding special effects that any of us had ever seen. For those of us that had grown up with the incredibly cheesy special effects of *Buck Rogers* serial reruns, *Star Wars* was an absolute revelation. Of course, in those pre–computer-graphics days, most of the *Star Wars* effects were created using the same basic technology that Petro Vlahos had perfected for *Mary Poppins*—the travelling matte, or what we often call *bluescreening* now.

Over the last twenty years, this technology has gone from being a rare specialty to the meat-and-potatoes of the filmmaking business. Particularly since the advent of the Cineon format and digital intermediates,

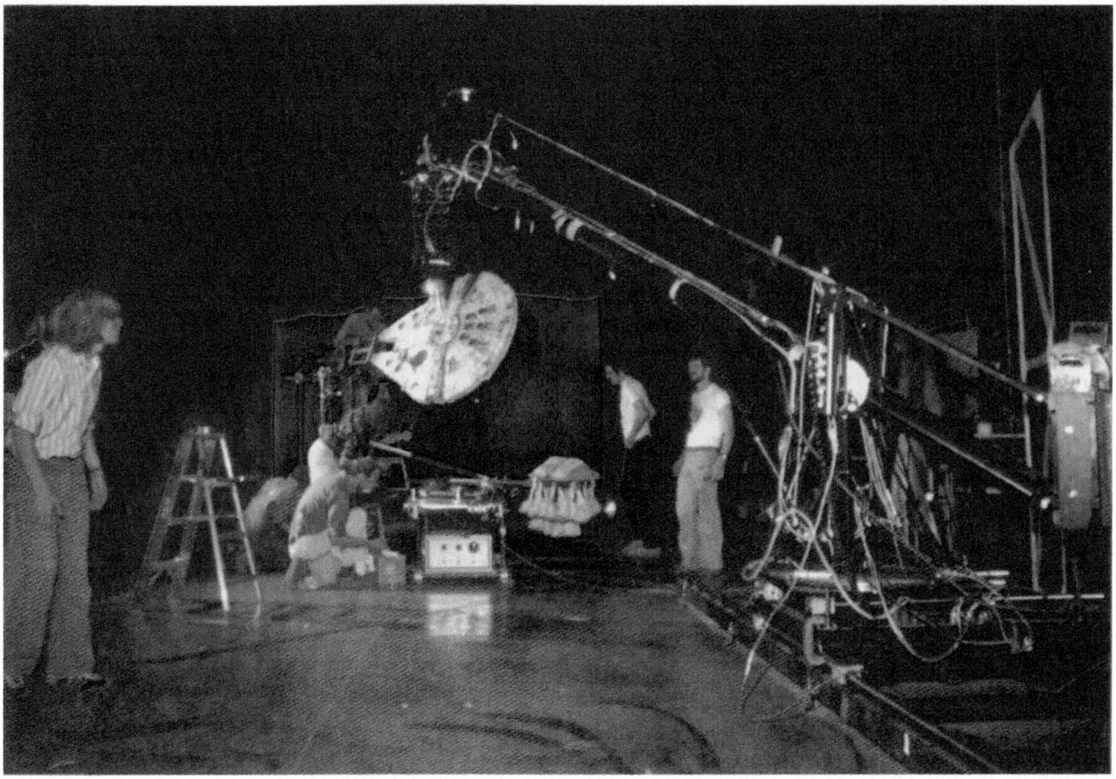

Figure 1.1 *Before the public ever heard the names of Darth Vader or Han Solo, the special effects team assembled by George Lucas created unparalleled movie magic for the 1978 movie* Star Wars *using bluescreens, handmade scale models, and motion-controlled cameras. Here the model of the Millennium Falcon is photographed in front of a bluescreen. Photo courtesy of LucasFilm.*

the use of blue and greenscreen in moviemaking has simply exploded, to the point that the technology is now used in all sorts of places where it wouldn't be expected. Shots that don't *seem* to be special effects may incorporate bluescreen compositing for budgetary reasons—for instance, to allow digital augmentation of a small and inexpensive set. All those automobile interior shots that used to be done with rear projection can now be done with blue or greenscreen—and they usually look the better for it! And while it's expected that *Spy Kids 8* would use a lot of greenscreen, the black-and-white movie *Sin City* (also directed by Robert Rodriguez) used the technology for every shot to provide the "comic novel" look.

Today, bluescreening and other forms of digital compositing are technologies available to anyone with a few bucks for a camcorder and a computer. To be sure, there are technological challenges to compositing with DV or HDV originated footage, but there are workarounds available that make this moviemaking magic economically accessible to more people than ever before.

But while the technology is easily available, making it work convincingly is still something of an art. Just as there is a huge gulf between home video and great cinema, there is an equally huge gulf between acquiring the technology for compositing and creating effective, believable composited scenes. In this book, my plan is to lead you through both the mechanics of the technology involved and the craft of actually creating a visual that "works" convincingly.

Like my earlier book on lighting, I've chosen to write for average users in the real world in a way that will move them toward expertise. There are other books available for specialty engineers whose entire working life is spent compositing. This book is aimed at the video professional who is already well versed in his or her basic craft, but would like to be able to delve further into this somewhat arcane field of special effects compositing. But even if you're a "just starting" beginner at video production or digital filmmaking, you should be able to read through this book and get started—and, I'm hoping, do a far better job than you would have been able to do through trial and error!

Because the book is not written for people who are already compositing specialists, we will be focusing primarily on the software that most "regular folks" in the business are using—most shops are using Macs or PCs, not SGI systems. And by an overwhelming margin, the software they are using are the Adobe products After Effects and Premiere Pro, and Apple's Final Cut Pro, and other software that operates on Windows XP or Mac OSX. So this will be our context! Illustrations and examples will come by and large from those software packages. I figure that tutorials based on software like Discreet Flame® (which runs on a quad processor SGI® Tezro™) will not be helpful to the majority of readers. And while we will touch on higher-end software like Apple Shake and eyeon Digital Fusion, illustrations and tutorials will be built around the more common software packages.

By the way, this also isn't a book on motion graphics. Though we'll touch on a few motion graphics techniques (such as motion tracking) we'll be looking at those only for circumstances of creating a realistic-looking finished shot, not flashy moving type and artistic effects. Besides, Chris and Trish Meyer have already written great books on motion graphics; you don't need another from me!

We will focus on the process of creating apparent realities that didn't exist in front of the camera. Ideally, everything you'll learn to do in this book will be so seamless that your audience won't notice that it was a carefully constructed special effect!

And that brings me to an important point (one that you are free to disagree with, of course). In my opinion, most special effects need to be accomplished in such a manner that they seem completely realistic—at least in the context of the film. Obviously, films aren't always about realism—even when they are supposed to be on the surface. Films are always fakery, but they must be fakery that is convincing and does not disrupt the audience's suspension of disbelief. This doesn't just apply to compositing effects, of course, but to lighting, sound effects, in short every aspect of the movie experience. If one of those is jarring or noticeably different in continuity, the audience's immersion in the story is disrupted. It's amazing what small things will do this—and what major flaws the audience will overlook! But overall, your special effects really must be seamless enough that the audience "buys" them in the context of the film. As soon as the audience says "Wow, what a great special effect," you've lost the battle.

Sure, everyone knows intellectually that the insurance folks won't let James Blond (played by Bill Bigstar) actually swing on a loose electrical cable over a glowing vat of molten iron. But if they've bought into the movie, if they have suspended disbelief, then they will say "Wow," but the "Wow" will be that James Blond made it safely, not astonishment that the special effects folks did such a good job! My aim here is to talk you through the process of creating effects that will seamlessly enhance your storytelling, not interrupt it with fizz and sizzle.

In the movie business, finding this mysterious balance between applying acceptable fakery and seeming phony is just awarded with the simple comment "it works." What it takes to make it "work" is to a great degree what we will be discussing, especially in the first part of the book. Everything we're going to be discussing is carefully constructed artifice—but all the technology and digital horsepower is a waste if you don't hit that magic balance with it.

The Basics of How Compositing Works

2

This chapter and the next one are the chapters lots of folks will be tempted to skip: "Hey, let's jump to the tutorials and the eye candy!" But I hope you won't skip them—or if you do at first, you'll come back to them later. If you don't understand how the process of compositing works, you won't be able to do much more than push buttons, and you'll be stuck with the most basic of effects. Understanding how various techniques work and which techniques work best for a particular situation will allow you to do better, more creative work.

Compositing is a sort of umbrella term we use to cover a number of different technologies that allow the creation of a new image (or *composite*) from multiple unrelated elements. These can usually be thought of as separate layers that are sandwiched together to create the new image. Anyone who has created a still graphic in Photoshop will be familiar with the concept of layers.

> Note: throughout the book, I will refer to bluescreen and greenscreen using the terms interchangeably for a color backing—which may actually be blue, green, or even red, depending on the color content needed in the foreground. This reflects the fairly casual usage of the terminology in the business.

But simply being able to combine separate layers isn't much use if you can't control what areas of each layer are "transparent." There must be some method of defining areas of transparency and opacity in the foreground layers, so that sections of the background layers can "show through." There are numerous technical methods for accomplishing this. Whatever the specific method used, the foreground layer with transparent areas is called a *key* in the television world, and is said to be *keyed* over the background. The hardware (or software) that handles the compositing is called a *keyer*. This terminology originated from the idea that the transparent areas of the foreground were sort of like an old-fashioned keyhole that you could look through.

Probably the most common use of compositing (or keying) in television is superimposed titling. Any time words have to be inserted into an existing picture, there must be some technical method of combining the title with the existing picture. In the earliest days of television, there wasn't a way to do this, so titles were simply printed or painted cards that were shot separately, rather like the dialogue cards in old silent pictures. Pretty soon, the engineers figured out a way to combine text into the picture through the most basic of video compositing techniques: the *luminance key*. In this very simple sort of key, any dark area that fell below a certain voltage in the analog video signal would become transparent; anything above that voltage was opaque. This allowed the creation of white-on-black title cards that could be easily inserted over the background image. In the 60s and even into the 70s, scrolling credits were often done with a large black wheel with white lettering stuck onto it. A graphics camera would be pointed at a portion of the wheel, the signal fed to a luminance keyer, and a grip would turn the wheel to produce the credits scroll at the end of the show. This practice, which started in the old black-and-white days, carried over well into the color era in many game shows.

Figure 2.1 *G. Méliès frame*

In the film world, exactly the same idea was being pursued but through a different technology and with a different nomenclature. While the earliest film magicians such as Georges Méliès had created compositing magic through simple double exposure, this approach had definite limits. It wasn't long before filmmakers wanted a more refined and controlled method of superimposing pictures together.

Filmmakers came up with a simple technique to create transitions or superimpose portions of two images together: the *matte*. In its earliest form, this was simply a plate of glass in front of the camera lens, with the matte area painted in black paint. This prevented the matted areas from being exposed; then the negative was rewound and a glass plate with the reverse of the original painting was used to expose the previously matted area with another image—usually a painting (see Chapter 4 sidebar on page 34).

Soon the process moved from in front of the camera lens to the lab, where a negative matte was used. This was simply an opaque mask that would be used in the printing process that allowed a portion of the film frame to be printed from one negative, while the balance of the frame (using a reverse of the original matte) could be printed from a second negative. By using a sequence of progressive mattes, each one slightly different from the last, the lab could create a *wipe* transition from one picture to another.

While the technology we'll be discussing in this book is far advanced from these early keyers and film mattes, the basic concept hasn't changed at all from the original idea! No matter how complex the latest digital Ultimatte keyer is, its basic job is the same as those early luminance keyers or film mattes: to define an area of the foreground layer as either transparent or opaque.

For most of the twentieth century, these two technologies remained pretty separate. The television world used keyers to create live composited images electronically, and the film world used optical printing techniques of increasing complexity to create composites in movies. In the last decade, however, there has been a convergence of the technologies and today nearly everything in both worlds is done digitally—though differences in technique, practice, and of course jargon remain. Nearly all movies today have special effects created using a digital intermediate, even if the movie was originally shot on 35mm film.

As the world of digital still graphics emerged in the 90s, various deep color file formats were defined (such as TARGA) that could include transparency information to facilitate compositing (or overlay) with other graphics. In the digital graphics world, this was known as an *alpha channel*. But it's basically the same as the film matte or the video key channel: a grayscale image that defines transparency and opacity.

Note this common basic concept for all composites, keys, or overlays! Though the jargon that grew up in each industry was different, the basic idea is the same. In addition to the basic visual that will be composited over the background, there is a separate and invisible graphic (whether it's referred to as a *key channel*, an *alpha channel*, or a *matte*) that determines what areas of the foreground are transparent. Generally, this separate channel will define white areas as opaque and black areas as transparent (or vice versa), while intermediate gray areas create various degrees of transparency in the foreground.

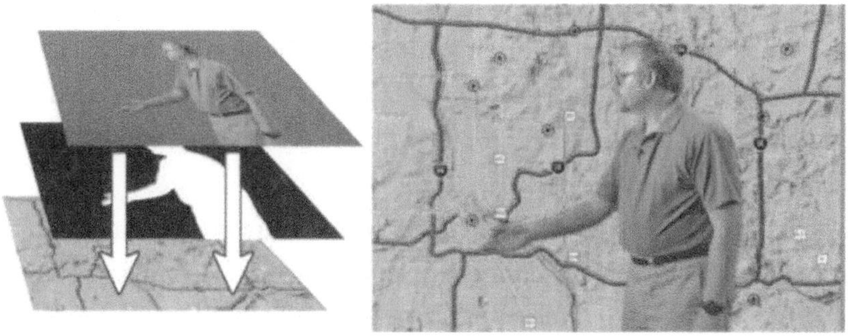

Figure 2.2 *The **foreground plate** (top) is made partially transparent by the **matte** (middle) so that the **background plate** (bottom) shows through, creating the **composite** (right).*

Now, this may at first seem confusing to those who have used built-in keyers in their editing software—because they never actually *see* the matte. It's invisible in the final composite, and often invisible to the editor as well! But trust me, the chroma key filter in Final Cut Pro is creating a matte internally based on the adjustments you make in the interface. Often you will not be able to "see" the matte unless you choose to. However, this basic concept of using a grayscale image to define layer transparency underlies nearly everything we will cover in this book, and so it's important to understand how it works. In each application, the specifics of how this transparency information is applied to the foreground graphic may be different, and there are a variety of means by which the matte may be created—but the underlying idea is the same.

Terminology

As you have already gathered, this basic idea has been used for many years in three different areas of production, each of which has developed its own jargon for the process. As these three previously discrete areas (video, film, graphics) have converged, the various nomenclatures have jumbled together to become a confusing mess for the neophyte. So before we go any further, we need to review the basic terminology that you'll run into and set out the terms we'll use for the rest of the book!

Video	Film	Graphics
Key	Foreground Plate	Foreground Layer
Key Channel	Matte	Mask / Alpha Channel
Background Video	Background Plate	Background Layer

Video keying technology is generally done live in hardware; and while there is a chapter later in the book on hardware keying, it really isn't the major focus of the book. And while we'll touch on issues of still graphics compositing, that also isn't the major focus here; there are plenty of fantastic Photoshop books already out there. The major emphasis in this book will be software compositing of digital video that is done in post-production (post), which is most similar to the techniques used in film production. For that reason, I'll lean more towards using the jargon of the film world for the rest of the book, unless we're specifically talking about live video keying or still graphic compositing:

- The various layers that form the composite are plates;
- The transparency information is the matte;
- The digital technique of defining the matte with the foreground plate is compositing;
- An image or image sequence saved with transparency information has an alpha channel;
- And the finished image is the composite.

However, this book will not deal with film directly. We will focus on digital video formats (HD, HDV, DV, etc.), though most of the techniques we will discuss are the same as those used with digital intermediates in filmmaking. We will discuss some issues related to film that affect digital video, such as creating "film" look, altering a background plate shot on film to match the look of the video foreground, and so on.

This is also not a book on image processing or color correction, but those issues enter into compositing quite frequently and so we will deal with those issues where they become important in compositing.

Okay, let's tackle a bit more of the jargon for this peculiar field. Here are some of the other terms you'll run into:

Background Screen: The physical wall or drape that constitutes the color background (usually blue or green) for a keyed shot that will be removed in post. See *Screen.*

Backing (or *Backing Color*): For chroma keying, this is the special background color (typically blue or green) that will be rendered as transparent. This will often be referred to as the "greenscreen" or "bluescreen."

Clean Plate: A shot of the background plate without actors present; or a shot of the backing color without actors or other foreground objects in the way. This can be used to correct uneven lighting and other problems with the backing. Audio folks, think "room tone" for compositing!

Chroma Key (or *Color Key*): A method of using a specific color (usually blue or green) to define areas of transparency in the foreground.

Composite: The end result of combining multiple images and their associated mattes into a single new image; in its simplest form, the combined foreground, matte, and background.

Cyclorama: A background wall painted the backing color that has smooth curves in the corners and at the wall/floor junction to create a smooth, shadowless background. Can also refer to a neutral color background drape.

Despill: A process to remove spill or flare from the foreground subject.

Flare: Colored light from the backing that appears over the foreground subject due to lens halation; or similar lens artifact from any light source on the set. Flare can induce *veiling*.

Garbage Matte: A simple extra matte that is used to block out "garbage" from the foreground such as mic stands or shadows on the backing.

Matte Choker: A software process to *choke* or reduce the area of the matte to eliminate colored halo around the foreground subject. Usually also includes the ability to blur the edges of the matte.

Print-through: Areas of the background that show through the foreground where they shouldn't.

Schmutz: The opposite of print-through. Okay, this really isn't the technical term, it's Yiddish for "dirt," but it's wonderfully descriptive of unwanted crapola in the foreground: areas that should be completely transparent—but aren't quite, so they are "schmutzing" up the background.

Screen: See *Background Screen.* The color background (usually blue or green) that will be removed in post. I will refer to this as the "background screen" in this book.

Spill: Color reflected from the backing that falls on the foreground subject—thus contaminating the foreground with the backing color. This can be caused by reflection from semi-shiny surfaces or by the bounce of colored light from the backing itself.

Track Matte: A matte made up of a drawn or extracted shape that allows a part of one picture to show through another. Figure 2.3 is an example of a track matte; the matte can be moved or "tracked," or even change size, but it will not change its basic shape.

Travelling Matte: A track matte that is animated across the screen and which changes in size and shape; or, in the original usage of the Vlahos/Pohl/Iwerks process, any matte which is extracted from motion frames and thus changes from frame to frame.

Veiling: The effect when internal reflections of light in the lens cause a "veil" of light or color to appear over the subject.

There's a lot more of this jargon to come, especially when we get to the various methods of combining graphic layers, but for now these are the terms you'll need to know for the basic compositing process.

Creating the Matte

There are a variety of methods for creating the matte—and thus defining the areas of transparency for the foreground. The simplest method is just to draw a black-and-white image that then is applied as a matte. For instance, you could draw a white triangle on a black background. When applied as a matte for either a still image or moving video, a triangle of foregound image will be superimposed over the background image in the final composite. In most software you can reverse the effect from the same matte, so that the foreground will be opaque at the edges and the triangle will be transparent. This method is useful for static composites (masking out a mic in picture, for instance) but is really pretty limited for any motion work.

Figure 2.3 *A simple static matte (here created by text) allows portions of the background image to show through the foreground image. If the static matte is moved or resized, then it is referred to as a track matte.*

That's why engineers in both video and film began to work on meth-

Green and blue aren't the only colors you can use as backing color! Back in 1998, I had the chance to talk with Dick Van Dyke about the filming of Mary Poppins. The original two-strip sodium vapor process that made the magic work used a yellow backing color. "It was a sort of sulfur yellow," Van Dyke said, "really intense, and a lot of the lights were yellow, too. So after a full day of shooting on the soundstage you'd walk outside and everything would have a blue tinge to it."

Vlahos' system used a modified three-strip Technicolor camera. Two strips of film were used, one color negative and the other a specialty stock sensitive only to a very narrow band of color (589 nm, sodium vapor yellow). A beam splitter was installed directly before the film gates to pass the image in the visible spectrum to the color negative while diverting to the other film the image carried in the narrow band selected to produce the matte. This sodium yellow system was superior to other systems tested at the time, which used diazo blue or red; these invariably produced fringing in the matte.

The 1965 Academy Awards gave a special Scientific award to Petros Vlahos, Wadsworth E. Pohl, and Ub Iwerks for the creation and application of the process, which was known as Color Traveling Matte Composite Cinematography. And of course we must remember Walt Disney himself, who was willing to back the new technology and use it in a feature film.

An animated penguin prepares to kiss Julie Andrews in the 1964 Disney classic Mary Poppins. The layered compositing of live action with animation was made possible by the development of a color-based travelling matte system invented by Wadsworth E. Pohl, Ub Iwerks, and Petros Vlahos. Image courtesy of Walt Disney Company.

ods of creating the *travelling matte*, a matte that is extracted frame-by-frame from live video or film.

The first really effective travelling matte for film use was developed by Petros Vlahos, Wadsworth E. Pohl, and Ub Iwerks for the Disney classic *Mary Poppins*. Dick Van Dyke and Julie Andrews were photographed in front of a colored backdrop; special film was used that was sensitive only to the narrow band of spectrum used in the color backing. When processed this film rendered the backdrop color as opaque and any other colors (the foreground subjects) as transparent. This roll of film served as the matte to composite "Mary" and "Bert" into the Disney artwork so they could dance with animated penguins.

Since those days, a variety of techniques has been developed for creating the matte from motion picture film or video. Most of these have come to utilize techniques of color differentiation using either blue or green as the backing color. These colors are used because they do not occur naturally in human skin tones. Other colors such as red can be used when the foreground must contain blue or green components.

Okay, enough basics. Let's move on to the various types of keyers and other forms of combining images.

Types of Keying Processes

3

If you're new at compositing, you may have the idea that this is all pretty simple: stick someone in front of a blue backdrop, click a couple of buttons, and bingo! Ming the Merciless is standing on an asteroid in space. Nothing could be further from the truth. For the most part, compositing using blue or greenscreen technology is a highly imperfect balancing act, something that can work well when all factors are just right—but that can go terribly awry if just one factor falls out of the compositor's control. Which is just about all the time!

As a result, a variety of processes have been developed over the years to create the travelling matte. Each has advantages and disadvantages, challenges and technical limitations. Some work better for certain situations, some work very well for very specific circumstances. Some that sound dandy on paper don't work that well at all in the real world, which after all is where we all have to live and work and play and do our compositing.

Whatever video editing or compositing application you use, it will likely have some form of built-in basic chroma keyer. Other third-party keyers are available for most software applications, and these may use a variety of approaches to creating (or "pulling") the matte. There are only a few basic keying techniques, each using slightly different methods of creating and applying the matte from the original footage. While you may run into variations on the names, here are the techniques in common use:

Chroma Key (or Color Key): The basic technology of selecting a specific color to become transparent. There are numerous variations, including proprietary keyers such as Primatte or Keylight that are based on the same basic idea with specific refinements. Some software will have keyers specifically for Bluescreen Key or Greenscreen Key. Color keying operates in the HSV mode (Hue, Saturation, Value) and allows the operator to select a specific HSV value as the "center" basic keyed color, and then specify a tolerance range around that color.

Variations on chroma key include Color Range (which allows the user to select a range of colors or hues) and Linear Color Key (which allows the user to select a very narrow range of color).

Color Difference Key: A more accurate and refined technique than the basic color key where the matte is created by having red/blue channels subtracted mathematically from the green channel. This technique often creates better edges and deals better with translucent foreground objects than is possible with the color key. Ultimatte is an example of color difference keying.

Difference Matte Key: This technique compares a static shot of any background (a clean plate) to footage of that background with a foreground subject in front of it. Ideally, the software should be able to detect the *difference* between the clean plate and the action footage, and create a matte from the difference. Sounds like a perfect solution, but doesn't work out in the real world all that well in many situations.

Image Matte: This technique applies a separate unrelated image as a transparency matte.

Garbage Matte: The garbage matte is usually a simple matte drawn to manually crop out unwanted areas of the foreground—the "garbage"—that the basic keyer cannot eliminate on its own. This may include microphones in the picture, uneven lighting at the edges of the backing, or shadows.

Luminance (Luma) Key: The luma key bases transparency on a selected value from the luminance (brightness) for the footage. Any values below (or above) a specified value will be transparent. Luma keying can be used with either a bright white backing or a dark backing.

Note that the difference between these types of keys is principally the methods they use to derive the matte from live footage. The most commonly used method today is some variation on the chroma key or the color difference key. As we'll see later, there are all kinds of variations on the specifics of accomplishing a chroma key.

An additional form of keying that is worthy of mention is the *spline key*, which uses curves and control points to define the areas of opacity and transparency. Some programs refer to this as *vector* keying. Spline keys are created and animated manually in After Effects and similar software, and a variation of spline keying is used to create smoother keys from highly compressed original footage in software such as Serious Magic's Ultra 2. Spline keying is the most common method for creating garbage mattes to get rid of unwanted foreground items such as light stands or mics in the picture.

Each of these basic techniques will usually have additional *matte choker* controls. In some cases, the matte choker is a separate module. The matte choker allows the user to contract ("choke") or expand the edges of the matte, and to blur the edge. Some now include additional controls for interpolating (mathematically recreating) missing information and thus eliminating the ragged edges of mattes derived from 4:1:1 or 4:2:0 material—usually video compressed by DV or MPEG codecs which remove color information as an integral part of the compression process.

Whatever process your favorite keyer uses, you must understand that the success and effectiveness of any of these keying techniques depends on a large number of factors being exactly right. A whole slew of production issues must all be within fairly narrow parameters for any of these techniques to work properly. So the advertised power and flexibility of a third party keying plugin may be entirely defeated by mistakes or inexperience in the studio! That's why the next several chapters, covering the complex production issues, are so important. No matter how expensive your software, you won't be able to do a good job on the final product without marshalling the production issues well.

Under the Hood

Most of us never have reason to pull a matte manually, because the software we have available does it so well. But it is helpful to have some understanding of what is going on "under the hood."

Blending Modes

Keying techniques are not the only story here. There are several other methods of combining layers together that involve mathematical operations rather than a transparency matte. Photoshop users will already be familiar with these *blending modes*, sometimes referred to as *transfer* modes. Apple's Final Cut Pro refers to these as *composite* modes. Technically, these aren't composites in the sense that we are using in this book; they are methods of having every pixel in a given image have a particular effect on the matching pixel in another image.

Each of these modes has a particular area of usefulness; for instance, the screen operation described below is the ideal method to put lens flares, glows, and other lighting effects like "laser beams" or "light sabers" onto an existing picture. Some modes you may never use; others you may find frequent use for.

Multiply: The multiply operation does just what it says: it multiplies the two images together. For this operation, white is considered to be 1, and black 0. All other colors are a proportional fraction of full scale. So if two light gray pixels (each with an RGB value of 190, 190, 190—or about .75 of full scale) are multiplied, the resulting pixel will be a darker gray of .56, or RGB 143, 143,

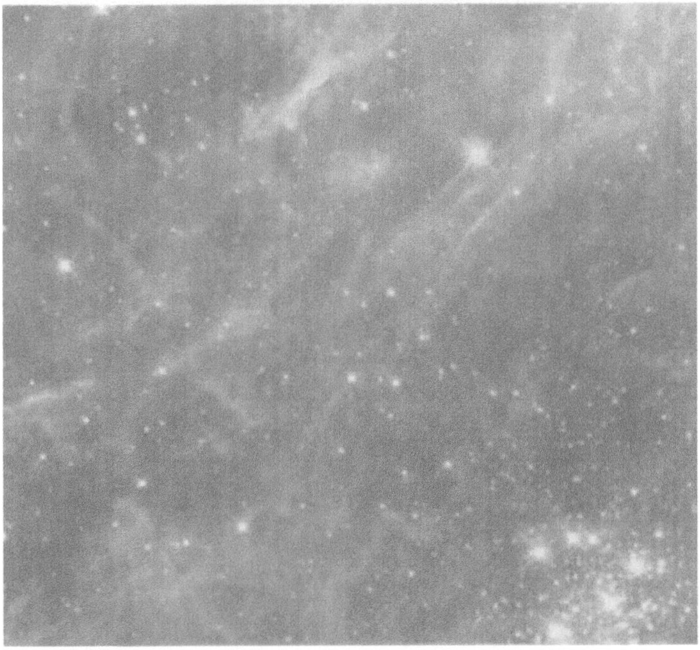

***Figure 3.1** We'll take two very different pictures (the girl and the Hubble space shot) and combine them using different math operations.*

143. Multiplying any color with black produces black. Multiplying any color with white leaves the color unmodified. In the multiply transfer mode, it doesn't matter which image is on top; the

results will be the same either way. The results of the multiply operation will always be darker overall than either original image. One common use for the multiply operation is to superimpose a dark line drawing over another background, while dropping out the white background of the drawing.

Figure 3.2 *Here we have applied the* ***multiply*** *operator.*

Figure 3.3 *Here we have applied the* ***screen*** *operator.*

Screen: The screen operation can be thought of as a method of overlaying a lighting effect onto another image. Technically, it's the opposite of the multiply operation: the screen operation multiplies the inverse of the value of the two matching pixels. Once again, white is 1 and black is 0, and all values in between are frac-

Figure 3.4 *Here we have applied the* ***minimum*** *(or Darken) operator.*

Figure 3.5 *Here we have applied the* ***maximum*** *(or Lighten) operator.*

tions of 1. The result is that areas of black in the blend image leave the underlying image unchanged; areas of white become white in the underlying image. Intermediate colors affect the underlying image proportionately and transparently. The end result is almost exactly the same as a photographic double exposure. The screen operation is ideal for lens flares, adding lights or glare to an image, or other effects that need to create an effect of glow or glare. The end result of the screen operation is always lighter than the original; like multiply, it really doesn't matter which image is on top. The most common use of the screen operation is the opposite of multiply; it's a great tool to superimpose light imagery while dropping out darker colors—as when adding a lens flare or similar lighting effect to a picture.

Minimum: The minimum operation (known as "Darken" in Photoshop and After Effects) compares the two layers and selects the darker of each pixel for the output. The pixels are not mixed or blended. Obviously, the operation results in a darker overall image than the original, hence its Photoshop moniker. Pretty boring at first glance, and not a process that you may employ often. But it can be very helpful in situations where you need to composite a dark subject against a light background into an image that contains light areas.

Maximum: The maximum operation (known as "Lighten" in Photoshop and After Effects), as you might expect, is the opposite of the minimum operation. Each corresponding pixel in both images is compared and the lighter one is selected for output. The situations where this will prove handy are the exact opposite of those where minimum is helpful: when you have an image with a light object of interest against a dark background, and you wish to combine this with a background that is also fairly dark—but not darker than the background of the other image!

Here is a list of the other blending or transfer modes that are available in Adobe's Photoshop and After Effects. These may or may not be present in other software packages, and in some cases may be called something different:

Dissolve: Think pixel-by-pixel dissolve as in a PowerPoint presentation! The resulting color is a random replacement of the pixels with the base color or the blend color, depending on the opacity of the overlaid image. While PowerPoint dissolves are pretty hokey, there are actually uses for this blending mode, such as simulating a rubber-stamped label where the ink has random gaps from the texture of the underlying material.

Overlay: Multiplies or screens the colors, depending on the base color. Pattern or colors seem to overlay the existing pixels while preserving the highlights and shadows of the background. The base color of the background is not replaced but is mixed with the overlay color to reflect the lightness or darkness of the original color.

Soft Light: Darkens or lightens the colors, depending on the blend color. If the blend color (sort of like a light source) is lighter than 50% gray, the image is lightened as if it were dodged. If the blend color is darker than 50% gray, the image is darkened as if it were burned in. The effect is similar to shining a diffused spotlight on the image. Useful for simulating lighting effects on the background.

Hard Light: Multiplies or screens the colors, depending on the blend color. If the blend color (light source) is lighter than 50% gray, the background image is lightened, as if it were screened. This is useful for adding highlights to an image. If the blend color is darker than 50% gray, the image is darkened, as if it were multiplied. This is useful for adding shadows to an image. The effect is somewhat like shining a harsh spotlight on the image.

Color Dodge: Looks at the color information in each channel and brightens the base color to reflect the blend color. Blending with black produces no change.

Color Burn: The opposite of color dodge. Examines the color information in each channel and darkens the base color to reflect the blend color. Blending with white produces no change.

Difference: Looks at the color information in each channel and subtracts either the blend color from the base color or the base color from the blend color, depending on which has the greater brightness value. Blending with white inverts the background color values; blending with black produces no change.

Exclusion: Creates an effect similar to but lower in contrast than the Difference mode. Blending with white inverts the base color values. Blending with black produces no change.

Hue: Creates a resulting color with the luminance and saturation of the background color and the hue of the blend color.

Saturation: Creates a resulting color with the luminance and hue of the background color and the saturation of the blend color. Overlaying gray (zero chroma) will result in no change.

Color: Creates a resulting color with the luminance of the background color and the hue and saturation of the blend color. This preserves the gray levels in the image and is useful for coloring monochrome images and for tinting color images.

Luminosity: Creates a resulting color with the hue and saturation of the background color and the luminance of the blend color. This mode creates an inverse effect from that of the Color mode.

It's worth having a basic knowledge of each of these blending or transfer modes. They each have very specific, narrow uses, and so you won't end up using them often. But they can each be a really handy tool when the right situation rolls around!

Simple Non-Action Compositing Solutions

4

Before we tackle the complexities of setting up a bluescreen studio, let's take a look at some of the other (often overlooked) kinds of magic that can be created with simple compositing techniques. Greenscreen is not the only type of compositing!

While blue or greenscreen techniques can be used to effectively extract what might be called an *action matte* (one derived from live action in the frames) there are some amazing effects that can be created with *non-action* mattes. We can't call these non-moving mattes, because we must sometimes move them through motion tracking or other techniques; but the matte itself doesn't usually change from frame to frame, and the matte is not dynamically extracted from live motion.

Compositing can be used to cosmetically alter existing video in post to get rid of problems (mic in picture, a flaw in the set) or to actually add impossibly expensive features to a relatively small set. It can be used to exaggerate depth, or to create subtle lighting effects when none were used in the actual shoot. How? Read on!

Fixing Flaws

This is an operation I have come to use frequently, usually in a planned manner. How often have you had to shoot a scene in a location that was absolutely perfect—except for one major flaw that was either difficult or impossible to change? For me, that's about every project! Since I do a lot of period pieces, I'm often challenged by glaringly modern intrusions into otherwise perfect settings. The intrusion may be a cell phone tower in an otherwise perfect seventeenth-century landscape, or it may be a red fire alarm pull box in a lovely eighteenth-century drawing room. Either way, they are intrusions that must be covered up, fixed, or removed somehow—or we have to find another setting!

How often have you had a shot ruined by mic in picture? The boom operator is struggling to keep the mic as close to the subjects as possible but just out of frame, and of course sometimes it slips in—and *of course* it's guaranteed to be on the take that was the best read for the actors! In many cases, you can actually fix this flaw digitally and use the take.

Here's how it's done. I'll use an actual example from a project I shot a couple of years ago, *An Uncommon Union.* We used the 1710 Buttolph-Williams House in Wethersfield, Connecticut, for several interior scenes. This house was the setting for the Newberry Award–winning novel *The Witch of Blackbird Pond* (Elizabeth George Spears, 1958), and was a perfect example of an early eighteenth-century New England home.

Figure 4.1 *The problem shot from* An Uncommon Union. *Note the emergency light in the corner. Right top, a close-up look at the anachronistic intrusion; right bottom, the room corner after our compositing magic is applied.*

Unfortunately, every room had a very modern emergency lighting system, as required by code for public buildings. Couldn't be tampered with, couldn't be covered up, and we had at least one shot where we just *had* to show that corner of the room. So we set up the shot as a *lock-down* shot[1] and planned to do a compositing fix in post.

With our camera shot set and locked, and the lighting set up, we rolled tape briefly without the actor to get a clean plate shot of the room. This

[1]A lock-down shot is a static shot where the camera doesn't move. The tripod head pan and tilt controls are "locked off" so the camera stays in exactly the same position.

wasn't strictly necessary, since the area to be "fixed" was above the actor's head, but it's a good practice. We then did several takes of the scene.

Back in the editing suite, I exported a still frame from the footage, and loaded it into Photoshop. Using the clone tool, I painted over the emergency light, creating an empty corner without an emergency light—a fairly easy fix on a static frame. I then created an Alpha Channel that allowed me to superimpose the small "fixed" area over the live video—effectively painting out the emergency light in every frame automatically!

You can try this with some of your own video. Either find a sequence you've already shot with a locked-down tripod, or go shoot one just for this exercise. Pick a scene that has some small isolated feature you wish weren't there—a radio tower or telephone pole, for example. *Make sure no live action happens in front of the feature you're going to remove.* Capture the footage into your editing program and then export a single frame—it doesn't matter which one—as a still image.

Now, open the still image in Photoshop and paint out the offending feature. The easiest way to do this, and have the fix look natural, is to use the Clone tool to clone sections of the surrounding sky or other background. Take some time and do this carefully so that the end result looks natural. Now we're going to take the small area you've painted and stamp it over the same pixels in the live video, effectively removing the radio tower (or whatever) from the video seamlessly.

The problem is that we only want to apply the fix over a small area of the finished frame, and allow the original motion video to be visible. We can't crop down to just the fixed area and paste it over the original video, because it's nearly impossible to position correctly. So here's where the compositing magic comes into play. We're going to retain the full fixed frame (which effectively preserves the exact positioning of the repainted area), but we're going to make everything else in the overlay transparent so that the original live video shows through.

To do this, we need to define which areas of the overlay will be transparent (most of the picture) and which areas need to be opaque (the small fixed area where you've painted out the telephone pole). We'll do this by drawing a simple grayscale image where white will be opaque, and black will be transparent. When embedded into a still image, as we will be doing, this is known as an Alpha Channel. When the grayscale image is saved separately and applied to motion video, it's known as a matte. We'll tackle separate mattes later in the book.

So here's how to do it. Once the offending bit of your still frame is removed through Photoshop magic, you have to create an Alpha Channel, which will act as a sort of cookie cutter, making most of the still image transparent and just the fixed area opaque.

In Photoshop, you've done the painting operation on a layer working in the Layers palette. However, to create the Alpha Channel, we need to work in the Channels palette. Click on the Channels tab to see the color channels. Normally, this palette will display the composite RGB image and the individual R, G, and B channels—a total of four channels. Click on the Add Channel button. The fifth channel will automatically become an Alpha, or transparency, channel. You can save this transparency information with the still image if you save the image in a 32-bit format that can include transparency. Now, follow these steps:

Figure 4.2 *In Photoshop, the transparency information is drawn as an extra Alpha Channel.*

1. First, copy the picture into the new Alpha Channel. We'll use it as a pixel-accurate guide for hand-drawing the transparency. To do this, click on any of the color channels above the new, empty channel to make it the active channel, then use Ctrl+A on a PC or Cmd+A on a Mac to select the entire frame, followed by Ctrl+C (Cmd+C) to copy the entire frame to the clipboard. Of course, once the entire channel is selected, you can also use the Edit>Copy command with your mouse.

2. Click on the empty Alpha Channel, and paste the clipboard into the channel using either Ctrl+V (Cmd+V)—or use the mouse for Edit>Paste.

3. Set the foreground color to 255, 255, 255 white and the background color to 0, 0, 0 black (the Photoshop shortcut for this is "D" to set

the default foreground/background colors of black (fg) and white (bg), then "X" to swap them). Deselect the channel and use one of the drawing tools (your choice) to draw an outline of the "fixed" area you want to be opaque in the foreground overlay. Draw directly on the monochrome image visible in the Alpha Channel. Fill the area with white.

4. Use the eyedropper tool to select the white area. Use Ctrl+Shift+I (Cmd+Shift+I) to invert the selection; or Selection>Invert.

5. Fill the selection—which should be everything other than the "fixed" area—with black.

6. The fix will generally be a perfectly undetectable overlay; but just to be sure that no hard edge gives the fix away, use Blur More (or Gaussian Blur set to two or three pixels) to soften the edges of the Alpha Channel. You could note that we are blurring the Alpha Channel only, not the original image! Save the image in a 32-bit format such as PSD or TARGA.

What you have created is a still image with an embedded "cookie cutter" that makes only the small area that we need to repair visible. When you import this image into an editing program, by dropping it in a timeline layer above the original live video, the hand-painted repair will be "stamped" over the problem area in every frame of live video. This technique is known as a "matted overlay."

Let's try it. Open your editing program, and import the original motion video and the 32-bit still image you just saved. Drop the original video into the timeline. Now, drop the still image in the next track, so that it is superimposed over the original video. Most current editing programs will automatically recognize the embedded Alpha Channel (in some older programs, you may have to set a matte control manually to recognize the Alpha Channel). Bang, you're done! Scrub through the video and you will see that the offending feature is magically removed. If you've done a good job with the painting, the fix should be virtually invisible—as invisible as the ugly emergency light in my finished footage!

This technique is similar to the glass paintings used in older films. It's a flexible technique that can be used in many instances to easily and cheaply fix something that would be expensive or impossible to fix in reality.

***Figure 4.3** The final composite, where the "painted out" corner is superimposed over live video. On the right, how the fix looked in the timeline of Premiere Pro.*

Obviously, this technique is quite easy with a lock-down shot. That's why *we plan a lock-down shot* whenever we know during production that there's an element in the scene that must be eliminated. But of course, this isn't always possible. When there is camera motion in the shot, this type of fix can still be used, but it becomes much more complex. The overlay must be motion-tracked to precisely follow the camera action. This is often necessary to fix a "mic in picture" problem, which is obviously unplanned. However, these are often brief intrusions rather than long portions that need to be fixed.

Motion Tracking a Matted Overlay Fix

Adobe After Effects (Pro only), Apple Shake, eyeon Fusion, and similar packages all have some type of motion tracker to aid you in this usually tedious procedure. Unfortunately, these motion tracker modules are all limited in their effectiveness in many situations. They do best when they have a nice, sharp, contrasty tracking marker to work with. In a planned tracking shot, some sort of marker (like bright red stickers) will be placed on an object in scene where the planned overlay will be. The stickers act as tracking markers for the software, and make the process much easier and more accurate. Unfortunately, a "mic in pic" shot is not planned, and so you won't have any of these handy-dandy tracking markers in the scene. You'll have to pick some existing feature in the picture and hope the software can stay on it. When this process works, it's fantastic, but it can be disrupted by many things: something passes in front of the mark you've chosen, or something with similar contrast/chroma characteristics passes too near, and the software picks up on the new object. Motion blur will lose the tracker every time. In these cases, you'll be stuck doing a lot of hand-tweaking until the wee hours—but hey, if it saves the one otherwise perfect take, you'll be a hero!

Let's take a classic example of the problem: the boom operator started to sag, or wasn't paying enough attention, or shifted position, and the mic drifted into the top of the frame for a couple of seconds. Unfortunately, it's during a camera pan so the spot we have to cover up moves in the frame.

Here's the fix: choose the frame with the most background material around the mic. This will be the frame in the sequence where the camera is the most tilted up. You need this as a starting sample so that when the matted overlay is motion tracked, the top edge won't dip below the top of the frame and expose the gaffe. Export this frame as a still, and follow the same procedure outlined above. It is actually a good idea to expand the canvas at the top by ten or twenty pixels and clone a little extra "wall" onto that area to create a bit of a safety margin.

Once you've created your matted overlay with the mic painted out, load it into After Effects (AE) with the footage you're going to correct. Make sure that the footage is set up right, with Interpret Footage set to the proper field order, etc. Now set your timeline cursor to a few frames before the incursion of the mic, and drop the matted overlay onto the timeline. Twiddle around with it to get it positioned *exactly* over the original piece of wall (or ceiling, or whatever). If the position is right, then you won't be able to see any difference at all flipping from the frame before the overlay appears to the first frame where it is present.

Now you need to pick a tracking point. It doesn't need to be anywhere near the area of the fix, but it does need a number of characteristics:

1. It needs to be very distinct from the surrounding pixels.
2. It's best if it has sharp edges and is in sharp focus throughout the segment.
3. It's even better if the color contrasts with the surrounding pixels.
4. Nothing should pass in front of this point during the critical frames.
5. The object needs to stay in the same relationship to the room or set throughout the sequence.
6. Ideally, the object should not have significant motion blur during the critical frames.

Okay, found a good tracking point? No? We'll wait. Still don't have one? Ahh, they can be nasty buggers to come up with sometimes! You may have to settle for five out of the six characteristics; just try not to ignore 4, 5, and 6 if you can help it—these can utterly disrupt the tracking.

With the layer you want to track selected in the timeline (this should be your main background footage), invoke the Motion Tracker by clicking on Animation>Track Motion. You'll be presented with a small square-within-a-square in the composition window. The inner square defines the "feature region" and should completely surround the selected tracking point. The larger square defines the "search region," the area in which AE will look for the distinctive tracking point. This shouldn't be too large, but should represent a good zone of ten or fifteen pixels outside the feature region. There will also be a tiny crosshair, which is the "attach point." The search box and attach point can be moved separately. To move the entire group to the tracking point area (remember, this is a distinctive spot in the picture that you will be deriving the motion from, not the point you wish to cover up), grab the edge of the inner box and drag. Once the outer boxes (search box and feature region) are over the appropriate search area, drag the center attach point to the precise feature you want to track.

In the Motion Tracker Controls dialog box, check that the settings are correct. The Motion Source should be set to the layer you want to track (your background layer). Track Type should be set to a simple "transform." Make sure that "position" is selected, but not "rotation" or "scale" for this operation. Next, click Edit>Target and set the Motion Target layer to the overlay image you created to cover the mic-in-picture; this image should already be positioned in the timeline as a layer above the background.

Now, position the timeline cursor to a point just before the frame where the tracking will begin. Now click on Analyze and sit back while you watch the software track your chosen point. If everything is dandy, it will track the point closely and you'll be happy. If not, try again—perhaps after repositioning the feature region if necessary. When you're finally happy with the motion (or you've gotten as close as you think you can), click Apply to set the control points to the target layer.

Figure 4.4*The double square marks the feature that will be tracked. The inner square defines the Feature Region and should completely surround the selected tracking point. The larger square defines the "search region." In this case, we are tracking special marks placed on the greenscreen specifically for this purpose.*

Now play back the segment, watching the matte overlay carefully. If everything has been perfect, the overlay will track closely without any excess false motion that will give the fix away. It's not unusual to have a few frames where the overlay seems to slip and then recover—or just slip and remain in the new position. If this is noticeable, you will have to go to those frames and correct the position manually. This is usually more fun than mowing your lawn with a pair of nail scissors, but not much. If the manual fix involves a lot of frames, you may want to dump the keyframes and start again with another tracking point.

Manual Tracking

If you don't have After Effects Pro (and thus don't have the Motion Tracker module) you can do a pretty fair job tracking manually, though it's not a load of laughs. The process is pretty simple, just tedious. Position your matted overlay at the start of the fix, and enable keyframing for the Position track of the matted overlay. Now move to the most extreme incursion of the mic, or some frame near the middle of the fix area. Reposition the overlay until it matches. Now move to the end of the fix, and again position the fix. Play back the fixed area. If it looks good, you've won the motion tracking lottery. Most likely it won't, and will slip noticeably between keyframes.

So now go back to a point halfway between the beginning and mid keyframes, and position the overlay. Each time you do this, of course, a new keyframe is created. Now go to the midpoint between the mid and end keyframes (about 3/4 of the segment) and reposition again. Now keep doing this, setting a new keyframe halfway between each existing set of keyframes (yawn) again and again, until the motion is satisfactory. Bingo, you've created a manual motion track. Do this two or three times

In *Gone With the Wind*, the wide shot of "Tara" early in the film is actually a glass painting. The building Tara is real, built as a set on the Selznick lot, but it was surrounded by other set pieces, not the rolling farmland of a plantation. So the sky, the trees, the grass, and the curving drive were all painted on a glass plate.

Glass painting could work two ways: either as a direct painting with a transparent area that allowed live action or real physical set to show through, or as a black matte that allowed later "replacement" of areas of the picture with a painting.

In the first variation, the glass artist would paint the needed enhancements to the scene, but leave a carefully registered clear area in the painting. When properly positioned in front of the camera lens, the illusion is near-perfect.

The second variation is more similar to the grayscale matte image that is used in digital compositing. A glass plate would be painted black, with a transparent area showing the real set and action. After the "real" action was shot, the negative was rewound and another glass plate (this one a reverse of the original matte) locked in front of the camera lens. The background painting would then be photographed, filling in the areas originally blocked off. This second variation allowed a larger painting to be positioned further from the lens than the first technique, thus allowing greater detail and realism.

This technique has been used extensively in movies made prior to the digital era. The scenes of Edwardian England in *Mary Poppins* often included only a few buildings on a soundstage; the rest of the scene was glass painting. Captain Nemo's island in *20,000 Leagues Under the Sea* existed only on glass.

There have only been a few specialized masters of the art of glass painting. One of the great masters of the craft is Peter Ellenshaw, who did the paintings for *Mary Poppins, 20,000 Leagues Under the Sea, Treasure Island, Davy Crockett: King of the Wild Frontier, The Black Hole,* and many other films. His son, P. S. Ellenshaw, did the matte paintings for the original *Star Wars.*

and you will quickly invest in an upgrade to the Pro version! But once again, if you save the only good take, you'll be a hero.

Digital "Glass Paintings"

Here's a bit of movie magic that most filmmakers don't think about, and which has been made much easier with digital compositing—the glass painting. As far back as classic movies like *Gone with the Wind*, glass paintings have been used to extend inadequate sets, fix problems with sets, or enhance the set with panoramic visions that don't actually exist. In *Gone With the Wind*, the wide shot of Tara early in the film is actually a glass painting. The building is real, but the trees, sky, and grass are all painted on a glass plate.

Today, of course, we don't have to use glass and the paintings aren't done in oils. Any sort of set extension or enhancement can be created in 3D programs, or through modification of real stills in Photoshop. In a lot of ways, this is just a planned extension of our matte "set fix" above, except on a larger scale. Rather than painting out an intrusive modern emergency light in an historic room, we can alter and enhance the set in a variety of ways. Here are some variations:

- You're shooting the exterior of a Victorian mansion, but you can't use a wide shot because it's surrounded by modern buildings. Solution: use a digital matte painting of other Victorian houses from another neighborhood.

- Your log cabin on the prairie has high-tension power lines visible behind it from several angles. Solution: use a digital matte painting of vacant prairie and sky. Of course this also gives you the opportunity of creating a fabulous sky with just the right sort of clouds, as opposed to the wimpy clouds and jet trail that were actually in the shot.

- There's a building that looks just perfect for an eighteenth-century English village, except it doesn't have a thatched roof. Solution: superimpose a digital matte painting of a thatched roof that covers up the modern fiberglass shingles the owner put on the property.

Okay, okay, these are all historical period examples, not much help for you fantasy and sci-fi producers. So try these:

- You've scouted a really futuristic-looking building that will work as a set, but it has a really ordinary parking garage on one side and a 1930s-era building on the other. Solution: create a digital matte painting of the rest of your twenty-fourth century city in LightWave to super over the ugly garage! Of course, you can go a step further than the matte painting here and also superimpose a layer of aircars flying by overhead if you wish.

- Your fantasy hero is trekking to an ominous-looking volcano to challenge the evil wizard that lives in its shadow. Only problem is, you can't find any ominous-looking volcanoes in your neighborhood. Solution? You get it now: find a great photo of an appropriate volcano, tweak and change it to taste, and then drop it into your shot, conveniently covering up the cell phone tower your actor is actually looking at!

As you can imagine, these techniques are much simpler with digital technology than they were in the old days, when there were only a few matte artists who could really pull off a glass painting well.

Let's tackle the futuristic city. We've set up a shot of our hero on a plaza in front of a modern building that could be futuristic as long as we don't show too much of it. The shot is planned so that there is a clean edge where the later matte painting will go.

In a 3D program (I used LightWave), create some futuristic-looking buildings composited in front of an alien-looking sky. Obviously, the frame should be the same size as the video frame you're compositing with, and you should work hard to create as much similarity as possible between the live foreground and digital background shots: the sunlight should come from the same direction, etc. Be sure to read the next chapter carefully before you actually try this.

Now, for variety, we're going to create the composite with a different approach than we used in the examples above. Here, we're going to create a simple matte image to punch a hole (transparency area) in the live video, and then we'll put the digitally created background behind the foreground to show through the hole.

Export a frame from the live video. This will serve as the base template for your matte. Basically, you need to carefully draw a black area to define the area of transparency and a white area to define the area of opacity, that is, the area of live video you want to keep in the final image. If there is a contrast or color difference between the desired foreground and the background you want to remove, this can often be done using the Magic Wand selection tool in Photoshop. With architectural edges, it's fairly easy to draw much of the defining edge with the line tool. When working in video (even HD) the edge created will be too sharp—so once the matte is defined, run a Blur or Blur More operation to soften the edge.

***Figure 4.5** The live video of a building that will work with our futuristic scene. Unfortunately, the buildings in the background don't cut it.*

You can do the compositing in a compositing program or any competent nonlinear editor (NLE). Place the background on a lower layer, and place the foreground (live video) in a superimpose track. Now follow the directions in your NLE to apply an Image Matte to the superimposed foreground; select the matte image that you just drew. Once the matte has been selected, if everything is set right, the undesirable areas of the foreground should now "show through" to the new background plate. In some programs (such as After Effects) you will need to import the image matte as an asset before it can be used; in other programs (such as Premiere Pro) you can select any file available on the computer, whether it has been imported as an asset into a bin beforehand or not.

Once you've tried this technique, you may begin scouting locations with a whole new eye and imagination!

Now, let's use this same concept to do some subtle effects on footage that just looks too bland. First, let's create an artificial depth-of-field effect, where the background in the distance (or the foreground) is out of focus. This particular example works realistically only with certain types of shots, but can be used as an effect in a variety of non-realistic ways. Let's tackle the realistic application first.

The sort of shot where this can work is where the picture content is

Figure 4.6 *The final composite where we have substituted futuristic buildings and a new sky. Live action can take place in front of the real building; anything you want can happen in the matte painting area. Want a space shuttle to fly through the scene? No problem!*

at an angle to the camera so that the distance from camera to background (and all significant foreground subjects) is greater on one side of the screen than the other. See Figure 4.7 for the type of shot I'm talking about.

The secret of this trick is a gradient matte, in which about the left quarter of the matte is black, the right quarter is white, and the middle quarters are a gradient. This is a separate graphic file (the same size as your video frames) that you will create in Photoshop simply using the gradient tool.

In either your NLE or compositing program, duplicate the video in your timeline or compositing window, so that you have two layers of the same material precisely synchronized. Now apply the gradient matte to the top layer. There won't be any visible change—because both layers are still identical. However, if you hide the underlying layer by disabling it, you will see that the top layer becomes transparent to the left.

Now enable the bottom layer so it's visible again, and apply a blur to that layer. You can use Gaussian Blur, Fast Blur, or Camera Blur (if your program has that). As you increase the blur level, you will see that the left half of the screen will appear to go out of focus while the right half remains in focus. Adjust the blur until you get the effect you want.

This technique can even be used to create a rack focus in post. In a shot similar to our illustration above that showed two men, one to the left of the screen (and far from the camera) and another on the right of the screen (and close to the camera), a simulated rack focus could be used to focus on the man to the right first, then focus on the man to the left when he calls after the other man. With the two layers of duplicate video on the timeline, one superimposed on the other with the Gradient Image matte, this effect can be accomplished by keyframing the Blur setting on each layer: first blurring the lower layer, then blurring the upper layer while the blur on the lower layer is reduced, bringing that layer "into focus."

Now, obviously, this technique is only going to work realistically for the specific type of shot used in the illustration. However, it can also

Figure 4.7 *A shot where the content on one side of the screen is further away than the content at the other side of the screen (left) allows a faked "depth of field" using compositing. The trick is applying a Linear Gradient matte (center). The resulting composite (right) roughly simulates a shallow depth of field.*

be used as a compelling artistic special effect to focus attention or convey a certain feeling. For instance, I have used this technique in several programs as part of a flashback or memory effect. This is similar to a vignette, except rather than having the edges of the shot fade to white, the edges of the shot are out of focus. This is done by using a Radial Gradient matte rather than a Linear Gradient.

A similar technique can be used to create subtle lighting effects—if perhaps more properly shadow effects. This is done exactly the same way as the illustration above, except rather than using a blur effect on one layer, that layer is darkened or brightened with image tools.

Here's an example from one of my documentaries. For interviews, I like to have the background lit about two stops down from the subject.

Figure 4.8 *The results (left) seem very much like the scene was shot with shallow depth of field. A variation of the effect (right) uses a Radial Gradient as a matte to allow the edges of the shot to be out of focus.*

This helps focus the viewer's eye on the foreground subject. This is especially true when the background is very busy and might seem distracting to the eye. This interview, with Darryl Stonefish, historian of the Delaware Nation, was shot in the tribal library with fairly flat lighting across the room. Nothing actually wrong with it, but the lighting didn't match the lighting of other interviews and, in my aesthetic judgment, threw too much light on the busy background.

Using the same technique outlined above, a matte file was created in Photoshop that had a diagonal slash of white (about 1/2 the screen width) with gradient fill to black in the diagonal corners. The video file was duplicated and laid on top of itself in the timeline, and the topmost layer had the matte applied. The background layer then was darkened using the brightness control until the corners of the shot appeared darker than the central area of the shot. The overall effect is sort of similar to when the background is lit with a barn door "slash" of light. It's not perfect, but the subtle effect made the interview seem more in keeping with the lighting of other interviews in the piece.

A similar approach (using a Radial Gradient) can be used to darken or lighten the edges of the shot in a vignette style or to simulate the darkening at the edges of a projected slide or film.

Figure 4.9 *The original footage (left) used flat lighting that did not match the lighting of other interviews. By using a hand-drawn image matte, two versions of the video were composited with the background darkened.*

So What's the Big Deal?

For some readers, especially new producers hankering after flash and sizzle, the examples in this chapter will seem like a big yawn. They don't *look* like special effects. But in many cases, that's the best kind of effect—one that is completely seamless and invisible, but which makes a problem shot work or helps create a set you couldn't afford. Any producer that has had the one perfect take ruined with a mic in frame can testify that the compositing technique here is the *real* movie magic!

Don't overlook the power of these sorts of "invisible" effects. They can save a scene or extend your budget—what more can you ask for?

Setting Up a Chroma Key Studio

5

Now that we've covered some principles of using *non-motion mattes*, let's move on to the issues of creating *motion mattes*, or mattes that are extracted from live action footage. While there are several ways to do this, by far the most common is to use a color-based system such as the chroma key or color difference key. And by far the most common technique for using these systems is to videotape your subjects in front of an evenly lit blue or green background. So the first and most obvious step in creating the original footage is to find a large blue or green wall!

In that phrase lies a key: *find* a blue or green wall. A greenscreen studio is not that difficult to set up, and there are several portable/temporary setups that we'll look at later in this chapter that can be quite serviceable for limited usage. But larger keying screen installations require a good bit of open space, and most producers only need a greenscreen studio for a limited period of time. It's worth looking around to find an existing studio to rent if your project only requires a few days of greenscreen shooting. In every major metro area, there will likely be at least one production company that has a green or bluescreen setup. If you don't have permanent space of your own, or space that you're using for free, there are some clear benefits to renting an existing studio.

Planning Your Studio

However, let's assume that you want to set up your own permanent studio with a green or bluescreen. This can range from a garage or converted office up to a full-fledged 50 x 50–foot space with electrical grid and heavy-duty HVAC. All you need is a can of green paint, right?

Figure 5.1 *A greenscreen studio with cyclorama wall. Photo courtesy of Pro Cyc, Inc.*

Well, maybe. Actually, you need some really specific paint or fabric —and you ought to answer a bunch of questions before you go off with hammer and saw and paintbrush. If you're an amateur enthusiast, you can skip the next section and go find some green paint for your garage wall. But if you're a pro investing time and money into a permanent installation, you need to take a look down the road at your potential use for the facility, and plan for the long run rather than next week.

You'll need to ask yourself a number of questions. Some good ones to start with are:

- How large a space do I really need?
- How many people are likely to have to be in a single shot at the same time?
- Will shots need to be full length, so that the floor must be green or blue as well?
- Will there be a repeated need for a full cyclorama treatment, where the wall blends smoothly into the floor?
- How often will the greenscreen be needed on a monthly basis?
- Will this area be dedicated to greenscreen use or must it be convertible to "normal studio" or other use?

- Is there going to be a permanent light grid or portable lights?
- And last but certainly not least: What's my budget?

In other words, before beginning construction, you really need to decide on the scope of the project, which will be determined by the formula:

(scope of the envisioned usage) x (budget) – (unforeseen problems)
÷ (Murphy's Law)

Okay, that's a bit tongue in cheek, but some serious reality checking needs to go into the creation of a specific-use studio like this.

How Much Space? How Many People?

Let's take a look at some of those questions and how the answers might define your studio. The first is a tough one, because the answer to "how much space" is always "more than you planned." Even when you get up to the large soundstage size, it's unbelievably easy to eat up the space and not have quite enough room for that wide shot. Many studios I've seen were planned without sufficient storage, and so there's equipment all over eating up already too-small space. But assuming that all other things are equal, and you have some flexibility on choosing or designing space, consider 30' x 30' a minimum. This will rapidly seem crowded on a routine basis; 50' x 50' or larger is better. One of the critical factors to consider is the amount of space in front of the color screen itself. You'll need about fifteen to twenty feet minimum from the front of the camera lens to the subjects if you plan full-length shots and need to show a group of people. Plus, you don't want the subjects right up against the wall; as we'll see in the lighting chapter, they need to be at least six to eight feet away from the wall to reduce spill and shadow problems. Then they need some room to move, of course! If you allow only 25 feet in front of the screen, you will be cramped for many shots and always wishing for those five extra feet. If you decide on creating a cyclorama (cyc) wall, the curved cove adds a couple of feet to this calculation.

But then, how much space do you *really* need beyond the basics? Do you really need the size of soundstages that George Lucas used for

Revenge of the Sith? Unless you must often shoot a whole crowd in front of the greenscreen, you may not need much more space than we've already described. As we'll see later, there are methods of shooting a group of people in a fairly small area and compositing them into an apparently huge setting. Action doesn't have to take place over a hundred feet to look like it in the final product. The greenscreen is really just a blank zone behind the subject that can simulate all manner of motion and angles through planned camera shots.

Figure 5.2 *A stationary keying background is all that is necessary for weathercaster-type shots. A similar setup works well for many academic and training applications. Photo of meteorologist Josh Judge in action at WMUR, New Hampshire, by Sabre Gagnon.*

Of course, the ultimate answer to this question for your situation may be "not that much space." If all you want to do is "weathercaster" work—one person pointing to computer graphics (without ever showing their full length)—you may not need much space at all. Local TV stations make do with fairly small bluescreens that are just barely larger than the shot you see on the news every night. This sort of setup can satisfy a lot of academic and training production needs—but as soon as you make a step beyond that simple usage, the space demands escalate dramatically!

So let's take a careful look at how many people you will need to fit into a shot at one time, full length, head to toe. For a tremendous number of movie shots, the answer to this might be four to six, tops. And this can be true for an epic production! Final editing decisions in recent years have veered much more toward tight close-ups and almost claustrophobic closeness to the actors. Even large groups are often shown in segmented close-ups. As an editorial aside, I think this trend has gone too far, and we need to rediscover the establishing wide shot. But the point I'm trying to make is that beyond that basic space requirement, you may not need a vast area even to accomplish an apparently "large" seeming shot.

> Warning: While you can make do with a fairly small background screen, the flip side is that it's also very easy to run out of background for dramatic shots. When the screen is lit separately from the talent, the talent is 10–12 feet away from the screen, and the camera then another 10–12 feet away, you'll be able to see beyond the edges of the screen. You have to be very careful that actors don't "go off" the screen with action or gestures.

Full-Length Shots? Do We Need a Cyc?

Again, if all you're doing is weathercaster shots, you won't need to have a green floor. But if you plan to do dramatic work, there will be many shots where actors must be shown full length and standing "on" the virtual set. To do that, the floor itself will need to be green—either temporarily or permanently. There should also be a smooth curved transition between the wall and floor so that a sharp shadow doesn't exist in a corner, a shadow that will cause problems in pulling a clean matte later. Again, this curve can be temporary or permanent.

It is possible in many situations to shoot full-length shots without a green floor. In those cases, the studio floor will become the virtual set floor. This is often workable, especially if only a few shots need to show the actors' feet. However, you will then be confined to the physical geometry of the break between the studio floor and the greenscreen wall. In most situations, the greenscreen will become a "replaceable wall," but not a true 360° "free space" where you can place the actor in any set in any orientation.

> Note: While using the visible studio floor may be somewhat limiting, there are imaginative ways around it. I did the special effects for one pilot where we concealed the break between studio floor and background plate by building in a "step up" to the multi-level virtual set that appeared to be visible "through" the green wall.

If you will need to shoot full-length shots only on occasion, you can paint just a wall and then add a temporary curve and floor cover using fabric. I even did one show where we used roll paper ("Apple Green" bulletin board paper from a teacher's store) to create an instant temporary cove and green floor!

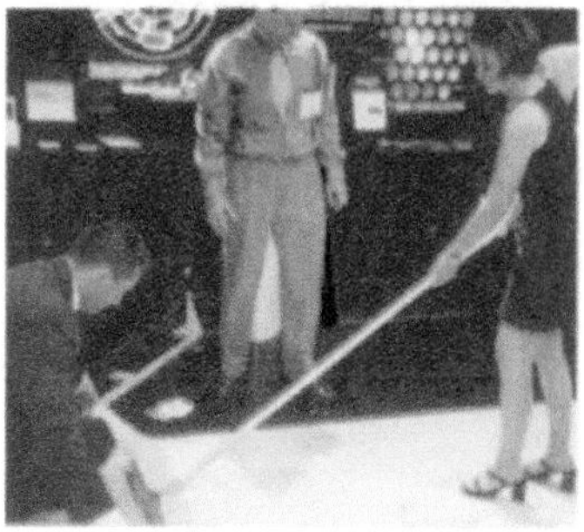

Figure 5.3 *GAMFLOOR is easy to put down and provides a solid reliable flooring surface in a studio. It is available in chroma key colors. Photo courtesy of GAM-PRODUCTS, Inc.*

GAM makes an interesting product called GAMFLOOR, which is a thick flexible vinyl flooring sheet that comes 48 inches wide in 100-foot rolls in a variety of colors—including chroma key blue and green. It can be applied to concrete, vinyl, wood, painted surfaces, glass, or plaster. It's supposed to stick to vertical surfaces, too—and it is designed for easy, quick installation and equally easy removal. If carefully handled, GAMFLOOR can be rolled up and reused.

If, on the other hand, you foresee regular use for the studio where full-length shots will be necessary, a permanent cyclorama installation would be more appropriate. This adds a permanent curved cove that creates a smooth transition from the wall to the floor. The entire wall, cove, and an area of the floor are painted to the chosen color. The cyc cove sections can be purchased premade, or a good contractor can custom build a lath-and-plaster cove for you. (See Appendix C for more information on building a cyclorama.)

How High Must You Go?

Here's another question that is often overlooked: how high does the color background need to be? If your usage will always be people walking or standing on the floor, and the camera always at or near their eye level, then you may not need much more than 10 feet high. If you need a wide shot that extends off the background screen, you can always garbage matte the non-color area in post.

If, on the other hand, you may need to build multi-level set pieces, you will need to anticipate this need and construct a higher background screen. You don't have to go nuts with this, since for most applications 16–18 feet will be sufficient. But with a 10-foot screen, you won't be able to have set pieces with stairs or multiple levels—or be able to set up a shot looking up at an actor from below. You'll run out of backing color.

Figure 5.4 *Pro Cyc System 4 FS is a modular cyclorama system that can be assembled in any studio space. Photo courtesy of Pro Cyc, Inc.*

How Often Used? Must the Space Serve Other Functions?

Let's get real. Unless you're planning a bunch of shows like *Sin City* or a sci-fi series, your weekly need for the greenscreen function of the studio will be much lower than your weekly need for regular studio space. For that reason, most studios are designed to be convertible. A bit of extra space is built in, and set pieces (or at least a curtain) can be used in front of the color cyc. If the floor is painted blue, special linoleum studio floor squares can be laid over it to convert it back to a regular floor. With thought and planning, a convertible studio can serve both regular needs and rigorous chroma key needs well.

Okay—you've decided how much space you need and all the other details. Now we get down to choosing what kind of paint or fabric to use.

Chroma Key Paint

I get at least one email a month from some startup hotshot who wants to create a greenscreen in his garage, and wants to know what shade of

Glidden or Dutch Boy to buy. And frankly, you can do it that way, but it won't ever work quite as well as the "real" stuff that is designed for chroma key work. The reason is that the hardware and software keyers work best when they have a pure color to work with, relatively uncontaminated by other shades. In other words, when you look at a color wheel, the keyer would like to see a green that is right smack in the "really green" zone, without any tint of extra blue or yellow. When you go to your local paint store, they may have some paint samples that look "really green" to you, especially next to all those zillion other shades of lime, oak leaf, waving grass, and baby poop—all of which are "green." But if you take your "really green" paint from the paint store and put it next to a swatch of real chroma key paint, you'll likely see that it has a lot of extra yellow or blue in it. And each deviation from the pure color is a variable that will restrict your keyer's range of flexibility later in the process. Some processes like Ultimatte are engineered for very specific shades.

So, you're on a really tight budget and a diehard do-it-yourselfer? Go on down to Home Depot or Builder's Square and take your best guess. Home Depot's Behr Paint #S-G-450 (Herbal Tea) is a workable greenscreen color, though not quite the same purity of tone as the specialty paint. It will work well enough for a lot of applications, but it may let you down for the finer work or those shots that are a real balancing act between colors in the scene. It's best to spend the extra bucks to buy paint that is specifically formulated for chroma key use.

Figure 5.5 *Chroma key paint from EEFX*

Rosco (the gel manufacturer) makes a line of paints for this purpose that are available from most lighting/video dealers. Other brands are available. Basic chroma key blue or green paints come in gallon cans for about $50. The paint is a high-quality water-based latex that has high pigmentation and so covers very well; in typical applications, a gallon will cover about 300 square feet of primed drywall.

Rosco has also worked with Ultimatte to create paints that have been specifically formulated to provide the correct luminance and RGB Values for optimum operation with the Ultimatte compositing system. The chart below shows the measured IRE values of the reflective paint when exposure is set for 100 IRE white with an 89.9% reflective chip on a Porta Pattern 11-step chip chart.

		Red	Green	Blue
#05720	Rosco Ultimatte® Blue	22	40	82
#05722	Rosco Ultimatte® Super Blue	7	18	72
#05721	Rosco Ultimatte® Green	29	84	36

Video levels when 89.9% white is at 100.

These values were measured with an Ikegami EC-35 camera with Plumbicon tubes. The iris was set so that an 89.9% reflective chip on a Porta Pattern 11-step chip chart was at 100IRE units. The gamma was set to 0.45 and the knee circuit was turned off. Different cameras may yield different levels even under the same conditions.

Fabric

So what about using fabric instead of paint? Chroma key fabric has a number of advantages over paint for certain situations, especially where flexibility is required. Fabric is available from a number of manufacturers in various widths and colors.

Westcott offers chroma key fabric in blue or green in 10 x 12 and 10 x 24–foot sizes, which is available from most video dealers. Rosco, Lastolite, and others supply similar sizes of fabric. Rose Brand in New York, which is a supplier of drapery, scrim, and fabric for the theatrical and film industries, carries large bolts of 10-foot-wide fabric in several colors of green and blue.

One type of fabric that has become popular in recent years is a foam-backed fabric that comes in 60-inch widths. The slight stiffness supplied by the foam backing means that the material is nearly wrinkle-proof, and can be easily hung entirely flat without draping or wrinkles. When properly seamed, multiple sections can be joined together to form a large backdrop with almost invisible seams.

Because you want an even, shadow-free backdrop, keying fabric is not treated the way normal drapery backgrounds are. The fabric must be hung so that it drapes completely flat; often fabric backgrounds are stretched on frames to create a completely flat and wrinkle-free surface. Canvas or foam-backed fabric can be mounted on a roller like many still photographic backgrounds are, and rolled up out of the way when not in use.

The obvious advantage to using fabric is the fact that it's somewhat more flexible for multiple-use space. Certain types of fabric setups are handy for portable use. But another advantage is that it's easier to have both blue and green available for different shots than it is with a painted cyclorama.

Figure 5.6 *Here the author has converted part of an office into a greenscreen studio by using a fabric on a roller and hanging simple electronic ballast shop lights for background illumination. After the need for the greenscreen was over, all that was required to return the office to original condition was a bit of spackle and paint.*

Paint, Tape, and Fabric

Rosco also offers a matched set of paint, fabric, and gaffer tape known as the DigiComp system, which is available in blue or green. Because the three products match very closely in chroma and luminance values, they should make it easier to pull an effective matte in post. The paint, like Rosco's other scene paints, uses a flexible vinyl acrylic binder with excellent adhesion to a wide variety of surfaces and cleans up with soap and water. The paint has a matte finish and is available in one-gallon and five-gallon sizes.

The matching DigiComp fabric is 100% cotton impregnated with color; the fabric is available in bolts that are 59 inches wide by 30 or 60 feet. The DigiComp tapes are a good quality of non-reflective gaffer's tape available on 50 mm x 50 m rolls.

While there are some advantages of closely matched keying colors in post, it isn't strictly necessary. I've found that different brands of chroma key green gaffer's tape, paint, and fabric are all close enough to work well. The more difference between the shades, the wider a range of chroma values will have to be selected by the keyer, but this is often more affected by uneven lighting than it is by minor differences in color between products.

One of the advantages of using both paint and fabric is that it extends studio flexibility. A single wall (without cove) can be painted the selected color, and then have fabric taped to the wall to cover the floor and create a temporary cove. Fabric extensions can be added to the sides of the painted wall, as well. These temporary additions can then be removed, the fabric laundered, and a "normal" backdrop or drape placed in front of the blue or green wall for normal usage.

Figure 5.7 *Rosco DigiComp line*

Background Lighting

We'll cover lighting in more detail in the next chapter, but there's an important point that needs to be discussed here. If you're designing a permanent installation for chroma key work of any sort (even if it's just in a garage) you should consider installing lighting for the color background. Of course, if you're designing a real studio space, you will probably be installing a suspended grid and control system for lights; specific lighting for the color background should be a part of this design. But even in lesser installations (a converted office, for instance, or a multi-function space that sometimes serves as a studio but must also satisfy other purposes) you should really install semi-permanent lighting for the color background.

The reason is that while your foreground lighting may vary tremendously from situation to situation, the background lighting won't. It needs to be even, that's it. And while some folks still use incandescent instruments to light these backgrounds, far and away the easiest and most efficient even lighting is going to come from fluorescent instruments. Since the painted wall isn't going to move, they can easily be mounted and wired permanently (or semi-permanently as in Figure 5.6) in almost any circumstance.

For most readers, the size of the area they will be illuminating will be small enough that it won't require complex setups to light it fairly evenly. A 10-foot-high screen can be lit well with single fluorescent banks mounted side by side across the width of the screen. A taller screen (18-foot) will probably need a second bank in each position aimed at the lower part of the screen.

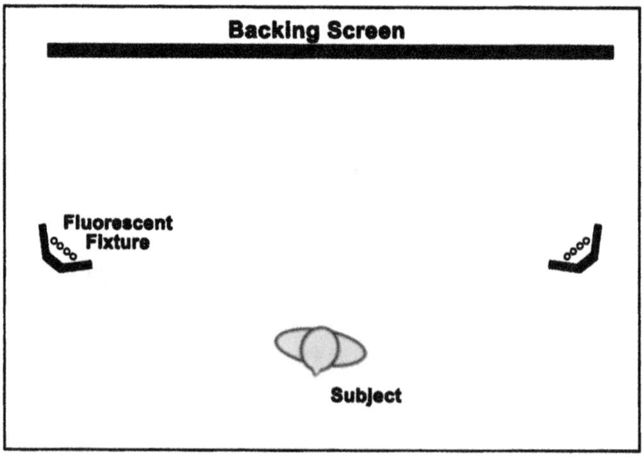

Figure 5.8 *This diagram shows one method of illuminating a small background screen with fluorescents. In some situations, a flag may need to be mounted to keep the background light off the subjects.*

In many smaller situations, an uncontrolled fluorescent light for the backing can act as a basic backlight for the subjects. This can then be augmented with other 'flos' (gaffer jargon for fluorescent instruments) or focused incandescent instruments. However, in other situations this

Figure 5.9 *A film soundstage set up for bluescreen. Banks of Kino Flo fixtures illuminate the backing screen from below and above, each bank carefully positioned and controlled from a DMX dimmer to precisely regulate the even illumination of the screen. Note the raised floor to the left which allows the actors to be above the lower light banks.*

Electrical and HVAC Considerations

If your ambition is to build a full-fledged studio, there's a lot you need to know that is beyond the scope of this book. Areas of particular concern are the electrical system, the lighting grid, and the heating, ventilation, and air conditioning (HVAC). Each of these systems must be designed by a knowledgeable person with some experience in the field. The needs of a video/film studio in these areas are completely different from the use that most contractors have experience with. Thousands of watts of lights generate incredible amounts of heat, which must then be removed by a very beefy HVAC unit that is also engineered to be extremely quiet. It's somewhat like running high-powered space heaters in a building and then attempting to cool it back down to normal temperatures without making any noise.

My book *Lighting for Digital Video and Television*, 2nd Edition (CMP Books, 2004) has a chapter on studio design and lighting issues. *The Small Television Studio, Equipment and Facilities* by Alan Bermingham (Hastings House, 1975) is a valuable resource. Though now out of print, it is available used and in many libraries. The best advice is to hire a consultant who has experience in the field, and who can give you guidance for the specific scope of studio you want to build.

will be inappropriate and the light spill from the flos will need to be controlled. This can be done with flags, nets, egg crates, or a combination. We'll discuss techniques for doing this in detail in the next chapter.

For larger installations such as film sound stages, the lighting must be carefully designed to evenly light a huge area.

Temporary/Portable Solutions

For a great many situations, a large permanent installation is not required at all. Smaller temporary solutions will do the trick for a lot less money and fewer headaches. I've already mentioned that fabric can be used in temporary setups. A bolt of fabric can simply be taped in posi-

Figure 5.10 *Fabric stretched on a frame (such as this one at the North Carolina School of the Arts School of Filmmaking) is a practical solution that can be set up temporarily and then disassembled for transport.*

tion and removed when the shot is finished. However, since most fabric (other than the foam-backed fabric mentioned above) will have fold marks and wrinkles, there will need to be some effort put into ironing or steaming these out for best results. The foam-backed chroma key fabric is ideal for this sort of tape-it-up-and-shoot use since the fabric does not wrinkle or sag.

There are a number of better portable solutions for temporary use. One is the use of a frame to stretch fabric on. Either the fabric can be grommeted for ties or special locking fasteners used that don't require grommets. The frame can be anything from a pro interlocking aluminum tube unit from Matthews to something cobbled together from PVC piping. The point is to be able to stretch the fabric flat to eliminate fold marks and wrinkles that will interfere with pulling a clean matte in post.

Another fabric-based solution is to mount the fabric on a roll, the same way still photographers do with painted canvas backdrops. This works best with heavier fabrics like canvas that won't wrinkle easily. Thinner cotton or poly fabrics will tend to wrinkle when they are rolled up.

Figure 5.11 *A chroma key green roll of photographer's paper can be mounted easily on light stands with adapters (Chroma-Key.com).*

Let's not forget the still photographer's old standby, the paper roll! Most still photographers use roll paper to provide all sorts of color backgrounds, and those rolls are available in chroma key green and blue. There are simple adapters to allow you to mount a 6- or 12-foot-wide roll on a pair of light stands. The paper creates a smooth cove when rolled out, and the portion with foot scuffmarks on it is simply trimmed off and discarded before the next use. These rolls sell for about $60 per roll for 107-inch-wide x 12-yard size. Larger and longer rolls are available, though they can't be shipped via UPS or FedEx. Savage Co. is one of the main manufacturers for these paper backgrounds, which are available from nearly all photo or video dealers. While roll paper works fine for product and talking-head shots, it is difficult to do any action or dramatic work with it.

A number of companies (Botero, Lastolite, Westcott, and Photoflex) make collapsible keying backdrops that are similar to their popular collapsible reflectors. These are typically about 5' x 7' and come, of course, in either green or blue. For a couple of hundred dollars, these units are a good portable solution for many smaller needs.

Figure 5.12 *A collapsible reflector (Lastolite) on the foreground image*

High-Tech Alternatives

Green paint and blue fabric are pretty low-tech, and haven't actually changed that much over the last 35 years. But in recent years there's been a high-tech newcomer in the keying background market, a glass-beaded fabric known as Reflec® (recently renamed Chromatte®). The product was also sold as the "Holoset" by the now-defunct Play, Inc. Manufactured in the UK, this fabric is very similar to the 3M Scotchlight® coating that is used on reflective signs and markings. The difference is that the Reflec® glass beaded surface has a very narrow angle of reflectivity. The Chromatte fabric appears gray to the eye in ambient light. It contains millions of tiny glass beads that act as reflectors, returning any light shone on them back to its source.

The system works by placing a ring of super-bright LEDs known as a LiteRing (in either blue or green) around the camera lens. The LEDs are controlled by a dimmer. After the foreground lighting is done and the exposure set on the camera, the color LEDs are brought up on the dimmer. When the directional light from Reflecmedia's lens-mounted LiteRing hits the Chromatte fabric, it is returned on the same path and back into the camera lens - so that the camera sees the otherwise gray fabric as a perfectly even blue or green background, no matter what the angle is between the camera lens and the fabric. The dimmer allows the user to find the "sweet spot" of color sensitivity for the camera. When the right lighting level is reached, the Reflec® fabric seems to fluoresce with the chosen color.

Figure 5.13 *Reflecmedia Chromatte studio setup. The author holds a Reflec® LiteRing which mounts around the camera lens (inset).*

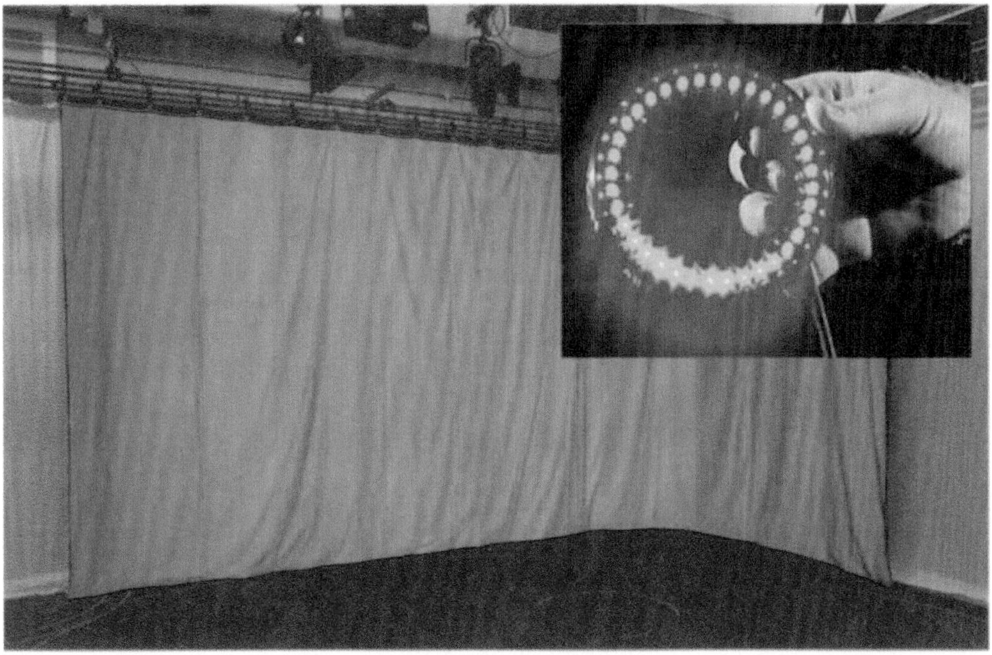

The result is a very even, strong backing color with no shadows that makes it quite easy to pull a clean matte in most keyers. The technology really works, and works quite well. But it's not without its downside. First, the fabric itself is quite expensive and will be out of the range of those on a tight budget—especially when plain ol' blue fabric is so cheap. The other downside is that the system can't be used with any shiny objects that will reflect the light from the LiteRing back at the camera. That means people with glasses—and in some shots even people with eyes! On close-ups the LiteRing sometimes creates a blue ring-shaped highlight in the subject's eyes that keys out in post. Gives rise to some interesting ideas for horror flicks, but for most shots the effect would be unacceptable.

Whether you decide to tape a piece of green fabric to the office wall, spend $75 to paint your garage wall blue, or invest $250,000 in building a full studio with fixed keying cyclorama, I hope this chapter has helped to home in on the keying background solution that is right for you. So now that you've built your studio (or opened up your Photoflex 5 x 7–foot green collapsible), we have to begin to work on lighting both the background screen and the foreground subject.

Lighting for Chroma Key

6

Now that you've painted a wall green or bought a Photoflex collapsible backdrop or built a $500,000 greenscreen studio, the next step is to light the color background and the foreground subject. While I've already touched briefly on lighting the background in the last chapter, now we need to delve into the details and make it happen.

First, a brief reminder of some of the basic principles of lighting. For those who would like a deeper discussion, pick up a copy of my book *Lighting for Digital Video and Television,* 2nd Edition (CMP Books, 2004). Lighting is incredibly important in creating effective composites, so if you're a novice please take the time to learn the basics!

Basics of Lighting

Probably the most critical point to understand about lighting for digital video is that the camera cannot "see" the same range of lighting that the human eye can. The ratio of light to dark in which the camera can record detail is known as the *latitude*. If the ratio of the brightest point in your scene to the darkest point in your scene exceeds the latitude of the camera, the camera will record solid black (if it's too dark) or solid white (if it's too bright). There will be no detail at all in these areas, no information to pull out with fancy shenanigans in post. The information simply isn't there because the camera could not replicate it. At the overexposed end, this is known as *clipping*. At the underexposed end, it's known as *crushed blacks*. So while a scene might look just dandy to your naked eye, it may be entirely too contrasty for the camera. A major part of the art of professional lighting is to compress the lighting levels into the range that the camera can reproduce effectively. This means that you will need to "knock down" (reduce) highlights and place more fill light into shadowed areas than might seem necessary to your eye.

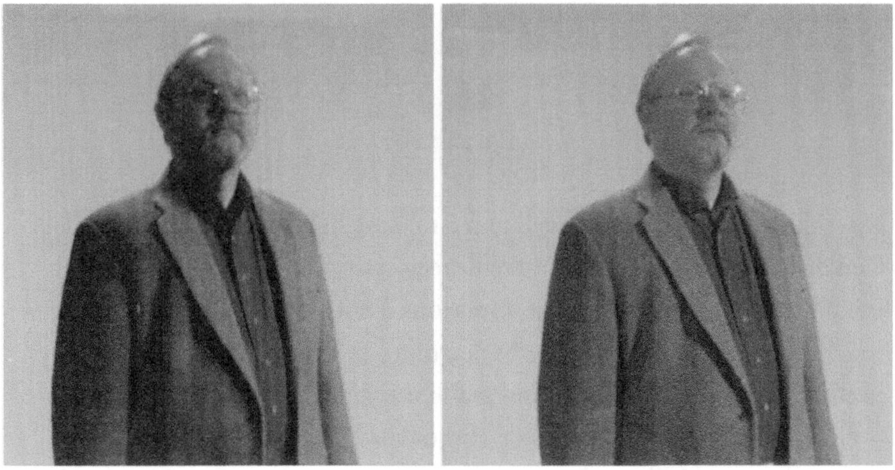

Figure 6.1 *This shot (left) was properly exposed for the highlighted areas. However, the shadows are too dark and will reproduce as crushed blacks in the camera. To fix this situation, you either have to reduce the level of the key light and change the exposure or, more likely, bring more fill light into the shadowed areas (right).*

While this situation has improved dramatically over the last decade or so, the latitude of even the best video cameras is still usually less than a quarter of what your eye can perceive—and in the case of less expensive cameras, it may be a tenth! For this reason, it is extremely important that you check the results of your lighting on a properly calibrated video monitor (see Appendix D) to see the effect of the lighting when processed by the specific camera you are using.

Another basic rule of lighting that must be understood is that of the inverse square law. This simply states that *distance* has a dramatic effect on *lighting levels*. At close range a small increase in distance causes the light hitting the subject to fall off quite rapidly. The further away from the light, the more gradual the change of brightness is over the same distance. If the distance is doubled between the light source and the subject (say you move the source from five feet to ten feet away from the subject), the light level on the subject will be *one-quarter* of what it was in the original position. This is pretty counterintuitive, since it would be normal to guess that doubling the distance would halve the light. This information is important because this phenomenon can make it very difficult to light the background screen evenly in some situations; however, we can actively use the effect to help create even lighting as long as we understand how it works.

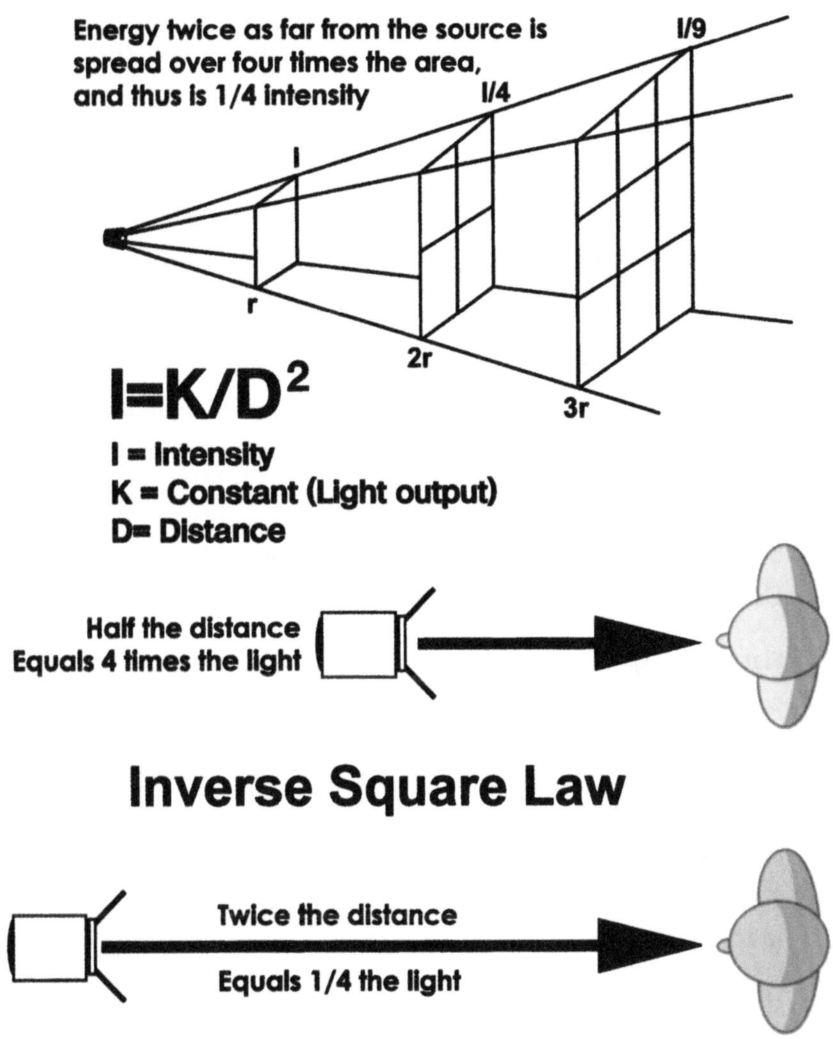

Figure 6.2 *The Inverse Square Law explains that lighting levels change by a factor of four when distance is doubled or halved. If you double the distance from subject to instrument, the lighting intensity falls to 1/4 of its original value. Conversely, if you halve the distance from light to subject, the intensity is four times its original value.*

Lighting for television or film is very artificial, and most architectural lighting is completely unsuitable for effective video work. In the case of color keying, we want to create completely even illumination over the background screen, but at the same time create very dramatic lighting on a foreground subject. While architectural lights usually shine down from above, video lighting must be set at a much shallower angle. We want the light to shine into the subject's face, not down on the top of her head! Shadows are carefully managed to not seem intrusive or unflattering; lights are carefully positioned to provide a little glint in the subject's eyes.

Here's a brief introduction to some of the lighting jargon that I'll toss around in this chapter:

Key Light: The principal (usually brightest) illumination on your subject.

Fill Light: A lower level of light thrown into shadowed areas.

Backlight: A light positioned above and behind the subject. Back lights can also be referred to as hair lights. When moved slightly to the opposite side from the key, it becomes a rim light due to the thin rim of illumination it places on the subject. If moved further to one side, it becomes a kicker.

Sidelight: Obviously, a light positioned to one side of the subject. Used to help define the edges of a subject.

Flat Lighting: Think local news studio. Equal amounts of light coming from every direction, almost completely eliminating shadows.

Low Key Lighting: Very dramatic lighting. The key light illuminates only a small portion of the picture while most other portions are very dimly lit (a key:fill ratio of more than 8:1). Film noir uses low key lighting.

High Key Lighting: The opposite of low key. The key light illuminates most of the picture, and the key:fill ratio is low, less than

4:1. Flat lighting is a variation of high key lighting where the key: fill ratio is 1:1.

The most basic lighting setup is the three-point lighting setup. This is pretty much "plain vanilla" video lighting. It's not a be-all and end-all, but more of a starting point. However, you need to understand the basic setup before proceeding to more advanced or complex setups. One point of the three-point setup that many beginners overlook is the use of the backlight. Professional video lighting and film-style lighting uses backlights, rim lights, and kickers everywhere to help define subjects and give a sense of dimension to the picture. These lights have particular benefits for lighting for matte shots that we'll get into later. But the neophyte would do well to start to watch the use of backlights and kickers in movies to see how they are used. One of the sure signs of amateur lighting is the underuse of backlights in a production.

One of the most common misconceptions is that chroma key lighting must always be flat lighting. While that's true for the background, it's definitely *not* true for the foreground! Flat lighting on the foreground will often give away the fakery, unless the background plate (the digital replacement background) happens to be flat-lit also. As should be clear already, we're going to light the background screen and the foreground subject separately.

Lighting the Background

Once you've selected the color backing you're going to use and set up your green or bluescreen, you need to come up with a method of lighting the background as evenly as possible. Remember earlier when I said that keying is an imperfect balancing act? The more variations in lighting level across your screen, the less latitude for pulling a clean key you will have in the keyer. Why? Because you'll have to include more and more shades of green in the selected zone for transparency, and eventually some of these will be too close to a color in your foreground subject. The more deviation you have from the perfect pure backing color, the harder the keyer will have to work and the more likely you'll have trouble pulling a truly clean key. The goal here is to light the backing screen as evenly as possible, and to a level that gives a clean, noise-free image in the camera. However, the lighting level is also a balancing act. You don't want the screen lit too brightly, because that can create problems with spill on the foreground.

Screens that are 12 x 12 feet or smaller are fairly easy to light. A row of fluorescents hung above and six to eight feet out from the screen will provide very even coverage. If you look back at Figure 5.6 in the last chapter, you'll see a photo of a temporary greenscreen setup that I was able to light with two electronic ballast worklights. Not very high-tech or fancy, but it was acceptable even if the illumination level fell off a bit toward the bottom of the screen. An improvement would have been to add a matching set of flos on the floor to balance lighting from top and bottom. In a permanent installation you would of course be more likely

Figure 6.3 *Fluorescent instruments positioned vertically on either side of the screen can provide very even illumination if the proper overlap is found.*

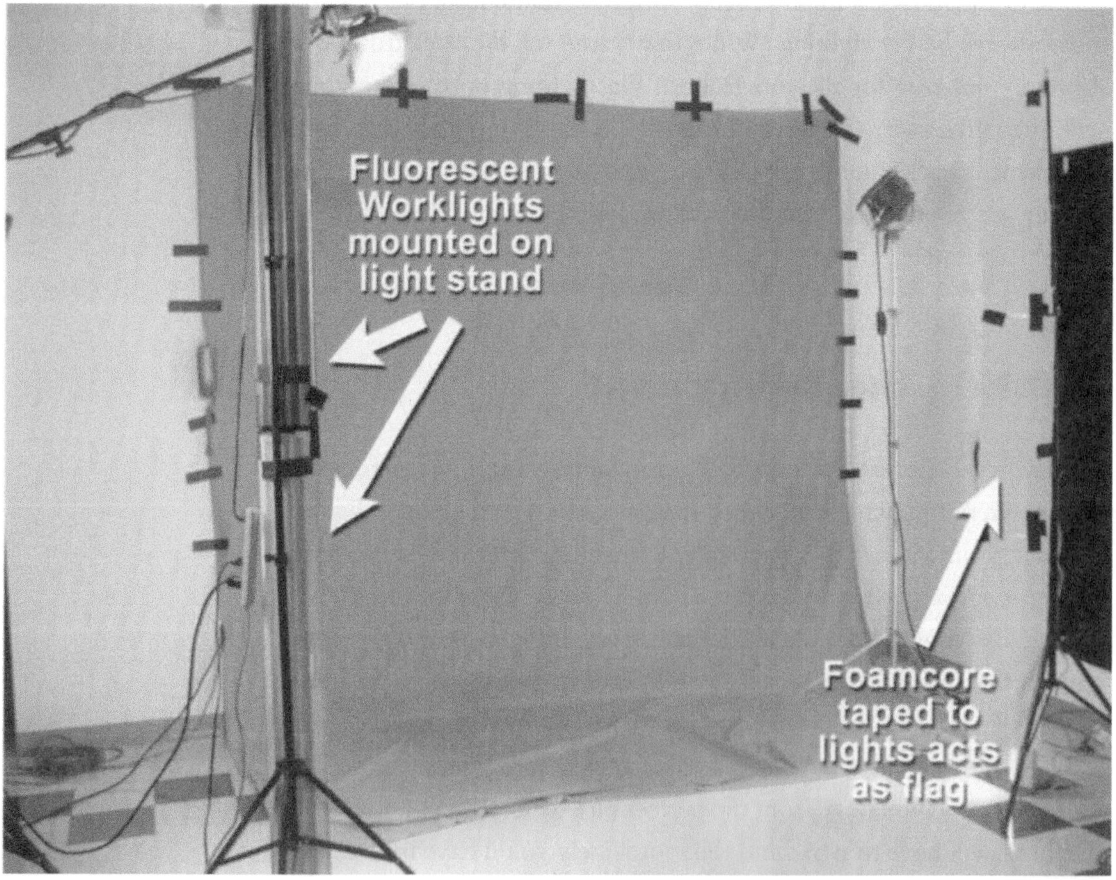

to use commercially made video/film fluorescent instruments that have proper mounting brackets for a light grid and professional controls. But this picture shows how simple it can be to light a smaller screen. By the same token, I've lit small screens of this sort from each side with incandescent softbanks as well.

For a larger background screen, two rows of fluorescents positioned vertically on either side of the screen and six to eight feet in front will usually provide excellent illumination. When the lights are positioned properly, the inverse square law will dictate that the light falloff from the bank on one side can be counterbalanced by the opposite bank. When the right overlap is set, the lighting level will be very nearly even across the screen.

Most lighting manufacturers make a fixture that is known as a *cyc light*, which is simply a quartz tube and reflector arranged to supply even coverage of a cyc. These can also be used in a vertical row to either side. When properly positioned and arranged, they can provide even coverage. The lights are arranged so that the beams overlap from either side; the falloff of intensity from the one side is mirrored by the falloff from the other side; the overlapped area ends up being evenly lit. You can also use scoops with diffusion in a studio setting, or banks of the simple Lowel Tota-Lites. Though still common, cyc lights really aren't nearly as good as fluorescents in this application, since they tend to have hot

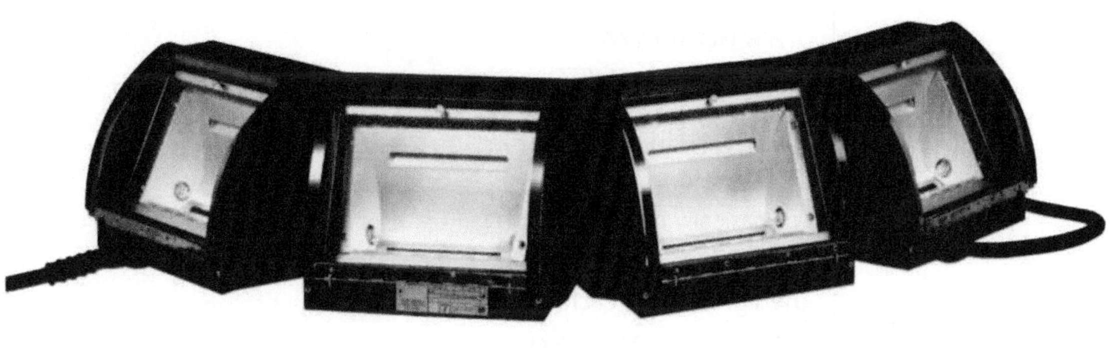

Figure 6.4 *Halogen instruments designed to evenly illuminate large areas are known as "cyc" lights, such as the Strand Orion units shown here. Courtesy of Strand Lighting.*

spots that are hard to manage without a lot of diffusion. I'm really quite a fan of fluorescents for background screen and cyclorama lighting.

With either incandescent cyc lights or fluorescents, you may need to place a flag along the lights to keep the cyc light off the foreground subject. This is especially true if you need dark or contrasty lighting on your subject.

So how brightly illuminated should the background screen be? A little like Goldilocks and the Three Bears—not too hot, not too dim, *just right*! Exactly what will constitute "just right" will vary a bit depending on your keyer and the color you've chosen.

As a rule of thumb for chroma key blue and green, the lighting level should read at about 50 IRE on a waveform monitor when shot with the selected camera aperture. It should *certainly* be about a stop lower illumination than the foreground. There's a good reason for this. A too brightly illuminated background screen will increase the amount of spill on the foreground. *Spill* is a combination of reflected color (shiny skin or fabric actually reflecting green/blue from the backdrop) and *radiosity*, which is actually colored light emanating from the backing surface. As the subject gets closer to the illuminated screen, you will actually have green/blue light illuminating the back of the subject. The higher the light level, the more radiosity; at lower light levels, radiosity falls off pretty

The video signal is measured on two devices, a waveform monitor and a vectorscope. Both are specialized, calibrated versions of the oscilloscope. Very often, the two functions are combined in a single unit.

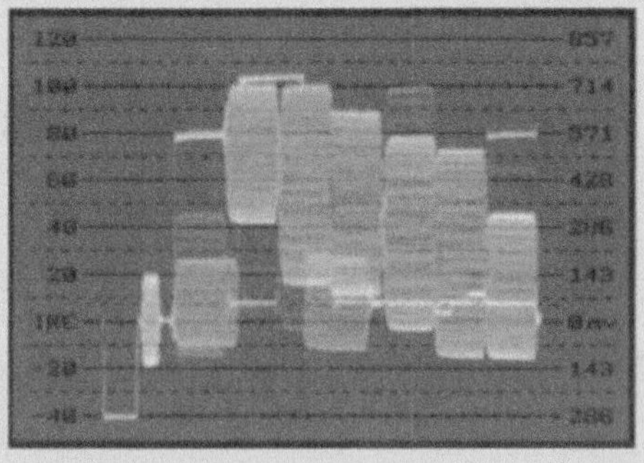

A waveform monitor displaying SMPTE color bars

The waveform monitor basically measures the varying voltage of the signal across each scan line. This accurately equates to the signal luminance, or monochrome brightness. Figure 2.2 shows the trace of a waveform monitor showing SMPTE color bars; Figure 2.3 shows a WFM displaying a sample of well-exposed

video. On the waveform monitor, the visual portion of the signal is measured from 0 to 100 units. This scale (traditionally known as IRE, after the Institute of Radio Engineers—now the Institute of Electronic Engineers) measures the range from black to full white. Actually, the US and a few other countries inject an oddity into this scale called pedestal or setup that calibrates black at 7.5 IRE in analog video. Digital video formats use 0 IRE black internally.

A waveform monitor displaying well-exposed video

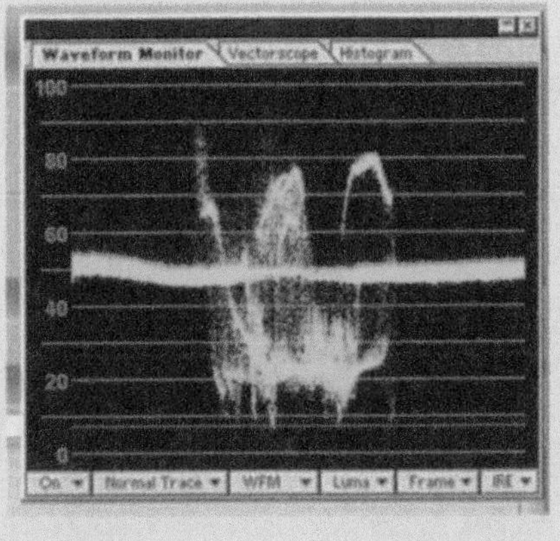

At the top of the range, 100 IRE should represent pure white. However, there is considerable headroom in the signal. Analog video formats will often display up to 120 IRE. However, digital formats will

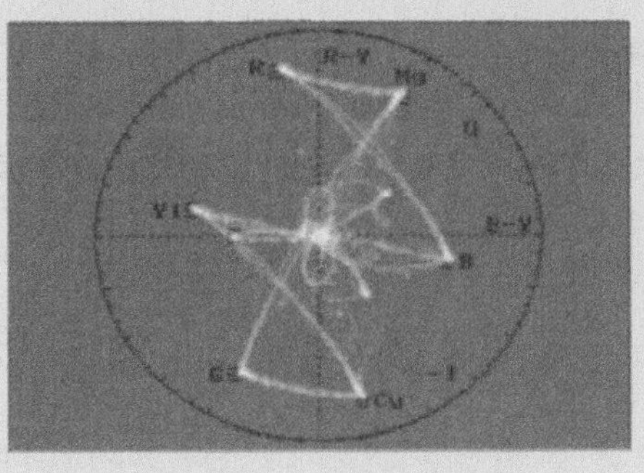

Vectorscope display of the SMPTE color bars; compare to waveform display in Figure 2.2.

clip at 110 IRE, the maximum level defined in the digital formats. This is important for lighting design, because it is essential to create a range of lighting that fits completely inside that compressed range. In other words, the hottest highlights ought to just kiss the 100 IRE mark, while the deepest shadows should just descend to 7.5 IRE, with most values falling somewhere in between.

The vectorscope works quite differently from the waveform monitor. Color in composite analog video is defined by the phase relationship of the portions of the signal; and that is what the vectorscope displays. You don't have to understand this, but it's a good idea to know what the display means. The phase of the signal is displayed by tracing vectors (hence the name "vectorscope") in different directions on the round display. In Figure 2.5, you'll see SMPTE color bars displayed on a vectorscope. The 75% saturation color chips draw peaks that fall within boxes known as targets. These are labeled (clockwise from top) Red, Magenta, Blue, Cyan, Green, and Yellow. The smaller target boxes labeled with lowercase letters are for the PAL system, which will display peaks in both boxes. You can tell that a video transmission is properly adjusted when these peaks fall in the targets of the vectorscope and the white and black levels display properly on the waveform monitor.

Reading a vectorscope is really pretty simple, though for some folks it takes a bit of getting used to. Remember that it displays color content only, not brightness. The more saturated (stronger) the color, the further from the center the vector trace. Washed-out desaturated colors will be closer to the center. Any traces that go outside of the outer circle are over limit and illegal. The one to watch most carefully is red, which will bleed terribly in analog displays. It's best to stay close to the 75% target with red, and not get too close to the outer perimeter.

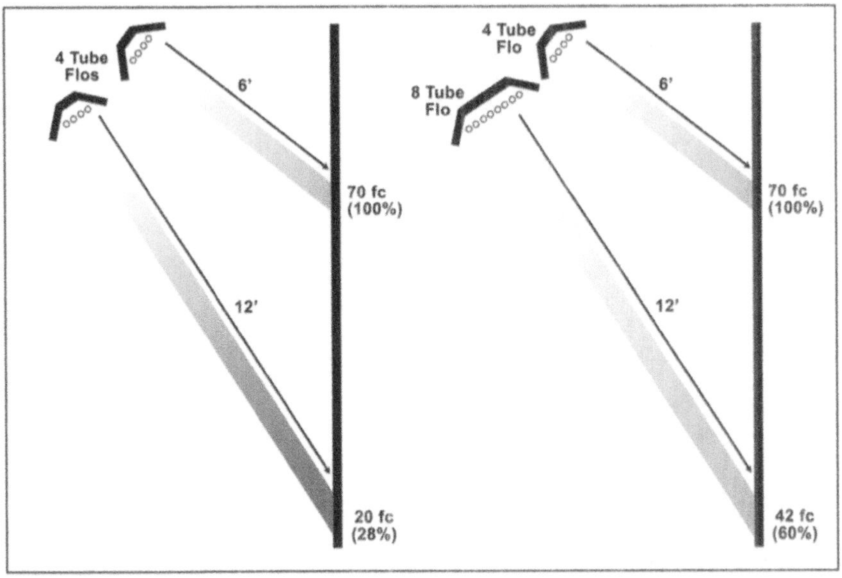

Figure 6.5 *On the left, note how the distance from each instrument affects the light level on the background screen. On the right, by changing the light power of each instrument in relation to necessary throw distance, we can produce a more even illumination of the background screen.*

quickly and isn't much of a problem at eight or ten feet. So you don't want the screen lit too hot.

But you don't want the backing lit at too low a level, either! At lower lighting/exposure levels, there can be a sharp increase in noise in the camera signal, which can create problems for the keyer in post. But additionally, a too-dark backing color becomes too close to shadowed areas of the foreground subject. There's less of a percentage difference between a green backing sample of RGB 12, 36, 14 and a dark gray foreground shadow of 15, 12, 18 than there is between that shadow and a solidly lit green backing sample of 24, 69, 32. The closer the backing sample gets to black, the more difficulty the keyer will have distinguishing it from shadows. It's a balancing act!

Now, the one situation where the suggested 50 IRE rule of thumb doesn't apply is when you are using an Ultimatte keyer and Ultimatte-approved paint or fabric. Ultimatte likes to have a slightly higher lighting level, approaching 70 IRE (I still tend to go under this a bit!) across the screen. This works in Ultimatte because of the company's sophisticated spill removal algorithm. But even with Ultimatte, it's still best not to have the subject standing too close to the background screen. If there is way too much spill on the subject, Ultimatte's software *will* still

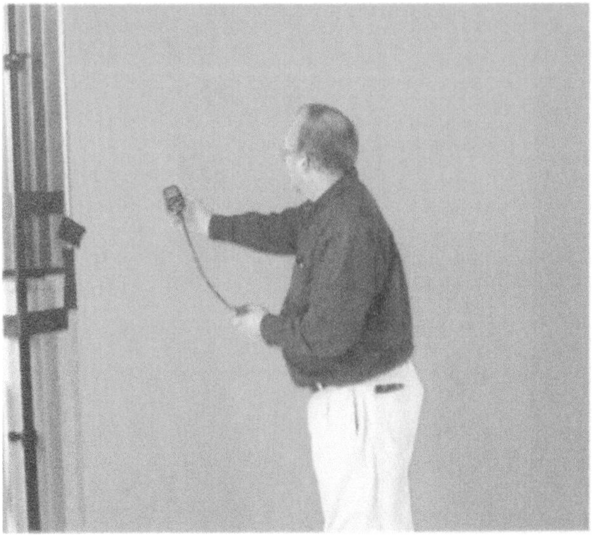

Figure 6.6 *The author measures the reflected light levels on a background screen with a light meter.*

remove it—but at the expense of shifting the color of the entire picture! No matter how good your keyer, it's *still* a balancing act!

If you are lighting a very large background screen—as in a soundstage—then you will need to use a somewhat more complex lighting strategy. Whether you are using incandescent or fluorescent instruments, each instrument can provide useful even illumination to only a portion of the large screen. Providing even lighting would be easy if we could position a network of fluorescents evenly across the surface of the background. But we can't do that, since many of them would have to be visible in the shot! Out of necessity, the lights must be above, below, or to the side—and so some of them will have to work at a greater distance than others.

The basic principle here is to use banks of instruments, each one illuminating a different area of the background screen, and overlapping enough to create an even illumination. This sounds easy enough, and it would be if not for that pesky inverse square rule! In the diagram below, note how distance affects the evenness of the lighting level.

As the distance doubles, the light output of the instrument must be increased to about four times the original power to produce an equal incident illumination on the screen. This can be done a couple of different ways, either by using more powerful instruments or by using multiple instruments trained on the same area of the screen. Care must be taken in the overlapping of the output of the instruments, since it is easy to produce dark areas by not overlapping enough, or hot spots where two instruments overlap too much!

The one situation where you can position fluorescents evenly across a screen is when the screen is backlit. This is typically a blue or green translucent plexiglass, and can be a very effective solution, but one that is difficult to do in a large-scale setup.

Checking the Evenness of the Lighting

So how can you tell when you've succeeded in achieving even illumination of the background screen? With a measuring device, of course.

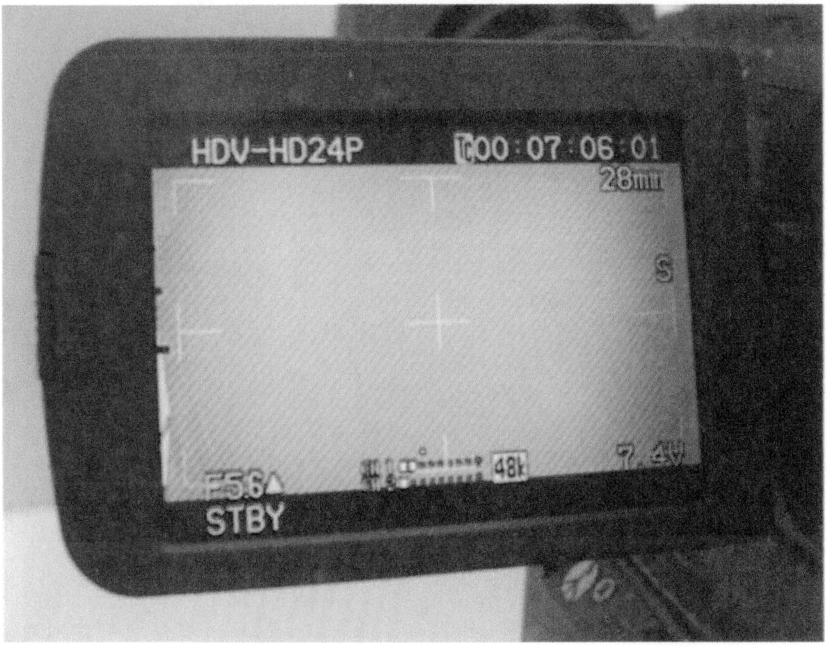

Figure 6.7 *The zebra display in the LCD viewfinder shows areas of brightness and where the background is too dark.*

"Eyeballing" it is not the best strategy unless your eyeballs have a *lot* of experience! There are three easy ways to measure the light on your background screen, depending on which technology you have available: with a lightmeter, a waveform monitor, or the zebra display in your camera.

To measure with a lightmeter, you can use either an incident or spot meter. If you use an incident meter (which measures the light falling on the screen directly), you'll have to take readings every few feet across the background screen. Although the idea is to get the lighting as close as humanly possible to even, don't be obsessive about it—perfection is simply not possible with a front-lit screen! If the variation is within a quarter or half-stop, you will have done quite well. If the variation is a full

Figure 6.8 *Phony as a three-dollar bill! A dramatically lit subject composited in front of a background plate that has fairly flat lighting. In the top image, the author looks like he's lit by a spotlight while everyone else around this fountain in Rome is lit by low-level indirect light. When the lighting is designed to match the background plate (below), it's not nearly as dramatic-looking, but it will look realistic when the author walks by the fountain. Background image courtesy of Wayne Jacobs, www.backgroundplates.com.*

stop or more, you probably need to do some more tweaking. Remember that a full stop represents a halving of the light level. If you use a spot meter (which measures a small area of reflected light) you can simply stand in the camera position and point the meter at different areas of the screen, while observing the readings.

Using a waveform monitor (WFM) is actually the easiest method in my opinion. Take a look at the WFM in the sidebar—you can easily see the evenly lit bar through the middle that represents the evenly lit color background. If the lighting is uneven, this line will dip in darker areas and spike in brighter areas. It's easy to see where light needs to be adjusted.

If you have a WFM in your studio, set up a camera shot that encompasses the entire background screen, or as much of it as you can get in the shot. Now select the exposure (f-stop) you are going to use for the shots. Observe the signal on the WFM, preferably with the chroma removed—this is usually called the *Low Pass* setting, which strips out the color subcarrier from the signal. In this mode, the WFM gives an accurate reading of the voltage of the luminance component of the signal. The WFM should read between 45 and 55 IRE all the way across if you've done a really good job. To check the vertical evenness of light level, set the WFM to measure a single line and then sweep through the

Figure 6.9 *Another phony shot—this one showing a subject with key lighting coming from the wrong side so the shadows are reversed between foreground and background. This can sometimes—certainly not always—be fixed by flipping the footage (below). Background image courtesy of Wayne Jacobs, www.backgroundplates.com.*

486 lines of the signal. This will show variations in illumination from top to bottom.

If you don't have either a lightmeter or a waveform monitor, but your camera has a zebra display in the viewfinder, you can use that to measure the lighting on the background screen. Turn on the zebra display and check which setting you are using—70–90 zebra or 100 zebra. The first triggers the zebra display at 70 IRE and turns it off at 90 IRE; this is typically used to bracket exposure on faces. The second triggers the zebra display at 100 IRE to indicate an overlimit signal. The exact "on" and "off" levels are adjustable on many pro cameras. Set the camera up as described above, except you will now open the iris wider than the intended exposure until you just trigger the zebra display. This will show angled black and white stripes on the "hottest" area of the picture, with darker areas showing no zebra. This will show visually the areas that need to be punched up a bit. In an optimal situation, the zebras will blossom across a lot of the screen quite suddenly as you open up the iris, and then will cover the entire screen when you open up just a tiny bit more—perhaps 1/4 stop. If you have to open a full stop to get the entire screen filled with zebra pattern, the lighting isn't even enough and needs to be fixed.

Figure 6.10 *Key and fill lighting by themselves leave the subject seeming rather flat (left); and the lack of white illumination from the rear means that spill may be prominent from the background screen. When backlight is added (right), the spill is killed and the subject seems more dimensional.*

Once you're happy with the illumination of the background, it's time to move to the lighting of the foreground subjects. We've spent a lot of effort making sure that the lighting on the background is even—but generally, this should *not* be the case with the foreground. This is an important point because many people have the mistaken impression that both the background and the foreground must be flat-lit for effective keying. In fact, the goal is to make the lighting of the *foreground match the lighting of the background plate* (the new background that will digitally replace the greenscreen) as much as possible. If the foreground subject is flat-lit and the background plate is lit like film noir, the composited results are going to look very phony indeed!

The first issue is the position of the subject(s) in relation to the greenscreen. *Please note that this bears no relation to the subject's apparent position to the backing plate*, which can be anything you want. If the subject is too close to the screen, you'll have trouble with spill on the subject and shadows on the background screen. Spill refers to areas of the backing color showing up on the foreground subject. Spill occurs in two ways, through reflection (the subject's shiny forehead actually is reflecting the background at an incident angle) and through radiosity (green or blue light actually bounced from the background and radiating onto the subject from the rear). Radiosity spill is most dramatic close to

Figure 6.11 *Using a gel that is the opposite of the backing color on the backlight or kicker can help counteract spill on the subject. The saturation of the gel (for instance, 1/4 minusgreen or 1/2 minusgreen for a green backing) should be selected in proportion to the amount of spill observed on the foreground subject.*

the screen, and when the screen is overlit. That's one of the reasons you usually don't want the screen reading at 70–75 IRE. If the lighting level on the screen is appropriate, and the subject is at least six to eight feet away from the background, radiosity spill will be dramatically reduced. We'll deal with reflections a little later. But also, if the subject is separated from the background by a few feet, you won't be troubled by its shadow intruding onto the background in the shot. While most software can handle shadows (either making them invisible or making them apparent on the background plate), most often it is best not to have shadows on the wall portion of the greenscreen.

Start by positioning the key light. To do this, you first have to look at the planned backing plate or have some role in creating it later. Where is the principal light coming from? It's going to look silly if the shadows lie in one direction in the background plate and the key light is obviously on the wrong side on your foreground subject. Set the key to more or less match the apparent main illumination in the background plate. The quality of the light (hard or soft) should also match the quality of the main illumination in the background plate. Is it harsh sunlight? Is it soft interior light? Moonlight? Make sure it matches!

Now, add fill light to match the level of contrast found in the background plate. Is the background very contrasty? Then you'll want a fairly low level of fill. Is it only moderately contrasty? More fill. As you might imagine, this is all easier to "eyeball" if you actually have the finished background plate available to you in the greenscreen studio. The precise direction the fill is coming from is less critical than the direction of the key light, but it ought to also match the lighting of the background plate. In many cases, the fill will need to be very diffused—so a soft bank or fluorescent would be a good choice. You can also use a hard light bounced off of a large white card or shot through a large sheet of diffusion material.

Now add the bits that separate the pros from the amateurs: backlight and a kicker or sidelight. These serve the same function that they would in a normal shot, to help separate the subject from the background and bring out detail that would otherwise be lost. But they serve an extra function here—helping to minimize spill. Pros will tend to use a bit more sidelight in bluescreen than they might in normal settings.

Here's a neat trick that will help counteract spill: gel the backlight with the opposite color of the background you are using. In other words, if you are using a green background, gel with a minus green (magenta) gel. If you're using a blue background, gel with yellow or straw. While this may look out of place to your eye (especially from other angles than the camera view), the colors will mix to seem neutral to the camera. *Do not use this trick if you are using one of Ultimatte's keyers*, since it will mess up their excellent spill removal algorithm.

It is worthy of note that while this backlighting trick is quite effective and commonly used, some professional visual effects artists prefer to avoid it. They have very sophisticated spill removal tools in their digital toolkit that can counteract the spill without it; and they complain that the backlight draws the eye unnecessarily to the "seam" between foreground and background in the composite—a seam they are trying to make as invisible as technologically possible.

Now, finally, you have to deal with those areas of spill that are caused by reflection. This can happen with shiny skin, shiny hair, or shiny fabric in costumes. If the reflection is too strong, it will literally cause that part of the subject to become transparent in post. So you must keep a keen eye out for these reflections and fix them *in production*. Do not assume they can be fixed in post—they can, but only with hours of tedious labor! It's always better to take ten extra minutes in production than many hours in post. Both shiny skin and hair can be dealt with through a light dose of the right tone of powder. If the skin is getting shiny due to a film of

Figure 6.12 *An example of luma keying in front of a black background. This works only if no area of the subject is darker than about 35 IRE. There are spots on this frame that may be problems since they are too close to the minimum.*

sweat, frequent breaks to dry off and repeated applications of makeup touch-up and powder will be needed. Remember how I harped in the last chapter on the heavy-duty HVAC you'd need in a studio? The heat build-up from lights will soon have your actors bathed in sweat if it's not efficiently and quietly removed—and that may create reflections of the backing color that will cause real difficulties in post. Make sure you watch the subject move through his or her entire range of motion, watching potential problem areas carefully: hair, forehead, fabric on shoulders. The only solution for shiny fabric is not to use it, so I hope that has been factored into the costuming process!

Lighting for Luma Keying

Up to this point, we've talked mostly about the specifics of lighting for some variation of color keying. That's because these are the most commonly used techniques. However, there are circumstances where *luma keying* can work better than chroma keying. In luma (or luminance) keying the background is either white or black. Very specifically, these are situations where the foreground subject can be lit with moderate contrast with no hot spots (for a white background) or extremely dark areas (for a black background). White or light clothing is obviously out of the question for a white background, and dark clothing—or film noir–style lighting—is out of the question for a black background. However, if you have a situation that fits in those parameters, luma keying can work pretty well, if it's approached with sufficient care.

Figure 6.13 *This luma keying example in front of a white screen works because the author has medium or dark clothing and no overexposed hot spots. A white shirt would render this shot unusable; reflections on the author's glasses will also become "holes."*

In fact, if you're shooting in a highly compressed format like DV or HDV, luma keying can be a real friend in the right circumstances. That's because while those formats only sample some of the chroma, they sample all of the luminance in a picture. So it's easier to get an accurate clean key without complex interpolation and smoothing algorithms with luma keying. If, that is, you can make the other issues work.

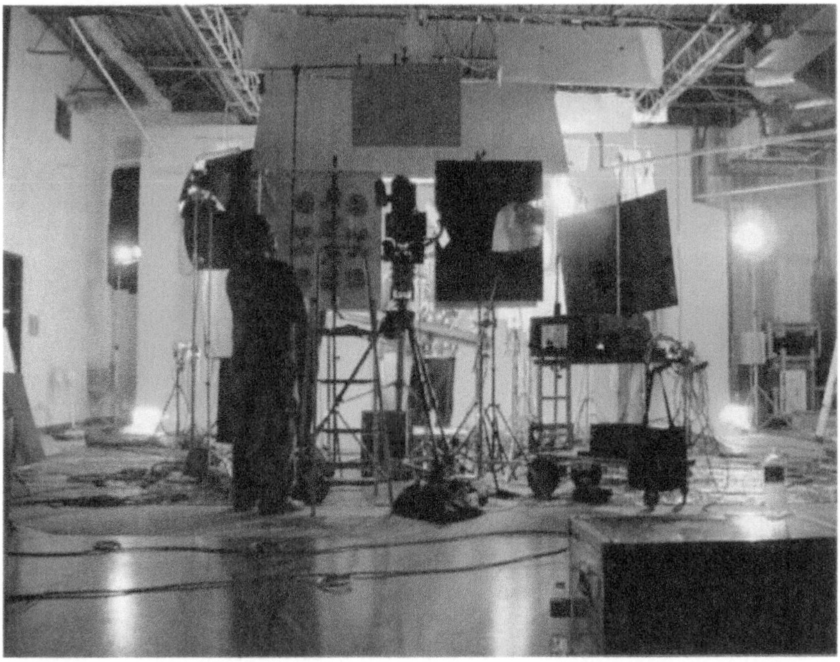

Figure 6.14 *The use of side and backlights in greenscreen work often also involves the use of a lot of flags to keep direct light out of the lens. Here Director of Photography D. A. Oldis uses a Thomson Viper camera to capture full HD video for PostHoles® prematted video clips. Note the use of fluorescent worklights to even out the lighting on the green floor. Photo courtesy of Leading Edge Video and PostHoles®, www.postholes.com.*

Let's set up two examples, first using a black background. Black backgrounds are easier to come by than blue or green; all you need is some dark fabric (it doesn't even have to be black!) in a light-controlled situation. In other words, there can't be any stray uncontrolled light sources such as windows. It's phenomenally easy to create an absolutely inky black background. All you have to do is not to put any light on it while properly lighting the foreground! When your exposure is set properly, the black background will fade into nothingness. Ah—one other secret. You have to have some space (eight to ten feet) between the subject and the background so that you have space to light the foreground fully while keeping all light off the background. If the background is right behind the subject, you'll have light on it and it won't be the solid black you need—rather it will be some shade of dark gray.

If you light the foreground subject professionally (be sure to use a backlight or kicker) *and* set the exposure correctly on the camera, *and* the subject is not wearing a navy blazer or Goth clothing, *and* does not

Figure 6.15 *Subtle lighting effects like the shadows cast on the foreground subject in this composite help to "sell" the integration of foreground and background. Background plate "Temple of Doom" courtesy of Patterlini Benoit.*

have black or very dark brown hair, you'll be able to pull a pretty nice luma key from the shot. Whoops, you have a subject with a blue blazer? And she has black hair? Suddenly you understand why chroma keying is vastly preferred over luma keying.

Okay, fine. You're stuck with the dark blue blazer and black hair. So let's set up a luma key in front of a white screen. Here you have the opposite situation. The white screen must be *very* evenly and brightly lit; any areas of shadow on the background will have to be clipped out of the later keying process. Sometimes this can be done with a garbage matte if the shadow is at an edge or corner, but usually those shadows will require you to key out a larger and larger range at the top end of the grayscale. This will quickly reach a point where you're punching transparent holes in your foreground subject as well! In this situation, however, the background can be lit so that it is actually overlimit for the camera (110–115 IRE) and you hit digital clipping, which will render the entire area a solid white (255, 255, 255 in RGB terms). This would be a no-no for a normal shot, but in this case it can work. But it's still a balancing act—you *don't* want the white background so overlit that it creates white reflections on your subject, as these will become transparent in post.

Once you've successfully lit your white screen, light the subject in a professional manner. Actually, since we're going to be keying out only the brightest values (say, everything above 240, 240, 240) and the darker values don't matter, you can have dark shadows, blue blazers, or black hair on this subject. The one thing you can't have is any hot highlight, white costume, or even light pastel color! Because of the strong spill from the lit white background, you may find you don't need much in the way of a backlight or kicker. Just a bit will do, and it's a mighty fine time to experiment with a color gel for the kicker, too!

Ah, whoops—you forgot that she has to be talking to a man wearing a white shirt! Odds bodkins, it's back to chroma keying! You can see from these examples that luma keying has definite limitations, and that's why most productions will use some version of color-based keying.

A Final Word About Lighting

As you experiment with lighting for blue or greenscreen, don't make the mistake of overlooking a problem and hoping you can fix it in post! Though the technology has come a long way, color compositing is still an imperfect balancing act of many compromises. There are plenty of factors (uneven background lighting, unexpected reflections, poor color choices) that can cause nightmares in the post process. You need to work to get the front-end production done as cleanly and as nearly perfect as you can, so that the necessary compromises in post won't be thrown off by unnecessary compromises made in the studio! And never overlook details in lighting effects that will help to tie the foreground subject together with the composited background. Little details, which may range from shadows that appear to originate from an object in the background or a touch of blue light from a window to orange light from a setting sun, help to "sell" the effect as much as clean compositing and convincing sound effects.

Finally, don't overlook *interactive lighting* in a scene. If the lighting in the background plate changes for some reason, *so must the lighting in the foreground plate!* If a meteor rockets by in the scene, there must be some change in the foreground to reflect that or the composite will just shout "fake!" When Buck Dodgers fires his ray gun in a darkened room, surely some light from the ray should illuminate his face from below; and of course, that light should be the same color as the ray itself. During shots of light saber battles in the *Star Wars* movies, lighting grips were just outside the shot swinging around appropriately colored fluorescents mounted to 1" x 4" boards to simulate the interactive light that would fall on the subjects from the interplay of the light sabers. This may be a subtle touch, but it is just this sort of touch that will put the shot over the line from "something's not right" to "that works!" While interactive lighting changes can sometimes be faked in post, it is never as good or as convincing as when the effect is planned and created in live production.

Costuming and Art Design for Color-Based Compositing

7

Professional compositors who spend their days in dark rooms trying to create new realities out of unrelated background plates and color screen shots have many horror stories. No matter how clear they have been with the other people involved in the production, it is almost always the case that one or more shots has violated a basic rule of production for color keying, either in lighting or design, in costuming, or simply in poor execution. The director, producer, and director of photography (DP)—indeed all the production staff—must understand that color-based compositing is a nasty tightrope of compromises that must be respected in every shot. Breaking the rules costs money and time and may render the best acting take unusable in post.

So as we turn our attention to the areas of costuming and art design, I'll start off with my favorite horror story. Years ago, I did the special effects for a TV pilot (which shall remain nameless) that required a number of greenscreen shots. The production team met in New York for preproduction planning, where each department weighed in on their special needs and issues. I explained the difficulties and challenges of greenscreen compositing and made very clear that there could be no green or green tones in any of the costumes of the characters involved in the greenscreen shots. I explained in pretty terrifying detail how a mistake in this area could explode the budget in post and render some shots unusable. I went over the lighting requirements with the DP, and double-checked that the designer and the director were quite clear about the issues. "OK, got it. Nothing remotely green in the costumes," said the director.

When I arrived on the live set, I was horrified to see that one of the principals had on an aqua blouse—aqua with more green in it than blue! Ten days of shooting were already in the can, and there was no way the costume could be changed at this point. I hauled the director aside in a private corner and had a quiet little conniption. "But it's not green," she said. "It's blue!" I tried to explain that they had picked the exact color for the blouse that would cause the most difficulty in either a green *or* bluescreen shot—and at that point we had already contracted with a greenscreen studio for the next week's effects shots. Once she understood the problem, she was quite apologetic—but there was nothing anyone could do at that point without seriously damaging the budget. So we went ahead and shot in the green studio with the aqua blouse. The studio owner was helpful and pointed out the color problem to me. "You know that's gonna be tough in post!" he said. "Why'd you pick that color?" I growled something grumpy.

Those days the software wasn't nearly as good as we have today, and so "tough" didn't really describe it. I was able to pull decent mattes (well, acceptable mattes that weren't absolutely horrid) on most of the shots without terrible trouble. But then I got to the scenes that just wouldn't work: a scene where each of the actors had to plunge through a magical portal, and then the matching scene where they came out the other side. In these scenes, during the motion toward and then out of the imaginary portal, the girl wearing the aqua blouse would develop a whopping great hole through her middle at the ideal matte settings for the rest of the scene. Adjusting the matte settings to fix the hole inevitably resulted in either fringes in other areas or loss of edges of other foreground subjects. After several abortive passes at different settings, I finally decided that the hole in the middle was easier to fix manually than edge issues on the other actors. So I pulled mattes for both scenes with a hole right through the girl's stomach—and then went back and hand-painted in the holes in every one of about 258 fields. More fun than crawling through the sewers of Paris, sure, but a tedious exercise I'll never forget. I learned to insist on having approval of costumes—and foreground set design—for any color compositing production.

By the way, the rest of that show was pretty nicely done; the directing was great, the other special effects worked dandy, and the child actors were a joy to work with. It was just that little glitch that marred the work I had to do in post.

Now, this was well over a decade ago and the software has improved tremendously in intervening years—and I have that many more years' experience at workarounds and matte doctoring. Some of the current software plugins could probably have pulled a fairly clean matte from that footage; and if they didn't, motion tracking has improved so much that it would be simple to motion-track a fix over any remaining hole. But the lesson is still valid even if we have better tools: don't assume that the art director or costume designer understands the technical requirements of color compositing! It's far better to be pushy in the early planning stages to make sure your technical requirements are respected than to fudge in post. Actually, this rule holds true for any of the production specialties, but it is especially true here. The more carefully you can control the parameters in the live shoot, the easier your job will be in post.

Horror stories aside, this principle applies not just to costuming but to a whole range of art direction and design decisions. Many of these are color selection decisions, but some extend to decisions about the texture and finish of set and prop materials as well.

Take a look at the color wheel here. This is a traditional way of visualizing which colors act as opposites—in lighting (transmissive or additive) terms, which colors would combine to form a near-white light. Of course, this works differently for reflective (absorptive or subtractive) colors where the opposites will make a muddy black. You don't have to select colors that are the opposite of your background screen, just colors that are not too close to the background color on the wheel. For instance, it is fine to use purple as a costuming or foreground set color when using a blue background; but as that color gets closer to a bluish-purple, pulling a careful clean matte will start to become more challenging. This fact will be aggravated by the fact that video systems often have difficulty reproducing purple well, and will often render them bluer than they actually are.

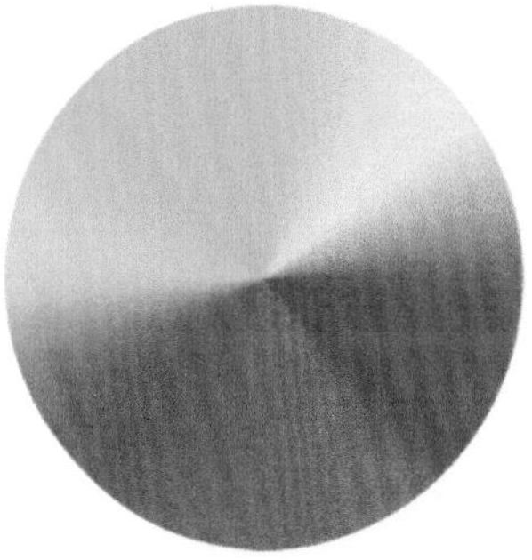

Figure 7.1 *A color wheel shows the relationship between complementary colors.*

It is at this point that lots of experienced compositors will be champing at the bit to tell victory stories—about how they pulled a clean matte with a blue costume in front of a bluescreen, and it looked just great. These are sort of the opposite of horror stories (some folks call them "hero stories"), and you'll hear a bunch of these from veteran compositors as well, because they're proud of the work they did on a difficult or even seemingly impossible shot. And those stories are true too! With better algorithms, 10-bit color, and advanced digital signal processing, we can make keys work today that would have been impossible a few years back. But the point I'm trying to make is that no matter how great your software and your working skills and technical trickery, *you'll still get a better end product if you're not skirting the edge of impossibility.* Careful art design and color choice in production will make the post process vastly easier and cleaner for the compositor.

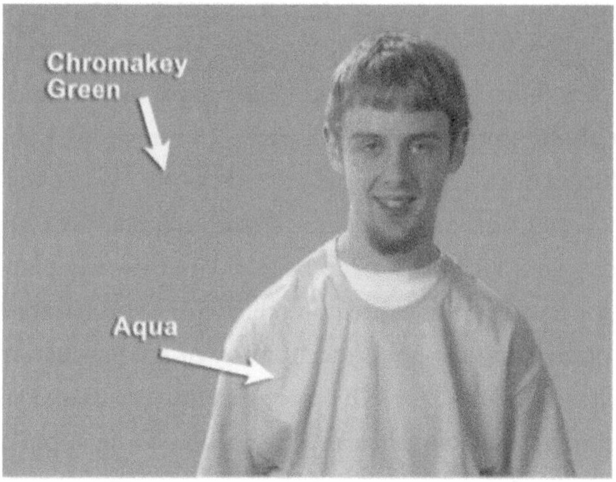

***Figure 7.2** An aqua shirt in front of a greenscreen might work if there are no other challenges—but it's close enough to the green backing to be a real test! Try this out—the file on the demo DVD is* aqua_grn.mov. *Attempt to pull a clean matte with crisp edges and no translucency to the shirt. You will probably be able to find a compromise that works, but it will be tough!*

Blue or Green—or Red?

So let's look at some of the color choices that must be made on a regular basis. These don't just involve costume and sets, but also the selection of which background color to use for a given scene. Let's actually start with that logic, since it usually involves colors we can't change—blonde hair or green bushes, for example.

In our online forums at DV.com, I'm often asked whether blue or green is a better choice for digital compositing. There's been a myth floated around internet forums (imagine that!) that green is substantially better for DV than blue, because the luminance (which is sampled for every pixel) is derived from the green channel. The logic sounds good, but is a fundamental misunderstanding. Actually, the green channel is extracted from the fully sampled luminance channel by a differencing of the blue and red channels in component video (Y, Y-R, Y-B); it does not mean that there is significantly more information in the green channel. Green has a tiny advantage over blue mathematically, but it is not substantial enough to override other color-based decisions, which must take precedence.

For example, it is fairly common practice now to shoot "outdoor" scenes on a soundstage with shrubbery, grass, and even trees in the foreground, with a bluescreen background, so that sky and clouds can be composited in later. Obviously, in this case a substantial amount of foreground material must be green—what other color can shrubs and bushes be?—and so it could be a real mistake to try and use a green background here, especially if some of the shrubbery is a light green. We can't and shouldn't change the color of the bushes (well, I suppose it might work in a sci-fi flick set on the planet Crustacia), so we may lean toward selecting blue or even red as the background color. This isn't a hard-and-fast rule, as you'll see when we get to the luminance exceptions below!

Another situation where blue is typically preferred as a background is when there is an actor with blonde hair. While it's not impossible to key blonde hair against green, it is slightly more difficult, since yellow is a strong component of green. But look at the color wheel—yellow is on the opposite side of the wheel from blue, so it will key much more easily. Actually, while this "blonde hair/bluescreen" rule of thumb is pretty commonly practiced, I haven't had that much difficulty using blondes in front of greenscreens. Some of these rules, while factually correct in their theory, actually are bent a lot in practice these days. They date back to the early analog chroma keyers, which were pretty much blunt instruments that needed as much help as they could get.

Conversely, if costumes or foreground sets must contain a lot of blue or near-blue tones, then a green (or red) background is the clear choice. There are instances when blue eyes will cause problems with a blue background, though it's not as much of a problem as the stories make it seem.

One great example of this problem is in the final sequences of the movie *Dragonslayer*, where Ralph Richardson's eyes turn white during close-

***Figure 7.3** Traditionally, it's considered best to place blonde subjects in front of a bluescreen (right), but a greenscreen is workable (left) if there are no other challenges—like an aqua blouse! Try this out—the files on the demo DVD are* blond_bl.mov *and* blond_gr.mov.

ups. The problem would only show up in close-ups, when it would be easy enough to fix the problem with a reverse garbage matte, or simply place a small greenscreen behind the subject for those tight shots. A pair of blue eyes probably shouldn't drive the decision—but a blue costume or lighting like they use in the CSI lab should!

In these examples, I've listed red as a second option. While certainly a usable color for background, it is less preferred for most situations because human skin contains a fair dose of red; skin tones typically have very little blue or green—unless the subject is about to be violently ill! Since human skin (whether pink, light brown, or dark brown) is a constant that we must accommodate, blue and green are the first choices. So when would you use red for preference? Typically in a scene where you have tones of both blue and green, or near colors in the foreground.

Selecting Foreground Colors

Okay, you've decided on a color for the background screen based on colors in the foreground that you can't or don't want to change. Now you need to select the palette of other colors that will be used in costumes and set pieces. By now you've probably gotten the idea—select colors that are on the opposite side of the color wheel from your background color. If you are using a greenscreen, then you have a whole range of blues, purples, reds, browns, and oranges to choose from. If you're using a bluescreen, then the range includes reds, oranges, yellows, greens, browns, and so on.

Aside from the color (chrominance) of the fabric, there's another issue to consider, and that is the brightness value, or luminance, of the fabric color. This is a factor when you have to use a color that is close to the background in chrominance. Bear in mind that most digital keyers use a fairly complex set of criteria to select the pixels to render as transparent or semi-transparent by way of the matte. While this is not true of all keyers, most will start from a limited color range defined by the operator—and the color range includes *both* chrominance and luminance information. Thus "close" colors that are significantly darker than the background color will not cause problems because they will be outside of the luminance range that the keyer is using to select transparency.

Let's look at an example. Suppose you are stuck using a greenscreen studio because that's what you've got available—and some part of the foreground simple must be green, such as a bush or some other sort of plant. As long as the color of the plant is significantly darker than the green of the background, most keyers will handle the task without a problem. Dark green boxwood will key just fine in front of properly lit Ultimatte green, for instance. The one exception to this rule is in very simple color subtraction keyers, which may subtract a substantial amount of the green tone from the plant, leaving you with brownish leaves. Most modern keyers, even those based on color subtraction, get around this problem without breaking a sweat. Back to my horror story at the start of the chapter—the aqua blouse was a disaster not only because it contained too much green, but because its luminance value was also very close to that of the background.

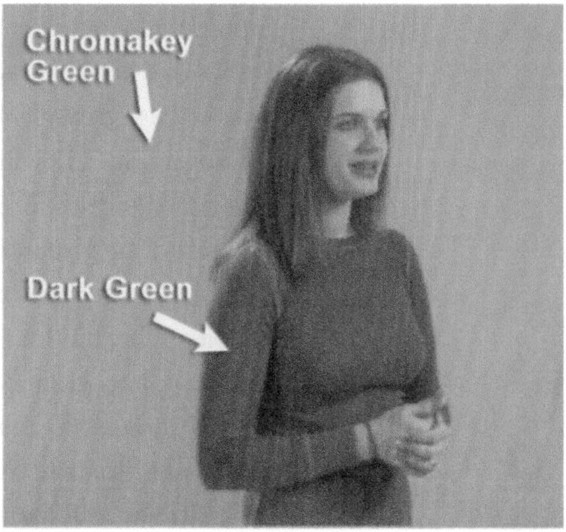

Figure 7.4 *Dark green in front of a greenscreen may be quite workable due to the luminance value difference. Try this out; the file is* dark_grn.mov.

However—having reassured you about the power of modern keyers and how easy it can be to use dark green and blonde in front of green, let me go back to my warnings earlier in the book. Pulling mattes is like walking a tightrope. Each cheat that requires careful tweaking of the keyer adds up. Cheat too much, and eventually there will be one that will make you fall off that tightrope—that's the one that leaves a big hole in the middle of your star's blouse! Careful craftsmanship requires that you not push the limits too far or in too many directions. Any shadows or underlit areas on your screen will cause problems with foliage or dark green wardrobe. The *lowest* luminance value on the screen must always exceed the *highest* luminance value (highlight) in any greenery or wardrobe item in the foreground—and prudence requires that it exceed it by a substantial amount!

Non-color Factors

Color issues aren't the only ones that have to be carefully watched in production design. The other factor that must be watched carefully is that of *reflectivity*. You simply can't have shiny, reflective props and set pieces in a color screen situation! Why? Because the main thing the prop or set piece will reflect is that whacking great huge brightly lit green or bluescreen! And when that happens, the portion of the table or phaser or antique book will suddenly develop a hole where the digitally composited background will show through.

Look at Fig 7.5, where a table with a highly polished surface has been positioned in front of a greenscreen. The horizontal surface of the table will reflect the greenscreen perfectly from almost any camera angle—and thus the top surface of the table will become transparent in the matte. Set pieces like this must be designed with matte (dull) finish so they don't reflect the background color. In fact, there are cases (especially with horizontal surfaces like tabletops) where even a matte finish will give too much reflection and angles will have to be carefully chosen to minimize the reflection. Similarly, manufactured props also need to have a dull finish. If the prop is supposed to be shiny, it's not unusual to create a shiny one for close-ups and a dull-finished duplicate for use in wider shots.

Of course, not all props are manufactured. If the actor must pick up a real book that has a shiny cover, there are a couple of approaches that work. One is that the shine can be knocked off the cover with dulling spray. The other is that angles and "business" with the book must be carefully planned to avoid actions or positions that will catch the reflection of the background.

Figure 7.5 *Here a table with a shiny finish has been used in front of a greenscreen. The reflective top picks up the green and is rendered as transparent in the final composite (left).*

Shiny props can't always be avoided, so when using them someone must be watching the monitor like a hawk, looking specifically for color reflections that will mar the post process. Those reflections can come in surprising ways in some situations. When I was testing the first incarnation of the Reflec® fabric with an LED ring that fits around the camera lens, I discovered that any shiny object would bounce back the light from the LED ring and become transparent. A shiny CD held up by the talent would become a transparent disc at certain angles. If the talent wore glasses that didn't have antireflective coating, the glasses would show a transparent spot. A glass of beverage would always have a little hole in it. That particular setup, which works well for head-and-shoulders interviews, has peculiar problems that are different from the standard color background!

The reflectivity factor is also important in selecting fabrics for costuming. You don't want to use shiny-finish fabrics such as silks or rayons in costuming, since they will invariably create the same problem by reflecting the background color. Duller-finish fabrics are always preferred.

Ah, but there's one more area where reflectivity comes into play—on the talent! Too-shiny hair or perspiration on a forehead can also catch

reflections of color background and create momentary holes. Watch out for shiny noses, foreheads, and cheeks—and avoid using shiny hairdos for shoots in front of a color background. Make sure that someone is present at all times with translucent powder and a brush to take the gloss off the talent's face!

Figure 7.6 *The heat is up in the studio, a bit of sweat has broken out on the talent's brow—and a part of his forehead has reflected enough green to become transparent!*

Figure 7.7 *Here Director of Photography D. A. Oldis uses a Thomson Viper camera to capture full HD video for PostHoles® prematted video clips. Note the use of fluorescent worklights to even out the lighting on the green floor. Photo courtesy of Leading Edge Video and PostHoles® www.postholes.com.*

Video Format Problems

8

Up to this point in the book we've talked about compositing and production issues from an almost analog perspective. We've talked about color, lighting, reflection, and production issues. These issues apply to all compositing, whether it is analog video, digital video, or film. But now we need to talk about the special issues that digital video formats (and their respective color sampling schemes) bring to the table. Digital technology has brought amazing advances to the field of compositing but has also brought some new problems that didn't exist in the analog world. While pure uncompressed digital video is a joy in postproduction, uncompressed full color video is not often what we deal with in the real world. In the real world, we not only have to deal with production shortcomings, but also with the challenges presented by real video formats in common use today. To understand the effects of compression and color sampling on our craft we need to understand a little bit about how digital video works.

Standard definition video in 8 bits creates a raw data stream that is over 30 megabytes per second (MB/sec). While we certainly have developed hard disk arrays and memory technology in recent years that can record and play back this data rate, it is definitely stretching the limit of most computer systems, disk storage systems, and certainly tape recording systems to accumulate this much data. For that reason almost every videotape format involves a heavy amount of compression and data removal. Let's take a look at how this works.

For standard definition using ITUR 601 video in a format such as Digital BetaCam, there are several stages of compression, or data reduction. In the camera, when the signal comes off the CCD imaging chips, it is basically in analog RGB (red/green/blue) signal. Each channel contains full video data for each pixel in the picture for that color. The first step in data reduction comes through conversion to the YIQ/YUV color space (see sidebar).

Broadcast TV and most digital video formats use a color space based on luminance and chrominance, which correspond to brightness and color. These color spaces are denoted as YUV and YIQ, both of which allow the transmission of full color and luminance information in a much smaller bandwidth than an RGB signal demands. The YUV space is used for the PAL broadcast television system used in Europe and the YIQ color space is used for the NTSC broadcast standard in North America. The two methods are nearly identical, using slightly different equations to transform to and from RGB color space. In both systems, Y is the luminance (brightness) component and the I and Q (or U and V) are the chrominance (color) components. These are the variables that are changed by the brightness, color, and tint controls on an NTSC television (the PAL system does not allow user adjustment of these in display).

The principal advantage of using YUV or YIQ for broadcast is that the amount of information needed to define a quality color television image is greatly reduced. However, this compression restricts the color range in these images. Many colors that appear on a computer display cannot be recreated on a television screen due to the limits of the YUV and YIQ standards.

Many video devices label inputs "Y Cr Cb," a designation that makes it easier to identify appropriate cables; and most video professionals will refer to "YUV" even when talking about the NTSC system, even though this is not technically correct. Very rarely will you hear anyone but video engineers refer to the NTSC system color space by its correct designation, "YIQ."

The RGB analog signal is converted to YUV color space, which significantly reduces the bandwidth of the analog signal, though the full-resolution video still contains luminance information and chrominance information for every pixel. This is referred to as uncompressed or 4:4:4 video. The YUV signal is then run through an A-to-D (analog-to-digital) converter, which converts it into a digital data stream of ones and zeros. This full-resolution data stream is manipulated by the DSP (digital signal processing) unit prior to data removal and compression. The digital data at this point has been reduced by about a third, to around 20 Mb per second.

The first step to reducing the data stream to a level that can be handled with inexpensive tape recording technology is known as *color decimation*. In this step the portion of the signal that records color data is reduced, usually to 1/2 or 1/4 of its original full sampling value. This can be done without significantly affecting the visual quality of the picture because the human eye is not as sensitive to color detail information as it is to luminance detail information. Most of our perception of detail comes not from the color channel but from the luminance channel (grayscale, or brightness) information in the picture. In ITUR 601 video, for instance, the color sampling will be reduced to half its original data. After the color decimation, the resulting reduced data stream is compressed using one of several methods of digital data compression before being recorded to tape. The resulting data stream has been reduced often by a factor of anywhere from 5:1 or even 8:1 or more before it is recorded to tape.

The various color decimation and data compression schemes that are used in different digital video formats are quite effective for normal video pictures, but create enormous difficulties for color compositing. Let's take a look at how these problems play out in specific formats.

In 601 SD video such as Digital BetaCam, a 4:2:2 color decimation system is used. This means that across each video scan line, every pixel is sampled for luminance (that's the "4") but only every *other* pixel is sampled for color (that's the first "2"). The second "2" indicates that the same color sampling patterns are used in the next video line; in other words, every other pixel will be sampled for color in the next line as well. The pixels that have not been sampled for color simply borrow the color value of the preceding pixel.

The now-ubiquitous DV format uses an even more aggressive color decimation system. In NTSC countries (such as the US and Canada), instead of sampling every other pixel, the DV format only samples every *fourth* pixel for color. This is referred to as 4:1:1 color decimation. In each video line every pixel is sampled for luminance (that's the "4"); every fourth pixel is sampled for color, with the following three pixels duplicating that color (that's the first "1"); and the next line repeats the same color sampling pattern (the second "1"). The PAL version of DV used in European countries uses a 4:2:0 color sampling system, which results in approximately the same data rate, but which works very differently than the NTSC system. In this system, every pixel in the first (or odd) line is sampled for luminance; every other pixel in that line is sampled for color, much as in the 4:2:2 system. However, in the next line (the even line) every pixel is sampled for luminance, but *no* pixels are sampled for color—that's the "0." The even line simply borrows or duplicates the color samples from the previous (odd) line. This 4:2:0 color sampling pattern is also used in MPEG compression in DVDs and digital broadcast streams; it is also used in the new HDV format.

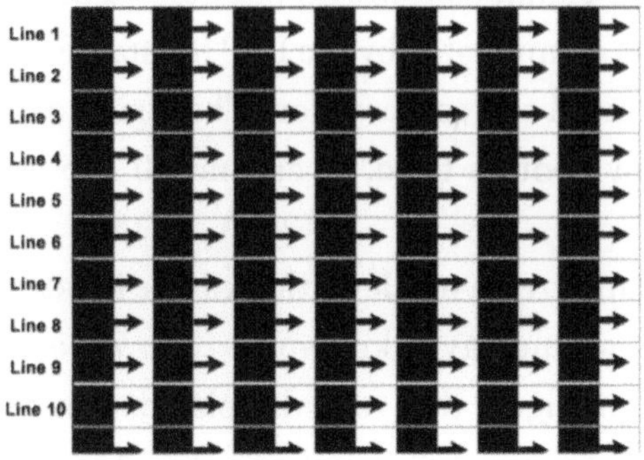

Figure 8.1 *In 4:2:2 color decimation, every pixel is sampled for luminance, but only every other pixel is sampled for chrominance. The unsampled pixel simply duplicates the color value of the previous pixel. The same pattern is used in the next scan line.*

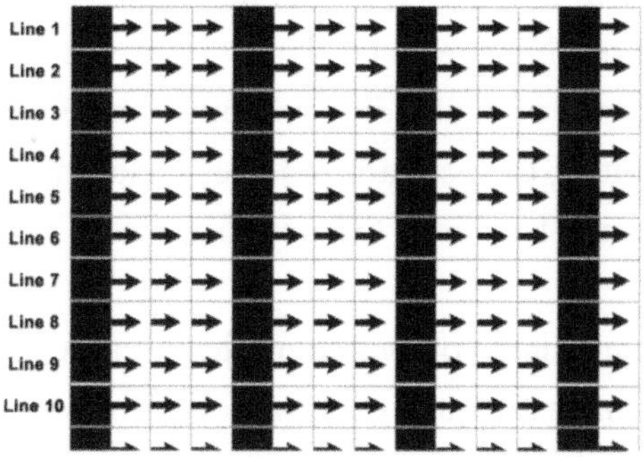

Figure 8.2 *In the DV format, 4:1:1 sampling is used, which closely parallels the characteristics of human vision—but which creates atrocious problems for color compositing! Here, every pixel is sampled for luminance but only every fourth pixel is sampled for color. The three unsampled pixels simply duplicate the chroma value of the last sampled pixel. The pattern is the same in odd and even scan lines.*

So how do these color decimation systems affect color-based compositing? Obviously, if the transparency matte is created exclusively from the color channel—no matter whether it is using green, blue, or red—the deleted (or decimated) information will have a dramatic impact on how accurate the resulting matte is. While 4:2:2 systems can key fairly well (though not perfectly) without unusual assistance or intervention, the odd patterns created by 4:1:1 and 4:2:0 decimation result in very strange, looking edges on foreground subjects (see Figure 8.2). This odd pattern, known as the *jaggies*, was a nightmare for compositing when these systems first came into use. In the early days of DV, most professionals would state flatly that DV could not be used for compositing because of these jaggies. As lower-end formats like DV became more common and widely used, however, software manufacturers and programmers began to come up with solutions for the jaggies. At first, the simplest solutions involved selectively blurring the matte to try and conceal the jagged edges. This was a less-than-ideal solution, though it worked for some situations. More advanced solutions began to actually recreate (or at least simulate) the missing data through mathematical interpolation. These solutions gave much better results; while not technically as accurate as creating a matte from full-resolution, full-color uncompressed video, it was highly effective for many situations, and produced an end product with clean, non-jagged edges that was nearly indistinguishable to the viewer from a composite pulled from higher-quality video. This trick of interpolation was "good enough" for many applications, and made color compositing with DV footage realistic. It's rather like the DV format itself—not perfect, but "good enough."

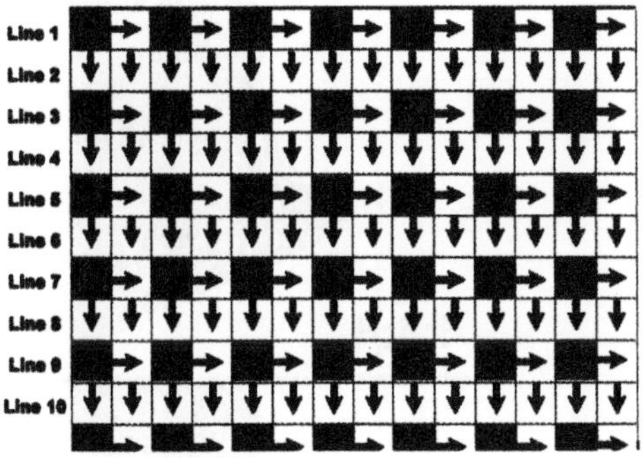

Figure 8.3 *In 4:2:0 color, every pixel is sampled for luminance. On the odd scan lines (1, 3, 5, 7, etc.) every other pixel is sampled for color, just as in 4:2:2 sampling. However, on the even scan lines (2, 4, 6, 8, etc.) every pixel is sampled for luminance, but no chroma samples are taken at all. The even lines simply duplicate the color values from the pixel directly above in the odd lines.*

Let's take a look at how this actually plays out in color-based compositing. Since the matte is being derived from a specific color channel (usually blue or green, but sometimes red) we are dependent not on the overall visual quality of the picture—a consideration central to most compression schemes—but the precise content of that color channel.

Take a look at Figure 8.4, which shows a raw matte pulled from the same original 4:4:4 footage in 4:2:2, 4:1:1, and 4:2:0 color decimation schemes. The distinctive color sampling pattern is immediately evident in the jaggies at the edge of the matte.

Probably the worst of these offenders in practical application is the 4:1:1 sampling of NTSC DV. While it is often possible to get a single frame keyed acceptably in 4:1:1, motion will immediately give the game away. Because most keyers work on a single frame, and do not predictively incorporate motion into their calculations, as a sharp edge moves between the four-pixel sampling points, the edge of the matte will seem to "snap" in four-pixel increments. This will be most evident with thin objects and slight motion, such as a stalk of wheat swaying in the breeze. In fact, the thinnest part of the stalk may simply vanish in some frames, appearing overly thick in other frames. The effect will also be evident in areas such as the talent's ear, the edge of which will move slightly back and forth as the head is rotated or nodded, thus showing a sharp edge that repeatedly crosses over a couple of four-pixel sampling areas.

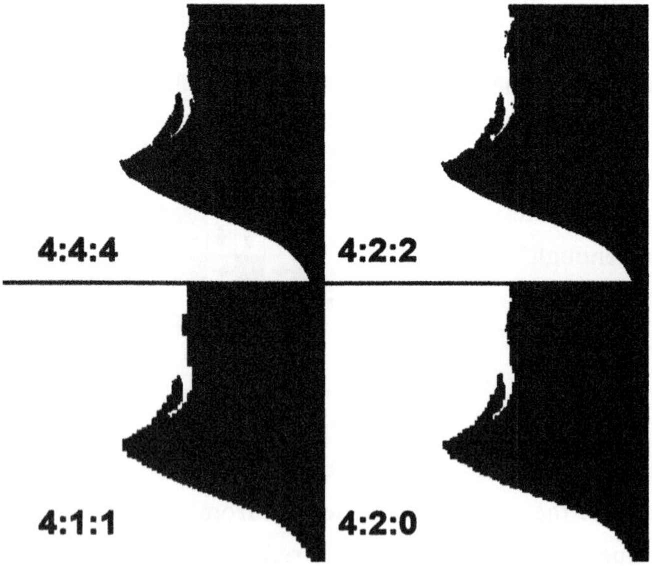

Figure 8.4 *This shows actual mattes pulled (with no choking or blurring) from 4:4:4, 4:2:2, 4:1:1, and 4:2:0 footage. You can clearly see the different jaggie patterns, particularly visible in the 4:1:1 sample.*

And Now...HDCAM!

If you're confused by all this, your reaction might be to throw up your hands and use HDCAM and the Sony CineAlta—after all, that's what George Lucas uses, and most of his stuff is color composited, right? Well, not so fast. HDCAM recorded to tape is nearly as bad as these other formats for high-end keying work. First, HDCAM is not full 1080 spec (1920 x 1080) but rather 1440 x 1080 displayed anamorphically (that is, with pixels stretched horizontally) and it uses a hybrid color decimation that amounts to 3:1:1. Not quite as bad as 4:1:1, but not as good as 4:2:2. When shooting the latest *Star Wars* prequels, Lucas may be shooting with a CineAlta, but shots that use green or bluescreen for compositing are recorded directly to disk in 4:4:4 uncompressed format. As far as I have been able to determine, LucasFilm and Industrial Light and Magic never use the HDCAM-recorded footage for color compositing. It is this issue that has given rise to the high-end market for cameras such as the Thomson Viper and others that are rumored to be in development as this book goes to press.

See for Yourself!

To see the different edge effects, try it out for yourself! On the DVD, we've included sample greenscreen footage rendered in 4:4:4, 4:2:2, 4:1:1, and 4:2:0 color sampling schemes. These are:

green444.mov
green422.mov
green411.mov
green420.mov

Remember, these files are in QuickTime format for maximum compatibility across platforms, so you must have Apple QuickTime installed on your computer to use these files.

Import the files into After Effects, and load in a background (either video or still) of your choice. Drop the background in the composition timeline first, then drop the 4:4:4 footage on top of it. Apply the Color Key filter. We'll use this one because it is the least sophisticated keyer and the one most likely to show flaws in the matte edge.

Use the Key Color eyedropper tool to select the backing color—in other words, click on a representative area of the green background to tell the software what color you want to render as transparent. Now adjust the Color Tolerance until most of the background disappears—but there is still a very slight edge of green around the young lady. In other words, stop before you begin to cut into the young lady's hair. Zoom in to 200% and examine the edge. Pixelized, to be sure, and still in some need of manipulation (blurring and choking) to become a workable edge.

Now, with the Color Key filter selected in the effects window for the 4:4:4 file, select Edit>Copy. This will copy the effect and all its current settings to the clipboard. Now, drop the color decimated files in the timeline, one after the other. Select each one and select Edit>Paste; this will paste the effect with identical settings onto each file. Now move the timeline cursor through each file and note the differences in the edges. Pay particular attention to the edges on the 4:1:1 file. Play that file back from the timeline, noting the effect on the edge of her hair as she moves her head slightly to her left.

Now, most of the keyers we'll be working with can do a better job than this, but this way you are able to see the raw problem undisguised by clever software tricks.

There are a couple of basic methods of disguising these jaggies. The first is to simply blur the edge of the matte and choke, or reduce the size, of the matte. This is sometimes workable but nearly always results in a too-soft edge. The second method is to use some sort of mathematical interpolation to predict where the missing data should be and fill it in. This, in effect, sort of averages the jaggies out to create a smoother edge. This is far more effective, but is something that can't be done manually; it must be built into the algorithm of the particular keying software you are using—so whatever format you're shooting on, make sure you pick keying software that is appropriate!

Creating the Plates

9

Let's stop for a refresher on some vocabulary. Typically, a basic color-based composite is made up of three elements: a background plate, a foreground plate, and the matte, which defines the transparency for the foreground plate. When creating a basic chroma key in a nonlinear editing program, the matte may be invisible (concealed within the effect plugin) but it is there nonetheless. Of course, these three elements are a minimum, because a complex effects composite may have many layers, each with its own matte channel. It's certainly not unusual to at least have a second foreground layer that is composited over the live action. There may be more than one background plate in certain instances, where the perspective effect of a dolly move or other motion must be simulated.

Most of what we've talked about so far has involved production issues for creating the foreground plate, since that's where most problems arise in real-world production. However, there are issues to watch out for in creating the background plate, whether it is actual footage of a real place or artificially created in a 3D program.

Previsualization

For most situations, it is advisable to start off with a storyboard or at least a rough sketch of the desired finished frame. This step, which

***Figure 9.1** Storyboard Artist is one example of a storyboard/previz program. Camera moves and blocking can be indicated for each shot.*

can be detailed and complex or just pencil on a napkin, is referred to as *previsualization* or *previz*. Whether the storyboard frame is complex and detailed or very simple, all major elements of the foreground and background should be represented, as well as any camera motion (dolly, pan, zoom, or crane) depicted with starting positions and ending positions.

There are numerous storyboarding programs available now that allow the non-artistic director to previsualize her shots. StoryBoard Quick and StoryBoard Artist from PowerProduction Software are excellent examples of storyboarding programs that use a sort of 2½ D rendering for previz. The programs come with prebuilt objects to create rooms, exteriors, and other environments as well as characters which can be rotated, positioned, and posed. Characters are selected from a stock set of angles and poses before they are placed in the scene and sized. They can't really be precisely rotated or reposed in the scene the way a 3D model could be, but you can build scenes pretty well for a storyboard. Add-on packs are available with more prebuilt content.

Another excellent program is FrameForge 3D Studio, which includes many predesigned objects in over 100 different categories including thirty-two fully poseable actors and everything you need to build exteriors, homes, offices, and far more. Such 3D-based programs are tremendously helpful for compositing previz because of their flexibility and the amount of detail that can be included easily in each storyboard frame.

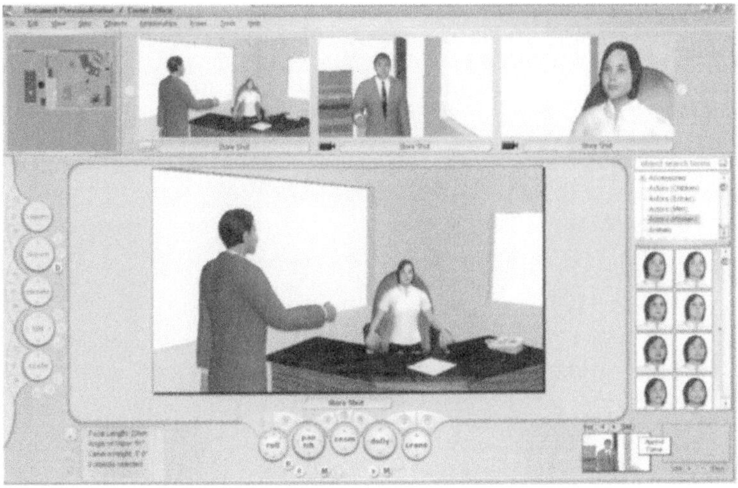

Figure 9.2 *Frame-Forge is a full 3D previz storyboard program with many options.*

There are many inexpensive and even free storyboarding programs available, but their limited features make them less useful for use in compositing previz.

Of course, even the non-artist can sketch crude stick figures in the correct positions. Though motion picture storyboards are often a work of art in themselves, it's not necessary that the storyboard be a creative masterpiece. What is important is blocking out the positions of the foreground objects and talent in relationship to critical portions of the background plate. Also as important (especially if different people are working on creating the foreground and background) are indications of key light sources and the quality of light that will illuminate the scene. For instance, is it harsh, hard, and contrasty (noonday sun) or gentle and warm (golden-hour sun)? Or is it fluorescent office light? While we can adjust the contrast and color balance in post, it's really impossible to change the quality of lighting. As I mentioned in the chapter on lighting, matching the light in plates is truly essential to creating an effective illusion in the finished composite. In fact, when the background plate is being created in a 3D program, it is probably a good idea to also draw up a basic lighting diagram that will be used for both the fictional background world and the real-world greenscreen studio.

Do you *have* to do a previz storyboard? Of course not. Particularly if you are creating all the components of the composite yourself, the previz

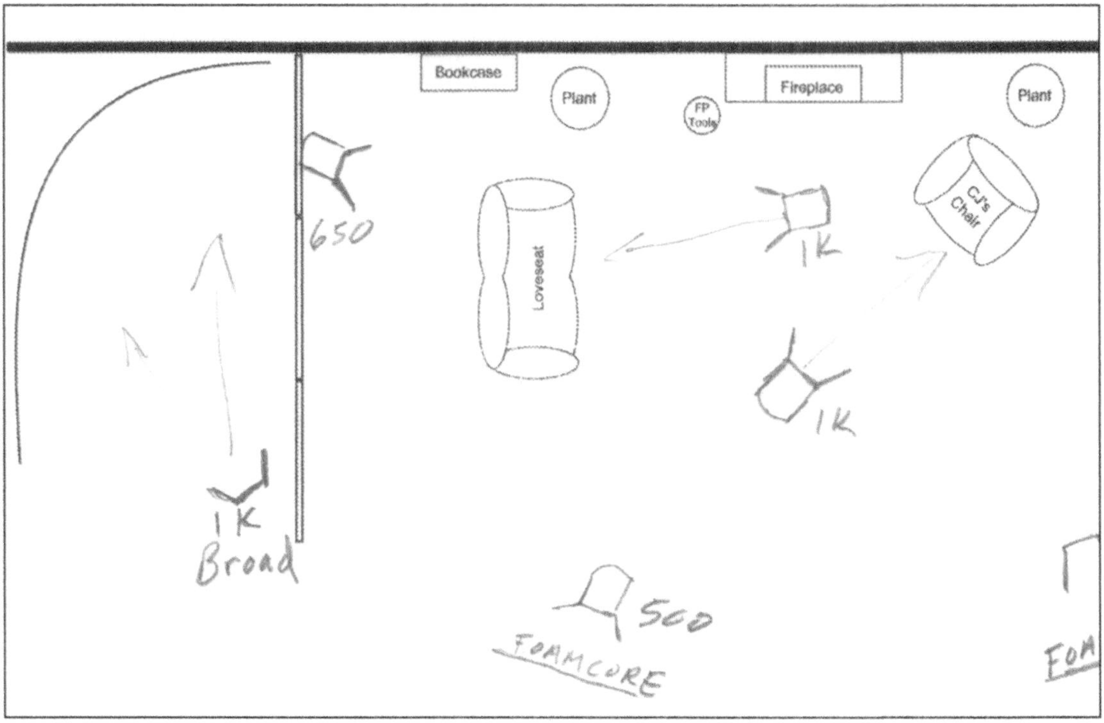

Figure 9.3 *A simple lighting diagram like this one can help coordinate the background plate with the foreground footage. Simple stick-figure storyboards can also help.*

in your imagination may be sufficient. But if various different people will be working on background, foreground, and post, the storyboard and lighting diagram is a road map that lets everyone know where things are in a consistent manner. The more people involved, or the greater the passage of time between creating the plates, the more essential and useful a storyboard becomes.

Creating the Foreground Plates

We've covered a lot of ground for creating the typical foreground plate—from decisions on the color of the background color and wardrobe to lighting. However, there's one thing we haven't touched on: matching the camera settings for foreground and background. When shooting the foreground plate, it is customary to record all the principal camera settings on a Visual Effects Data Sheet so that they can be matched for the background plate. The sheet should include (of course) the title of the production, shot number, scene number, take number, and date of shooting. It should indicate whether the scene is a day or night shot, and probably should include whether it is interior or exterior and a note about what the intended prevailing conditions were: sunny, cloudy, etc.

The sheet should then record the focal length of the lens, the f-stop of the lens, the height of the camera, the distance to the subject, and the tilt of the camera. If your tripod does not have a tilt indicator, you can make a rough estimate, use a protractor to make a more precise estimate, or measure precisely with an inclinometer (some compasses have these).

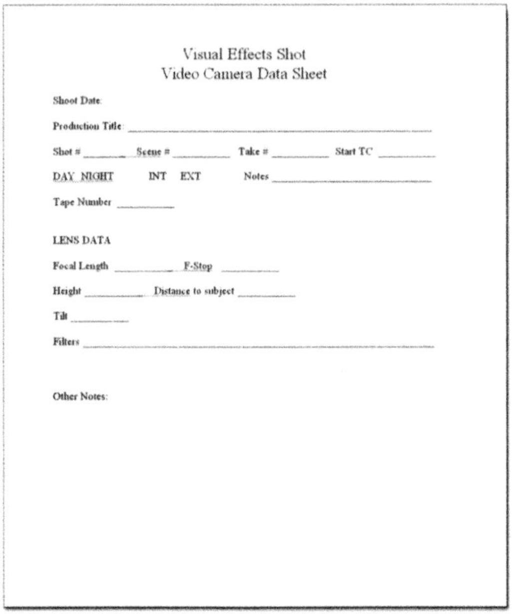
Visual Effects Shot
Video Camera Data Sheet

Shoot Date:

Production Title: ____________

Shot # ______ Scene # ______ Take # ______ Start TC ______

DAY NIGHT INT EXT Notes ____________

Tape Number ______

LENS DATA

Focal Length ______ F-Stop ______

Height ______ Distance to subject ______

Tilt ______

Filters ____________

Other Notes:

Figure 9.4 *A simple Visual Effects Shot Data Sheet will help match camera settings for foreground and background plates.*

When the background plate is shot (or created in a 3D program) in an ideal world these measurements will all be duplicated in the camera—whether it is a real camera or a virtual one. While a convincing composite can be created without having every setting match, the best final look will be achieved when the settings are at least close. Dramatic differences in the focal length of the lens between foreground and background can create the vague impression that something is "not right" in the composite, even if the viewer is not able to identify the problem.

Real-World Background Plates

Though fantastic 3D worlds are the stock-in-trade of the movie business these days, a great number of composited backgrounds are actually shots of real locations. Typically, these are used in several situations:

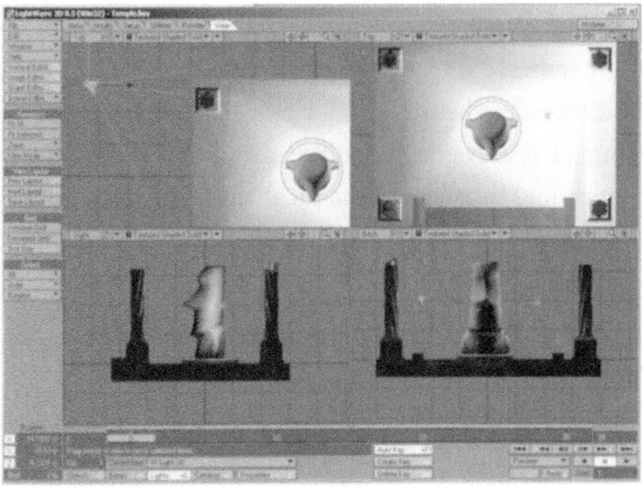

Figure 9.5 *Many directors will create previz in a full 3D animation program such as NewTek's LightWvave.*

- When having the actors at that location for production is costly or logistically difficult.
- When the actual situation represented in the shot would be dangerous—stunt close-ups of the principal talent are often done as composites, for instance. It's also common to composite moving backgrounds for "moving car" interior shots, or motorcycle close-ups.
- When augmenting a set or real-world scene with enhanced features (such as a particularly glorious sunset) that can't be counted on for a shooting schedule.

For instance, if you are shooting a low-budget film and you need your main character to have a flashback to a romantic weekend in Rome, it is possible to purchase quality background footage of Rome from a company such as Backgroundplates.com, HD24.com, or Stockfootageonline.com, and composite your hero in Piazza Navona! In these situations, it is necessary to match studio lighting (direction and quality) to the lighting of the stock footage, which of course cannot be altered.

Composites are commonly used in dangerous situations, and may in fact be required by insurance for key talent. The definition of what constitutes a "dangerous" situation is pretty squishy and has changed over time. *Vertigo*-style shots from high towers or cliff edges are one example; raging infernos or explosions might be another.

Figure 9.6 *Using a real location as a background plate combined with live action foreground. Background plate of Rome from Backgroundplates.com.*

A very common use for compositing is the *moving car shot.* While it might not seem dangerous to the novice to drive a car and act, it can in fact be very dangerous (not to mention illegal in most situations) to have an actor actually piloting a car while acting. Since the camera must often be mounted outside the car window on a grip frame, the entire contraption is too cumbersome for use on a public road. One solution for this is to mount the camera-rigged car on a flatbed truck. The flatbed truck then drives along a closed road while the actors act, the camera operators operate, and the director directs.

However, a more common solution is to use color screen compositing. By hanging a blue or greenscreen outside the car windows, the moving exterior can be composited in later. When done well (realistic slight motions and shaking of the car, a well-matched background plate, effective lighting), the illusion is nearly perfect. When done poorly (clearly artificial motion of the car, a poorly matched background, or inconsistent lighting) it's as hokey as a weeping televangelist.

It's not hard to create an effective background plate for this situation. The camera operator can simply work from the back seat of a car, with the camera mounted on a tripod. While the driver drives at a fairly sedate pace, the camera simply captures the view out of the window. Since it's common to need reverse shots (of the passenger) and rear-facing shots, a second run captures the scene out the passenger side of the car and a third run captures the view from the back window.

Figure 9.7 *Simple greenscreen setup for a moving car shot*

The footage will be most effective if the road is smooth and the driver maintains a fairly slow pace. Remember, you can always speed it up in post, but little bumps can put quite a jump in your footage at 50 MPH. It's those bumps that often give the fake away in the final composite. If there's a bit of a jump in the background plate footage, there needs to be a precisely matched bump in the car, as well. This is usually accomplished by having grips push on the front and rear bumpers of the car. If the background jumps and the car and actors remain perfectly stable, the viewer's mind will immediately cling to the inconsistency and the illusion will be lost. Of course, in post, we will be able to slide the background footage around to match the background bump with the simulated foreground bump.

The third example, augmenting existing scenes with enhanced backgrounds, is much more common than it used to be. This can be adding

In the good ol' days, of course, the "moving car" shot was typically accomplished in front of a rear projection screen. A projector with the background footage was synched to the camera, and Cary Grant would drive his convertible while a fan blew his hair and grips simulated bumps in the road. Or Sean Connery would drive his motorcycle at insane speeds along a curving country road. While the audience accepted these shots, they were typically quite obvious fakes because the contrast of the background was always too low and the color did not match. The gate weave of the background was sometimes obvious. In many movies, only limited effort was made to match background motion and foreground motion, as well. Color-based compositing gives so much better results that rear-screen projection has become an obsolete technique.

The technique has been resurrected in a new form, however, with the advent of cheap and high-output video projectors. Some low-budget films have used video projection outside a car to accomplish the shot without resorting to compositing in post. The technique can be effective, especially for moving car shots, as long as light is kept off the projection screen to maintain contrast. Throwing the background image slightly out of focus can also help, as if the live camera were set for a shallow depth of field. It's my understanding that this technique is used for all the driving or helicopter shots in the TV series *24*. Once regarded as an obsolete method, digital projection has brought this technique back into play in an improved form that allows spontaneous handheld camera shots and zooms. It's also a technique that is great for undersampled formats like DV, because it bypasses the chroma compositing problems altogether.

a real sky and distant background to an "exterior" studio set, or it can be augmenting a real exterior shot. Nature is fickle, and it can be quite difficult to schedule one of those spectacular sunsets to coincide with a tight production schedule. But it is possible to capture the fabulous sunset (or license any one of thirty thousand stock shots of a great sunset) and key it behind the live shot. Just as commonly, the director may want great marshmallowy cumulus clouds in the sky, and on the shooting date the sky is stubbornly clear.

These "real world" backgrounds are easy to composite into a studio bluescreen shot, slightly more difficult to composite into a real exterior. However, it's often possible to use the clear sky as a backing color and successfully composite in improvements.

Working in 3D Programs

Of course, the stock-in-trade of special effects compositing in films is not just improving reality or putting different bits of reality together, it is creating new or perhaps impossible realities. While pre-digital films like *Star Wars* did this with bluescreens and models, most of this is done in advanced 3D programs today, often with amazing results. However, just as with any other type of plate, careful matching of detail and various qualities of foreground and background plates are essential to create a convincing illusion. Any one of a number of factors can give away the fake if they are not carefully controlled.

There are a great many 3D animation programs available today, ranging from inexpensive consumer programs to more professional programs like Maya, LightWave, and 3DS Max. The details of modeling and work in these programs themselves are beyond the scope of this book. There are excellent books available from Focal Press and other publishers that delve into the button-pushing and techniques for each program. We're going to assume here that you are competent at creating scenes in the 3D program of your choice, or you are working with a specialist who is. We're also going to assume that you (or your animator) can model, texture, and light background scenes that look breathtakingly realistic.

But even once you've achieved a phenomenal level of realism in creating virtual 3D worlds, there are still several factors of image quality and content that are critical when the 3D image is being composited with a live production image. And these issues hold true across the board, whether the live foreground plate was shot on film or in HD, HDV, DV, or PixelVision! These factors are:

- Lighting and contrast
- Chroma content and color balance

- Resolution
- Aspect ratio

Lighting

We've discussed the issues of matching light and exposure in an earlier chapter. These issues apply just as much in the virtual world as they do in the real world. Essential elements of lighting that must match between the background and foreground plates are:

1. Quality of light. Is the key a hard light source or diffused? How large is the key source? How close is it to the subject? The apparent size (a combination of the actual size and the distance to subject) determines the wrap of the diffused light, or how far around a curved surface the light reaches. A single fluorescent fixture is diffused, but is small when compared to a cloudy overcast day, which constitutes a virtually infinite light source.

2. Position and intensity of key light. While this does not have to be precisely matched, it needs to be close—and certainly not from another direction altogether. Since in real-world light sources (or real-world modeled sources) the intensity falls off dramatically as distance increases, the distance is a factor as well.

3. Position and intensity of fill light. Fill position is somewhat less critical than the position of the key, but must still match generally.

4. The intensity of the fill light, particularly in relation to the key, determines the contrast of the picture. While this can be adjusted somewhat in post, it needs to be close to start with.

Chroma Content and Color Balance

This is an area where many less experienced 3D animators make serious mistakes. I've seen some excellent modeling and beautiful animation with chroma content that may have been technically legal for broadcast, but which was far hotter than any real video would be. The result is a cartoonish, oversaturated look that simply doesn't look natural even on its own. When combined with live footage, an over-saturated background plate will simply shout "fake." While chroma levels can be adjusted in post, it's best for the animator to start off with a color palette that is close to that of the camera being used for foreground footage.

Each video camera also has a certain color matrix, and often has a bias in terms of color balance. These characteristics can be adjusted in professional cameras, but the stock settings of different brands are fairly familiar. Canon cameras tend to be more magenta than reality, and Sony cameras skew towards blue. It's best if the animator is able to see some test footage from the camera. For the most part, color balance will need to be precisely matched in post by a skilled colorist. A foreground with a magenta tone composited over a background plate with a blue tone will also seem artificial.

Resolution

It should be obvious that the animator ought to create the background plate at the same spatial resolution (pixel frame size) as the foreground footage. This might be 720 x 480 for NTSC DV footage or 1280 x 720 for 720p footage. The background plate should also be created at the same *temporal resolution* (frame rate) as the foreground. This could be 24 fps, 25 fps for PAL footage, or 29.97 fps for NTSC footage. That much is clear.

However, there is another resolution issue that is often overlooked, and that is *sharpness*. Sharpness is a separate quality from resolution, though it is affected by resolution. Computer-generated graphics are always far sharper than real-world video or film footage because they are created artificially and are not affected by the physics of glass lenses and lens coatings, or the limits of CCD imaging chips. Standard definition NTSC video, for instance, cannot legally transition from a black pixel directly to a white pixel without intervening antialiasing. Computer graphics can do that without breaking a sweat. Inevitably, the computer-generated background plate will need to be blurred slightly to match the sharpness quality of the foreground footage. This is typically done by examining a sharp, high-contrast edge in the video and blurring the background footage until a similar edge matches. Novices will be astounded by how much blurring is necessary to match a CGI background plate to, say, HDV-originated foreground footage. The end result appears nice and crisp when displayed on an HD monitor or projector; it is only when the raw, sharp CGI file is placed next to the "natural" video that the video appears blurry. Take a look at this in Figure 9.8. On the left, the HD foreground plate looks slightly soft because of the sharp-as-a-tack edges of the CG background. After we blur the background pate (throwing in a little phony shallow depth of field as described in Chapter 4), the final composite is much more satisfactory.

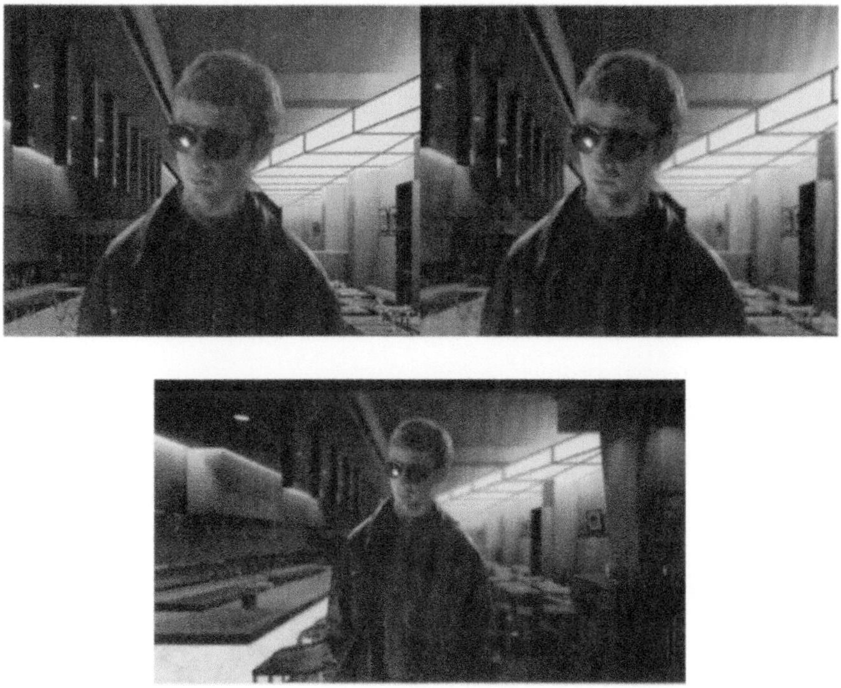

Figure 9.8 *A common beginner mistake is to use a crisp CGI background plate without blurring it to match the foreground footage. This makes the finished shot look like the foreground is slightly out of focus and calls attention to the fake. Background plate "Coffee Room" courtesy of Chen Qingfeng, chen3d.com*

Aspect Ratio

Just as it is fairly obvious that the animator should be working at the same spatial and temporal resolution as the foreground footage, it should also be obvious that the background plate should be created at the same aspect ratio and pixel shape as the foreground for best results. There are many circumstances where fudging the aspect ratio later will create a less-than-desirable end product.

Problems in Post

10

Now we get down to the real nitty-gritty of the work in post—pulling and cleaning the matte. There are many plugins (particularly in NLE programs) where the matte is pretty much invisible to the user—but trust me, it's there. The matte is the intermediary workhorse graphic that will determine the look and quality of the final composite—it's the heart of the compositing process. That's because it is the matte that determines what areas of the foreground are transparent, translucent, or opaque, and how soft the edge transition is. Of course, there are other factors that come into play (notably spill removal), but it is the matte that is at the core of the process.

Creating the matte is typically referred to as *pulling* the matte in the compositing business. The precise technique for pulling the matte varies from plugin to plugin, and depends in part on the precise process the plugin uses to define transparency and edge quality. However, there are similarities. Every software plugin will need to know what backing color you are using. Extremely simple plugins may just give you a choice of generic blue or green. Most will include a sampling tool, usually looking like an eyedropper that allows you to sample the exact values of blue or green that your real-world shot includes. This is far better than just selecting a generic color, since the actual backing color may deviate quite a bit from the theoretical RGB model of 0, 128, 0 or 0, 0, 128. It's very difficult to achieve those values with a real camera in a real-world setup when various factors such as lighting temperature, exposure, and the simple vicissitudes of life are factored into the equation. A real-world green backing might sample at 41, 132, 35; a nicely lit blue backing might sample at 38, 52, 128. So the first stage in pulling a matte will be to sample the actual backing color to define the "center" color that will become transparent in the foreground of the final composite.

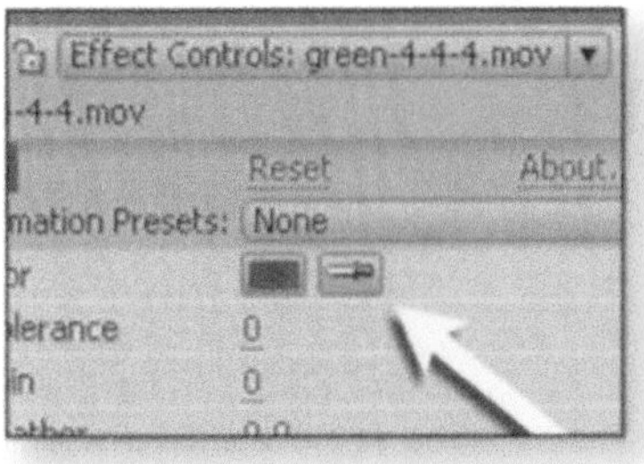

Figure 10.1 *Eyedropper sampling.*

Usually this sample is fairly narrow and will only match a few areas of the backing color. The next step is to expand the range of luminance values (brightness) and chrominance values (color) that need to be included in the transparency region. This will be accomplished in some programs by dragging separate slider controls for luminance and chrominance. Other programs (such as the Color Range Keyer in After Effects) will include Add and Subtract eyedroppers to include or exclude specific tonal variations. Other programs which use more complex calculations may include a single slider to increase *range* or *fuzziness*. These will allow the program to include a wider range of tonal variations on either side of the sampled set in the transparency area of the matte. See the tutorials in Chapter 12 for specific details on different plugin controls.

At this point, many plugins are still now showing the matte itself, but default to showing the final composite output. Most allow you to select display of the matte; after making your initial sampling and range inclusions, it is a really good idea to look at the matte. This is because the composite of a single frame against a background may look dandy; but it may also contain all kinds of schmutz that will become painfully obvious in the final motion video. Usually at this stage, the actual matte is not refined enough for high-quality output. The transparency region (usually black, though it is white in some software packages) is actually dark gray with areas of variation that change from frame to frame due to video noise. These areas will show up in the final composite. The foreground may be almost opaque (totally white) but may contain areas that are light gray—and thus semi-transparent. Again, these areas may look fine in a single frame but will become quite obvious if the subject passes in front of a contrasting color that then tints the area of transparency. Edge problems from color sampling are also easily visible when viewing the matte directly.

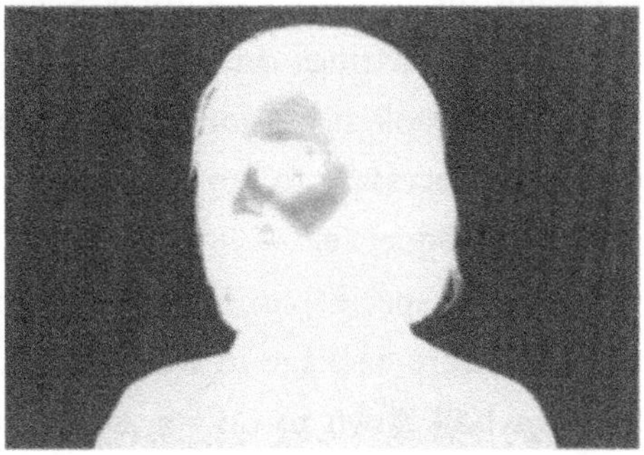

Figure 10.2 *A matte that isn't quite ready for prime time!*

While viewing the matte, you may be able to tweak those basic controls a bit more and hit a home run. However, it's more likely that you will have to look at some other controls. Sometimes these are labeled "Foreground" and "Background" or something similar. These will operate as image-processing tools on the matte to boost the light (but not quite white) areas of the foreground to full white, and the dark (but not quite black) areas of the background to full black. If your original footage is well-lit and clean, you will probably be able to create a nice clean matte at this stage—a solid black background area that will define transparency (the area of the original backing color) and a nice solid white foreground area (your foreground subject). The edge between black and white may need some cleanup or blurring or choking, but the basic matte has been defined. You'll still want to flip back to the final composite view to see how that looks.

Cleaning Up Those Edges

If you are dealing with uncompressed video and have a fairly sophisticated keyer like Ultimatte or Keylight, you may be done! However, the likelihood is that you are working with video that is 4:2:2 or, worse, 4:1:1 and you still have some ugly jagged edges where the background transitions to foreground. These will be cleaned up either through selecting the proper logic (à la Ultimatte or Primatte) or using a geometric blurring tool (à la zMatte or After Effects Matte Choker) to reduce jaggies. The resulting edge will likely be blurred somewhat and perhaps choked (reduced in size) to eliminate excess material at the edges. Again, the precise controls to do these processes will vary from software to software but the processes themselves will be similar. Once you are happy with general settings on a specific frame, remember to scroll through the file and look at motion and how the settings affect different frames. It is often necessary to keyframe certain controls and vary their settings through a sequence.

While the specific controls and even the names of the controls vary from software package to software package, the basic edge cleanup operations boil down to only a few: geometric blurring or mathematical interpolation to smooth out undersampled color, matte blurring, and matte choking. Let's look at these in turn.

Eliminating Jaggies

While the purists with huge budgets can stay in the uncompressed world of 4:4:4 video, most of us have to live in the real world of undersampled color. Whether the undersampling is moderate as in 4:2:2 or severe as in the world of 4:1:1 DV, it is important to do some cleanup of the jaggies that result from the undersampling if you want to have an effective composite as the end product. As I mentioned above, it's often possible to produce an acceptable-looking key in 4:1:1 while looking at a single still frame. But as soon as the video begins to move, the extremely jagged nature of the edges becomes apparent. For an effective composite, we have to smooth the jaggies out by creating artificial data to fill in the missing areas. In a purely digital matte, this can be done through mathematical interpolation, a technique of averaging the curve of the stairstepped edges. However, most software does this through a process that is part interpolation, part blurring. Some software such as Ultimatte AdvantEdge has specific algorithms built in for different color decimation schemes. Most require you to adjust a slider to achieve a level of smoothness that is acceptable.

Let's take a look at the Geometric Softness function in the After Effects Matte Choker as an example—we'll look at it in greater detail in the Tutorial on AE's Color Range Keyer.

In After Effects, load in the sample picture *green411.mov* and apply the effect labeled Color Key (Effect>Keying>Color Key, not Color Range). Drop in a background file of your choice; this makes it easier to see the results of what you are doing. Use the Key Color eyedropper to select the green background, and turn up the Color Tolerance until the green background is almost entirely transparent, with the exception of a tiny jagged fringe around the woman. Now apply the Matte Choker (Effect>Matte>Matte Choker) and note how the edges instantly clean up. The default setting for Geometric Softness is 4, with an Iteration of 1 (the bottom setting). For the time being, just look at the top of the settings (Geometric Softness 1) and ignore the second set of controls below.

Play with the Geometric Softness slider to see what effect it has. You'll see that it averages the jaggies to produce a smoother edge, but the effect has a penalty. As you increase the value to smooth the jagged edges, note that inside corners (where her shoulder meets her collar, for instance) that should be a sharp angle become rounded. Note the very artificial effect on wisps of hair above her shoulders. You need to be aware that this sort of cleanup does not come without a cost, one that will be more obvious in some pictures than others.

Now play with the Choke 1 slider. Positive numbers choke (shrink) the matte, while negative numbers grow (expand) the matte. Notice how choking the matte just slightly into the foreground image can make the edges seem more realistic in some areas, while making edges worse in other areas. Particularly note how even a slight choking will virtually eliminate small edge details such as wisps of hair.

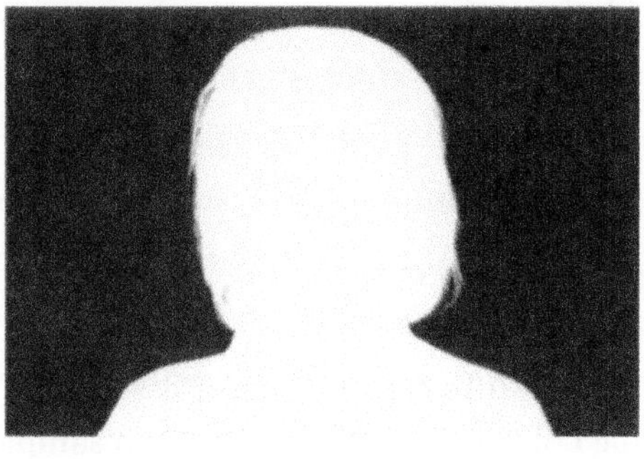

Figure 10.3 *The matte is now crisp and edges cleaned up, blurred, and choked.*

Geometric averaging is not a perfect solution to undersampled video. It creates artifacts (unintended visual consequences), which can be mitigated but not eliminated. It is not a replacement for fully sampled video, but a compromise that comes with a cost. There is no method of accurately recreating the vast amount of edge data that is lost with 4:1:1 color decimation!

Removing Spill

The matte has now been defined and cleaned up to precisely define areas of transparency and opacity, and a satisfying transition between them defined. But what about that bit of green spill on Harry's forehead, or the silver coffeepot that is catching a bit of blue reflection? Since we don't want these areas to become transparent, the matte really can't fix them. We have to use an image processing technique that removes enough of the offending color in those areas to make the final image look normal, with no odd patches of green or blue spill or reflections in the foreground. Again, each plugin will have a different method of spill removal, some more effective and others less. Many will begin to change the overall color of the subject when applied too aggressively; others are more selective and use sophisticated algorithms to aggressively remove spill color in certain areas while having less effect in other areas.

Most keying software has some sort of spill removal. Probably the most sophisticated are programs like Ultimatte or Primatte. Most color difference keyers (such as Keylight) will remove a lot of spill simply through their basic methods of operation, though it's not unusual to have to apply additional spill removal in certain situations.

Let's try a basic pass at spill removal. In After Effects, import the still file *grnspill.jpg* from the DVD, and a background of your choice (I used *ROME_BR.jpg*). The *grnspill.jpg* foreground is a frame from lighting setup when we had the screen overlit, thus creating spill on the model. Follow the procedure outlined above using the Color Key and Matte Choker effects to create as clean a key as you can. It won't be perfect; you won't be able to get really smooth edges and there will be clearly visible green spill on the girl's hair and blouse. Now, apply the After Effects Spill Suppressor (Effect>Keying>Spill Suppressor). You have to tell the Suppressor what color you want to suppress; use the eyedropper to sample the green swatch that is displayed in the Color Key control. Another method is to temporarily disable the Color Key to make the backing color visible again, and then sample from the actual background. Be sure to enable the Color Key control again!

The Spill Suppressor will remove most—but probably not all—the spill on the foreground. It will be a vast improvement over the original image. You can play a bit with the limited controls, and try sampling slightly different shades of green to see how it affects the end product.

That's the process for pulling a basic matte, cleaning up edges, and then implementing spill removal. If your original footage was clean and crisp, well exposed, and well lit, count yourself lucky, you're done! But what if you're not so lucky? What if the scene includes the shadow of the mic boom or, worse, the mic itself in frame? What if the greenscreen was unevenly lit? What if the screen is too small and the subject's hand extends off the backing color? What if the main character has on an aqua blouse and gets a hole in her middle when you pull the matte? What then?

Fixing Problem Mattes

Here's where we get to the nitty-gritty and hard work of creative compositing—where we separate the James Bonds and Emma Peels of compositing from the Casper Milquetoasts and Valley Girls. Those of you who never want to do more than click on a single filter in your NLE and slide a single adjustment can stop reading now. Those who won't accept anything but visual perfection and are willing to work to get it, read on!

I think I've made clear in earlier chapters that a significant proportion of the work for creating a good composite is in the production phase: good lighting, good color choices, sharp focus. However, the reality is that you will often be presented with less-than-ideal (and sometimes downright awful) footage that you have to work with. And that's where some of the techniques we're going to tackle here come in handy.

First, experimentation with the various keying programs will quickly show you that some keyers are stronger in one area than in others. One keying technique may work really well to create nice edges on under-sampled color, but doesn't do so well on preserving colors that are too similar to the backing. Another technique may do a great job on an unevenly lit background but creates sloppy edges on the foreground subject when used aggressively. So the first step in dealing with any scene is to decide which keyer is the first choice for dealing with the specific issues presented in the scene.

However, that's only the beginning. Very often, we will find that no individual keyer will really do the trick. That's where we start to choose multiple keyers and combine multiple mattes to create the final composite. Remember the non-color-based compositing techniques in Chapter 3? These are known in After Effects as *Blending Modes*, or *Transfer Modes*. The modes of Multiply, Screen, Minimum, and Maximum can prove very useful in combining various mattes, each of which will play a role in the final matte. Let's walk through a real example of combining mattes.

First, we'll use a sample that is on the DVD, *green422.mov*. This is the file compressed to 4:2:2 color sampling, and there are some sections that are a bit difficult to get details (especially the edges of the subject's hair) to key accurately. The background is a bit noisy due to the compression that was used on the file, which complicates matters just a bit. This isn't really a horrible problem file, but we'll use it to illustrate the technique of combining multiple mattes.

There is no single keying software that is best for all situations. In fact, since each keyer handles the image processing differently, you may find that the plugin that produced stupendous results on the last shot simply can't create a clean matte for another shot. So the first step in solving problems is to try several different plugins and observe how each behaves. Some will be better at producing clean detailed edges but can't create a clean background (the black area of the matte). Others will be adept at producing a clean background but will massacre the edge details. Another may do both well, but at different settings! The setting that produces clean edges leaves schmutz in the background. The setting that produces a clean background leaves sections of the foreground transparent. This is where you will want to pull two or more mattes and combine them in a manner that will give the final matte the best features of each.

Let's walk through the process a step at a time. Once you get the hang of how to do it, there are numerous variations to the technique—which matte is on top, how it is composited with the ones below, and so on.

First, experiment with several keyers and see how they behave with the file. Here we're going to pull two mattes and composite them. The first will be created with the Color Difference Keyer, which can create very clean edge detail. However, this is also the keyer that on this file will leave some of the foreground transparent when adjusted to give a solid background (see figures below). So we have a couple of choices:

1. Using the Color Difference Keyer to create nice edges and a clean background, and using another keyer to fill in the foreground; or

2. Using the Color Difference Keyer to create nice edges and a clean foreground, and using another keyer (or a second version of the Color Difference Keyer using different settings) to fill in the background.

We'll try option 1. Drop the footage in the composition. Now duplicate it twice. Doing it in this manner ensures that all three layers are synched; and if for some reason you need to update the footage later it will update through all layers in the same way. For the time being, turn the bottom-most version off (invisible) by clicking on the eye to the left of the name.

Create a *pre-comp* of the two layers on the top. To do this, hold down the Shift key and select both layers, then select Layer>Pre-Compose. You can also hit Ctrl+Shift+C (Apple Cmd+Shift+C). In the pre-comp requester, rename the new composition to "MATTE." Now double-click the pre-comp MATTE in the project window (not in your existing timeline) to work on the files.

Make the top version invisible, and select the lower version. Add the Color Difference Keyer from Effect>Keying. Follow the instructions in the After Effects Help file to set the black and white points of the matte, concentrating on achieving a clean background. Set the View to Matte Corrected so that you are working with the matte, not the composite view. You will probably need to play with the Matte In Black and Matte In White controls, and possibly with the various Gamma controls. You will end up with a clean black background with nice detailed edges, but a schmutzy foreground with transparent areas where you don't want them. This will be your edge/background matte.

Now, make the uppermost layer visible and select it. Try another keyer that gives a good solid foreground easily, such as the Color Range Keyer. Follow the instructions in the After Effects Help file to set the black and white points of the matte. You will probably end up with a clean foreground and background, but junky edges. Note that this keyer does not have selection to view only the matte, so you are seeing the final composite where the background is transparent and the foreground is opaque showing those areas of the original file.

But for a matte, we need pure white and pure black with grays for translucency—no color information. So here's where you bring in some trickery. Apply the Levels control (in Effects>Color Correction in AE 7.X and above, in Effects>Adjust in earlier versions). Now set the Output Black control to 255, something you would never do in normal image processing. This will change the foreground area from full-color video to pure white, which you can superimpose over the edge matte to clean up the foreground! However, the junky edges on this matte overlap the clean edges of the other matte in some areas, so we may wish to Choke this matte to make it smaller. Apply the Matte Choker (Effects>Matte>Matte Choker) and adjust the choke values and edge blur until this white overlay exists just a pixel or so inside the foreground area of the edge matte. Applying edge blur (Gray Level Softness) so a soft blurred edge just overlays the crisp edges of the edge matte is often ideal. (Note: You can use the Simple Matte Choker in this way in many cases.) This matte is often referred to as a Core Matte.

Bingo, the clean foreground is automatically composited over the edge/background matte. The resulting combination is better than could have been created at a single setting.

Figure 10.4 *The first matte, or Edge Matte (left), the second matte, or Core Matte (center), and the composited final matte (right).*

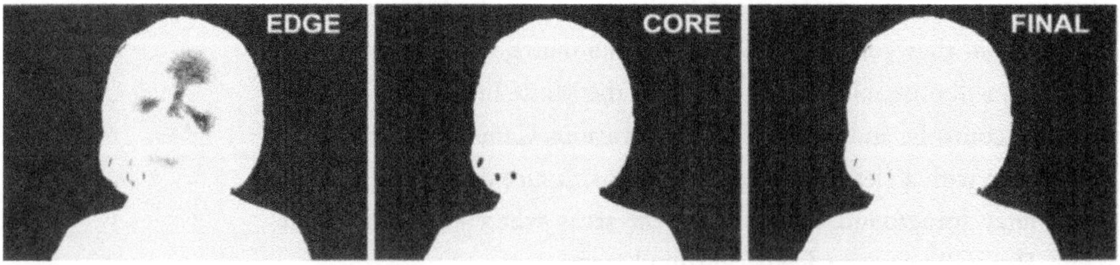

Now, back in your main composition the MATTE pre-comp will appear as a single item in the timeline above the original footage. Make the MATTE pre-comp invisible by clicking the eye to the left of the name. After all, we don't want to actually see the matte, we want to use it invisibly.

Load in a background (either still or video), and place it on the bottom line of the composition timeline, just below the original footage. Make the original footage visible, and make sure the Modes column is visible. Now, in the Trk Matte column for the original footage, select Luma Matte. Bang, your footage is now composited using the precomp MATTE to create transparency! If any green spill remains in the final composite, use Effects>Keying>Spill Suppressor to remove it.

Figure 10.5 *The final composite using the combined mattes in the precomp.*

This gives you the basic idea for the process. It's not unusual for professional compositors to pull four or five mattes in this sort of process, each one contributing a specific narrow attribute to the final matte. A background matte (one with a clear background with the edges just outside those of the edges matte) can be placed on top of another matte with a gray and schmutzy background and composited using the Darken (minimum) transfer mode. This will overlay the black of the background matte—but the white areas of that matte (which are not its best feature) will be unused. Conversely, a clean foreground matte can be composited on top of an edge matte using the Screen or Lighten (Maximum) transfer modes. There are many techniques that will work with this approach—try them all!

Incidentally, if I had known how to do this ten or twelve years ago, the horror story from Chapter 7 about the girl with the aqua blouse and the hole in her middle would have turned out much better! This very technique would have allowed me to set up a foregound matte just for her in the troublesome frames, and composite it over the matte with the "hole" in it. Ain't experience wonderful?

Live Keying

11

Much of what we have discussed so far in this book really has primary roots in the world of filmmaking special effects, where artificial realities have been composed from various components in a post-production process. However, in the television world, chroma key compositing is primarily a live process that happens electronically in a switcher or Special Effects Generator (SEG) before the signal is recorded to tape. This process, operating off of the component signal directly from the camera, is in fact technically superior to any post process that deals with compressed video. The analogue component signal from the camera is

Figure 11.1 *An older Sony production switcher*

uncompressed, has not been color decimated, and typically has a higher horizontal and vertical resolution than the studio's recording format can retain on tape. So, if all the production variables are cared for properly, mattes pulled electronically from this originating signal tend to be far more accurate (that is, reflecting actual details of the original picture) than a matte pulled in post from a compressed recorded signal.

The major use for live keying in the television world has of course been for weathercasting. What would the Weather Channel or your local station do without live keying to allow the meteorologist to point to a map and explain the Doppler radar? But while every local station uses live keying for weathercasting, there is another application for live keying that has grown in recent years, and that is the use of virtual sets. We'll take a look at both applications in turn; but first we need to understand the basic hardware that is in use in live studio production.

Switchers, Special Effects, and Keying

The heart of any live production studio or production truck is the production switcher, often referred to as an SEG, or special effects generator. This is, in effect, a video signal mixer; in fact, in Europe, the term for these units is *vision mixer* or *video mixer*. All camera and graphics signals are fed to this unit, which allows the operator to switch between signals, mix multiple signals in dissolves or wipes, superimpose titles (a keying process), or create color-based superimpositions via chroma key process. Of course, in these digital days, most switchers/SEGs have all sorts of other effects and bells and whistles, some of which will hardly ever be used in normal practice. Let's take a brief look at the anatomy of a standard switcher.

The Production Switcher

The basic concept of a production switcher is the *bus*, which is a bank of buttons that each represents an individual video source (camera, videotape, or CG). Selecting a particular source sets it as the output for that bus. Traditional analog switchers were set up with two main busses, usually A and B, with an additional keying bus. The transition bar, or T-Bar, would manually control a dissolve or wipe between buses, and the position of the T-Bar dictated which bus (either A or B) was output

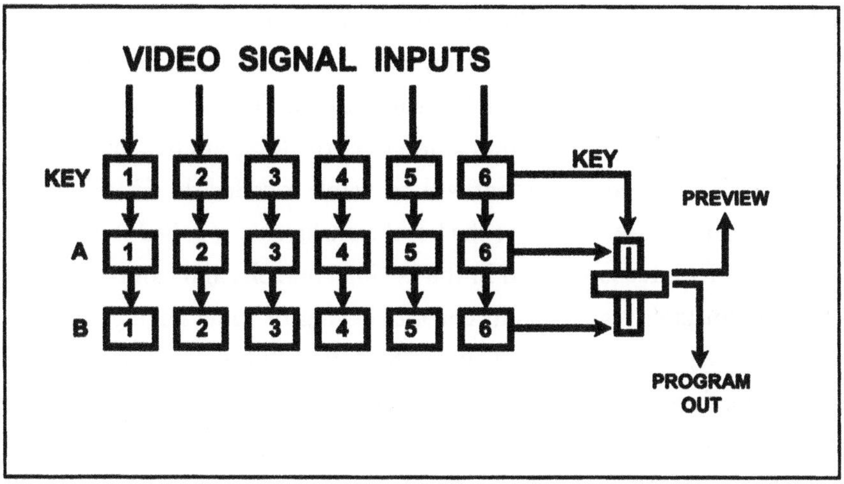

Figure 11.2 *A traditional analog switcher function diagram. The position of the T-Bar determines which bus outputs to Program.*

to the main, or Program bus. The opposite, offline bus would automatically be switched to a Preview monitor. These units are known as *A-B switchers.*

Digital switchers are set up a bit differently, since the actual switching and mixing of signals occurs in microchips and is no longer directly controlled by the rotation of physical components. Most digital switchers have a set Program bus (usually the middle bus) and a Preview bus

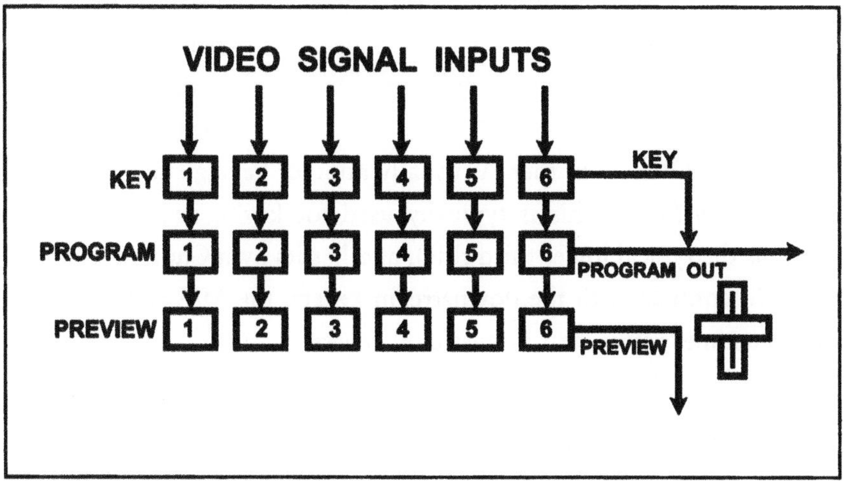

Figure 11.3 *A digital Flip-Flop switcher diagram. On a flip-flop switcher, the position of the T-Bar simply swaps (flips) the selected input on the Program and Preview buses.*

(usually nearest the operator). The transition between buses can be set in advance and previewed offline; while a T-bar still exists to manually control the speed of a transition, most of the time the transition is preset and a Take button initiates the transition. Following the transition, the selected sources of the Preview bus and Program bus reverse or flip; for this reason, these units are known as *Flip-Flop switchers*.

The third bus is the Key bus. A mixer can actually have more than one of these sharing a single set of control buttons. The Key bus signal can be selected for digital superimposition over the Program bus image. The portion of the keyed image that will be visible is called the *fill*, while the matte (or mask) used to create the keys' translucence is called the *source*. The type of source is selected in the keying controls, and can be derived from the original signal (as in chroma keying or luma keying) or supplied by a separate source (an alpha channel, a CG pattern, etc.).

The Preview, Program, and Key buses together are called *Program/Preset* or *P/P* section. The P/P section is sort of the basic component of switcher architecture. Larger production switchers may have several P/P sections, which can be preset and selected for program output. These are collectively called *Mix/Effects* or *M/E* sections, and they are usually numbered. Any M/E section can be selected as a source in the P/P stage. Effects can be set up in advance, for instance, a key can be set up and adjusted offline and then taken "live" at the push of one button.

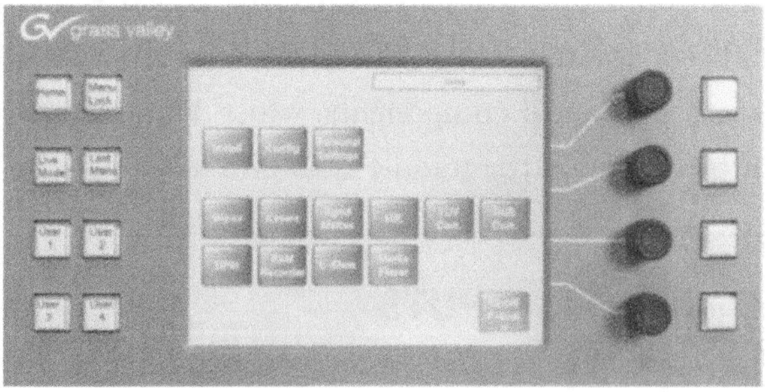

Figure 11.4 *The Special Effects control panel of a Thomson/Grass Valley Kayak switcher*

After the P/P section, there is usually another keying stage called the *downstream keyer*. This is typically used for keying text or graphics (such as the typical lower third title), and has its own Cut and Mix buttons. To contrast with the downstream keyers, the M/E section keyers are sometimes referred to as *upstream keyers*.

Switcher Trivia: In the original 1977 *Star Wars* (now known as *Star Wars Episode IV: A New Hope*) the "control panel" for the Death

Star is a Grass Valley production switcher. A gloved hand reaches for the T-Bar, switches from Bus B to Bus A, there's a buzzy synthesizer sound effect, and bam! No more Alderaan!

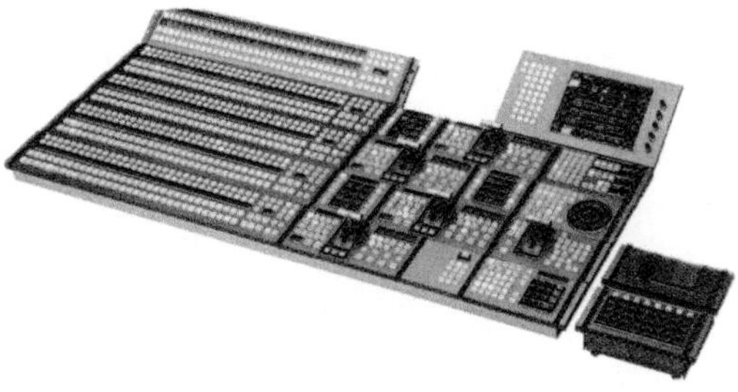

Figure 11.5 *The Sony MVS-9000 production switcher in full studio configuration*

In larger live production studios, production switchers can become very complex. Various components comprising M/E sections can be ganged together to control feeds from studio cameras, satellites, and other sources as required by the installation.

Digital Video Mixers

Just a few years ago, the production switcher was a discrete component that really required a roomful of other equipment to operate. *House sync* was supplied to cameras, switcher, and decks from a sync generator. Videotape sources had to pass through a separate time base corrector (TBC) locked to house sync before they could be fed into the switcher. Most full-blown studios are still set up like this; but as digital technology evolved, in the mid-nineties there appeared a new version of the production switcher, a self-contained portable digital version sometimes called a *video mixer*. What made these different were frame synchronizers on each input, allowing unsynced camera and tape signals to be mixed together without external TBCs or sync generators. These usually incorporate a small audio mixer to make the unit a portable production studio. Most incorporate some level of chroma key capability with the quality and flexibility of control paralleling the price pretty precisely. These units range in price and features widely, from simple two-input units like the Sima SFX-9 Video Mixer with a street price of under $500 and the four-input Edirol/Roland LVS-400 at $1500 to much more substantial professional units such as the Panasonic AG-MX70, which can range from $6000–$10,000 depending on accessory boards and effects

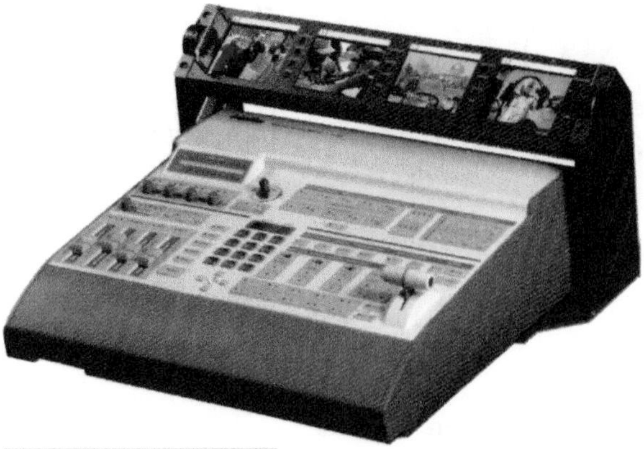

***Figure 11.6** The Datavideo SE-800 provides four-channel video switching with chroma keying capability and IEEE-1394 (DV) inputs.*

configuration. Some, such as the Datavideo SE-800, include IEEE-1394 (DV) inputs.

These units are quite portable and can provide live keying options on location that (in the higher-end units) rival the quality of studio production chroma keyers. Obviously, the difference in price between a sub-$1000 unit and a $10,000 unit plays out in performance. Don't sink cash into one of these specifically for keying work until you've tested one to see that it meets the standards for your intended usage. Lower-end units may not produce sophisticated or difficult keys cleanly.

Video mixers are no longer limited to standard definition video. Units such as the Edirol V-440HD (around $12,000) provide full 1080 and 720 switching and keying capabilities.

Toasters and 'Casters

There is a third, and very important, category in the live switcher market, and that is the computer-based switcher system. The two most recognizable names are the NewTek Video Toaster and the Globalstreams GlobeCaster. Both are really integrated turnkey production packages

The Panasonic AG-MX70 is an excellent example of a full-fledged professional video mixer with full chroma keying capability. The MX70 is the latest version of a fairly long-lived line of Panasonic video mixers.

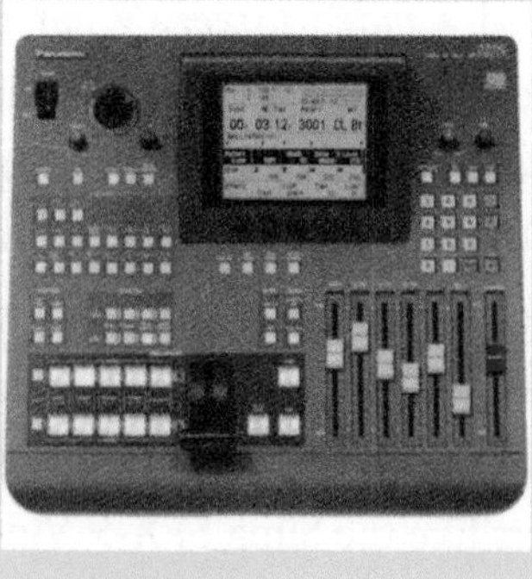

- Designed for live events and full-fledged digital post-production Compact unit with a 2-BUS, 8-input video switcher, high-performance, multi-functional digital video effects unit and versatile audio mixer.

- 4:2:2:4 digital component picture quality, 16:9 wide and 4:3 aspect ratio capability (the fourth digit represents an embedded alpha channel)
- Creates more than 600 2D effects patterns including transitions, key patterns, mosaic, paint, trail, and multi-images
- Digital chrominance and luminance keys
- Downstream keyer
- Optional AG-VE70P 3-D effects board delivers over 1600 effects including page-turns, accordion, spheres, and ripples
- An easy-to-operate joystick allows users to position and size effects as well as select and adjust colors
- Tally outputs for up to eight cameras and 2-channel frame synchronization permitting special effects in each of the A/B program busses
- Large LCD control panel for easy operation and monitoring of system status
- Five-row matrix menu display with five rotary switches makes it easy to set the units multitude of functions
- Inputs including composite, Y/C, component, or Serial Digital Interface (SDI)
- 30-frame graphics buffer for roll, crawl, and logo animation; and a USB interface makes it easy to download graphics
- RS-422A and RS-232C remote-control terminals standard and a GPI terminal to permit the AG-MX70 to team with video editing devices

that include every basic function, special effect, and utility that a small live switching setup needs.

If you've been around video production for fifteen or twenty years, you know that the original Video Toaster really made desktop video a reality. Based on the then-revolutionary Amiga 2000, it did stuff back in 1990 that looked (almost) like a multi-million-dollar postproduction suite. Blew us all away, and really revolutionized the lower-end video business. Today, the Video Toaster 4 (or VT[4] as it is now referred to) is PC based (the Amiga went away after Commodore's bankruptcy in 1994) and provides functions and effects that truly rival high-end set-ups. The basic VT[4] is operated by mouse and computer keyboard, but NewTek also offers a hardware remote control, the RS-8, that makes the switcher handier to use. Turnkey versions of the VT[4] are available from dealers for under $10,000, and provide everything you need from titler to paint to switcher/seg and keyer.

The GlobeCaster is an interesting product that began its life as the Play Trinity, a product that was so long in development and so long on hype that most of us suspected it of being pure vaporware for a long time. By the time the Trinity actually came to market, the company was bankrupt, and the technology was spun off to GlobalStreams, which has continued to develop the core product. The GlobeCaster is designed as a live switcher that can stream out multiple formats, including streaming web video. The GlobeCaster (from its Trinity beginnings) has always had an integrated virtual set function as part of the chroma keying section. While no real motion tracking is available, the virtual sets do include features such as shadows and virtual reflections.

GlobeCaster now also has a tactile control surface, the CS-1000, which makes the unit as easy to use as a regular full-size production switcher. The CS-1000 is larger and more substantial than the VT[4] remote, and is configured much like a pro switcher. A base GlobeCaster with four input modules starts below $20,000, but there are many options that can take a full-blown package price up to near $40,000.

Dedicated Keyers

Most local television studios use the built-in chroma keying capabilities of their production switcher for live keying. However, there are several standalone hardware units available that provide more sophisticated keying management that networks and better-equipped stations will use.

While dedicated hardware keyers have come and gone, and companies with them, the company that stands out in the history of hardware chroma keying is clearly Ultimatte. Founded by Petros Vlahos, one of the creators of the compositing technology used in *Mary Poppins*, Ultimatte has been at the forefront of continuing development of hardware color-based compositing technology. The current crop of Ultimatte

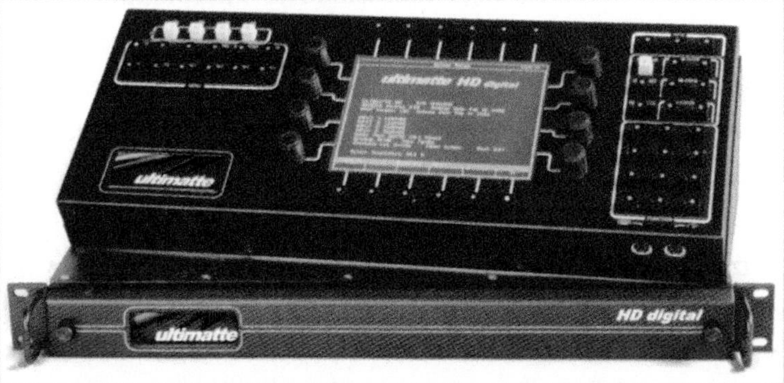

Ultimatte's High Definition matte compositing system has been designed to meet the needs of visual effects production with digital cinema technology. With advanced features like dual link 4:4:4 I/O, internal 4:4:4:4 image processing, external matte input, automated ambiance color adjustment, field upgradeable software, support for all Broadcast HDTV and Digital Cinema 24p/psf image standards, as well as production-proven compatibility with Sony's CineAlta™ digital HD cameras, the Ultimatte HD is the perfect choice for real-time travelling matte generation.

The Ultimatte HD digital is part of the third generation of Ultimatte's all-digital compositing devices and features the Emmy®- and Oscar®-winning technology. A fully linear matting system, it produces totally realistic composites even when the foreground contains smoke, shadows, soft edges, and other translucent and transparent qualities. Ultimatte Corporation is the world's recognized leader in blue/greenscreen compositing technology and has been in business for over twenty-five years, continually refining, enhancing, and improving the craft of travelling matte generation.

hardware ranges from the UltimatteDV, a unit optimized for 4:1:1 video and accepting IEEE-1394 i/o (under $6000 street) to a high-end HD unit ($85,000).

***Figure 11.7** The Ultimatte 400 provides sophisticated color-based keying for local studios at an economical price.*

An excellent example of a standalone keyer that might find use in a well-equipped SD studio would be the Ultimatte 400, which is available in single-channel or dual-channel versions. Designed around 4:2:2 SDI video, the unit internally *uprezzes* the video to 4:4:4 through mathematical interpolation, and pulls the matte at fully pixel-sampled 10-bit resolution. The resulting composite is known as 4:4:4:4, the fourth 4 representing a full-resolution matte; this is as contrasted to a matte pulled directly from 4:2:2 video, which essentially has half the horizontal resolution as 4:4:4, or a matte pulled from 4:1:1 DV, which essentially has one-fourth of full horizontal resolution. Ultimatte keyers have a sophisticated spill removal algorithm and can replicate clean shadows on the set.

Weathercasting

Without a doubt, the major use for live chroma keying is weathercasting. Nearly every local station in the nation uses chroma keying for this purpose, and many don't ever use the capability for anything else. The ability to put the meteorologist right smack in front of a satellite shot or radar map, allowing her to point out specific areas of interest and then easily switch to the next graphic, has been one of the most effective visual additions to local news.

As with any specialty, meteorology is a niche world with its own culture, jargon, and unique technology. There is a whole specialty market of hardware and software packages specifically for local station meteorologists—graphics packages, control systems for integrating maps and Doppler radar, and lately sophisticated motion tracking systems that allow the meteorologist to change graphics with certain hand motions instead of using a hardware remote. These are the sort of specialty niche products that if you're in the meteorology business, you know about and

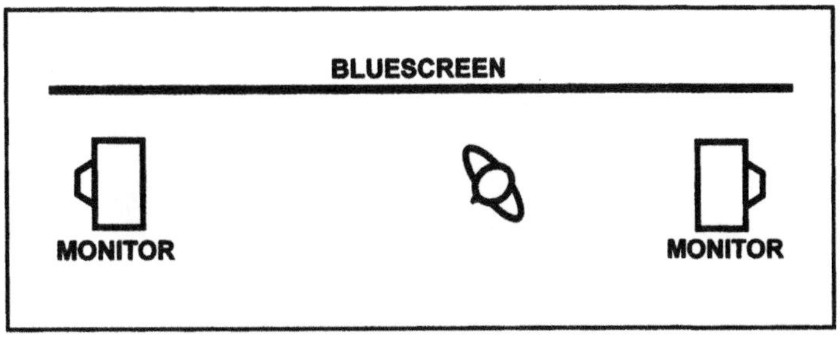

Figure 11.8 *A diagram of the typical studio setup for a local weathercast. Monitors offscreen on either side display the composited signal, allowing the meteorologist to see herself in action interacting with the computer graphics and satellite images. Usually, the meteorologist carries a remote control that switches views.*

keep up with the latest developments on each one; and if you're not in that business, you've never heard of. While interesting, these specialized products are really beyond the scope of this book, so we're going to stay clear of them and focus solely on the actual keying technology.

As I mentioned above, most local stations simply use the integrated chroma key function in their production switcher to set up the weathercast. Better-equipped stations may use a dedicated keyer such as one of the Ultimatte line.

Virtual Studio

Until recently, weathercasting comprised almost 100% of the use of live keying on broadcast television. However, over the last decade the development of virtual sets has changed that, and today numerous network programs are shot on virtual sets.

At its most basic, a virtual set is simply a static CG set used as a background plate behind live talent. Simple sets can be prepared in any 3D program showing different angles from different camera positions; the live foreground can be shot using static cameras in similar positions, and the effect can be quite convincing.

However, the true virtual set allows full camera movement through the set, including pan, tilt, dolly, and zoom motions of the camera to follow live action. Some systems use complex sensors on the camera to detect every motion of the camera and change in the lens settings and send those changes to a real-time 3D rendering engine, which matches the changes in the virtual camera. When the real camera zooms in and tilts up, the virtual camera zooms in and tilts up at the same amount. Thus, the 3D set changes and moves just as it would if being photographed by the real-world camera. The live output of the 3D rendering engine is sent to the production switcher, where it is used as background; the live

Figure 11.9 *Meteorologist Josh Judge in front of the blue screen at WMUR-TV in Manchester, NH. The inset shows the composited signal. Photo courtesy of Sabre Gagnon and WMUR-TV.*

host, photographed in front of a blue or green screen, is sent through the chroma keyer and the resulting composite looks exactly as if the talent were standing in the fictitious set.

Creating a simple set with locked-down camera shots and no camera motion is quite easy, and can be done with the most basic equipment. It is the camera motion that has always been the complex technical challenge with virtual sets. There are three basic approaches to matching the camera motion for virtual sets.

Software Motion Tracking

The simplest (at least mechanically!) is basically a software-intensive version that uses a tracking grid on the set. Tracking software in the package is able to translate the on-screen changes of this grid pattern (usually a lighter blue) into camera moves and zooms in the virtual camera. One example of tracking software that works with this style of set is Orad SmartSet.

Hardware Sensor Motion Tracking

There are a number of hardware-based motion tracking systems for virtual sets. These range from mechanical sensors connected to the camera head and lens to complex infrared (IR) systems. Many combine both technologies. In all cases, the combined technologies work to feed the rendering platform camera data for camera position, tilt, angle, and lens settings.

Mechanical sensors are the most basic form of camera position tracking for virtual sets. THOMA, Orad, and Vinten manufacture tripod heads with built-in sensors and remote data feeds for lens settings.

One of the most widely installed virtual set systems at the time of writ-

Younger folks have never seen a weathercast done without chroma key, but of course it hasn't always been done that way! In the 50s and 60s, television weather forecasts were done with physical diagrams ranging from whiteboard-type maps with marker, or magnetic shapes moved around on a map. Additionally, the local personality delivering the forecast rarely had any education in weather forecasting—they were simply regurgitating what had come in on the teletype (another obsolete news technology!). David Letterman and several other "names" in television today got their start doing local weather.

Once chroma keying technology really took off in the 70s, it wasn't long until it found nearly universal adoption—from high-end networks on down to the smallest local television station. Pretty soon every station had chroma keyed weather, and they began to compete on the basis of more accurate forecasts. That's when local stations began employing actual meteorologists and installing their own radar; but again, that's a story for another book and another market.

I remember clearly when WRAL-TV in Raleigh, NC, first began to use chroma key for the local weather. I remember just as clearly when WGAL-TV in Lancaster, PA installed a new Ultimatte unit that could handle shadows, so that the weathercaster's arm cast a realistic shadow on the weather map rather than an area of unkeyed blue. How cool was that?

With the improved quality and brightness of plasma monitors and "video walls," some stations and networks have recently moved to using videowall installations on the set for weathercasting. However, the graphics are far less legible and good chroma key remains (in my opinion) the strongest presentation mode for weather or other graphics that must be combined with a live presenter.

ing is the Orad Xync system, which uses IR LEDs mounted on the camera and mounts IR motion tracking sensors around the studio. Orad also manufactures camera pedestal head sensors and a proprietary rendering platform that is switchable between SD and HD output.

Another IR tracking product is the THOMA Walkfinder Tracking System. In this system, an odd-looking array of reflective balls is mounted on each tracked camera, and a set of IR motion sensors placed on the grid of the studio is able to track the position and orientation of the camera. The advantage of an IR system like this over mechanical sensors is that it can be used with hand-held or SteadiCam mounted cameras.

Figure 11.10 *A Pro Cyc virtual set. Note the gridwork on the back panel, which is a lighter blue than the base chroma key blue. Software tracking is able to translate changes in this grid, which reflect the motion of the real camera, into matching motion of the virtual camera.*

IR position systems like these can capture camera position, tilt, and pan but must still use a lens sensor to send lens data to the rendering engine.

A similar system developed by the BBC and known as the Free-D tracking system mounts an infrared emitter/mini-CCD camera package on the rear of each camera, which illuminates and tracks grid-mounted reflective targets. The image from the tracking camera is processed by a Free-D unit to calculate the exact position and orientation of the studio camera. This is done by real time analysis of the image to identify each target. Knowing the physical location of the targets, Free-D calculates the position of the camera to a very high degree of accuracy. The zoom and focus axes are monitored by high-resolution optical sensors mounted on the camera lens. Combining this data allows the Free-D processor to calculate the Pan, Tilt, Roll, X, Y, Z, Zoom and Focus parameters to accurately pinpoint the studio camera position. The system is licensed to Vinten Radamec Robotics.

Robotic Motion Control

The third and slightly different approach to virtual set motion tracking is to combine robotic control of the real-world camera and the virtual camera. Once the real and imaginary cameras are calibrated together, the remote control panel sends identical data to both cameras; both then move in sync based on the received signal. Rather than tracking the motion of the physical camera, both the physical and virtual cameras track the signals of the remote control operator. The Radamec Robotic Track-

Cam System is an example of this sort of virtual studio system.

As the technology has matured, the use of virtual sets in television broadcast has recently exploded. In many local markets, sets that appear quite real are in fact virtual. While the initial investment in equipment is higher than the cost of building a traditional set, it has numerous advantages, not the least being the ability to apparently have multiple, very complex sets for different shows, all shot in a single (fairly small) bluescreen studio—a trick not easily accomplished with traditional set construction!

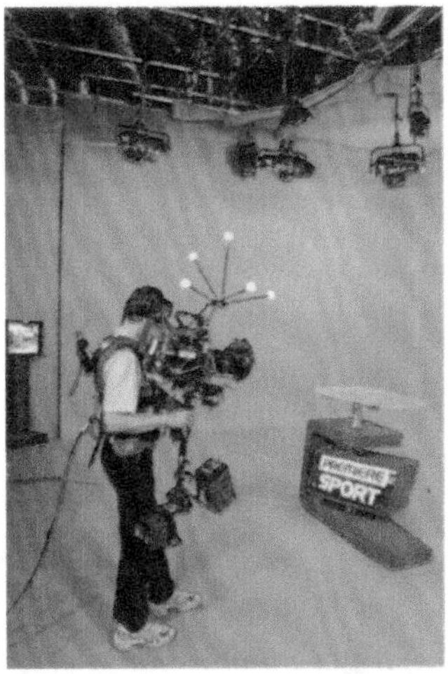

Figure 11.11 *The THOMA Walkfinder Tracking System attaches an array of reflective balls to each camera, allowing IR emitter/sensors to track location and orientation.*

While most special effects compositing will continue to be a post-production process, live keying has an important spot in television broadcasting, a role that will only grow in the future.

Manufacturers of Virtual Set Equipment

http://www.orad.co.il/
http://www.3dk.de/tracking.html
http://www.thoma.de/
http://www.vinten.com/
http://www.ddgtv.com/

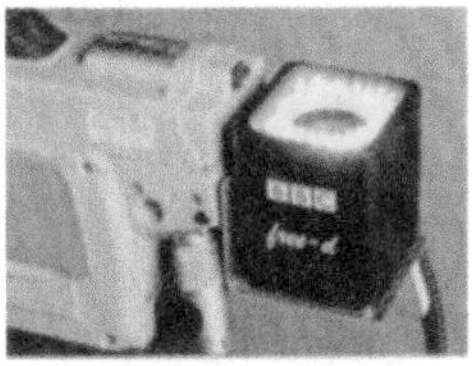

Figure 11.12 *The BBC Free-D IR LED emmiter and tracking camera package mounted on the rear of a studio camera.*

Research & Development

http://www.ist-matris.org/
http://www.bbc.co.uk/rd/projects/index.shtml

Virtual Set Graphics

http://www.ddgtv.com/
http://www.getris.com/
http://www.3dvideobackgrounds.com
http://www.litesets.net/LiteSets.htm
http://www.istudiostv.com
http://virtualsetworks.com/

Not-So-Live Virtual Sets

Serious Magic ULTRA 2

Since we are discussing virtual sets here, this is the place to mention the Serious Magic ULTRA 2 system, even though it is not a real-time system. This is probably one of the most popular "low-end" virtual set systems due to its relatively low buy-in price and ease of use. Any basic color screen shot can be placed in one of the included virtual sets, each of which includes several different basic shot angles at wide, medium, and close-up variations. Within each of these shot angles, the virtual camera view can be moved and zoomed to some degree while still retaining a sense of realism. Of course, this is not a live system and the results must be rendered before they can be used.

Serious Magic has several add-on packs of virtual sets, and there are several third-party companies that now supply sets in the Serious Magic format. Some of these sets are quite impressive some are pretty cheesy. Just as with certain popular suppliers of royalty-free clips and music, the nice sets will soon get overused.

Since the sets are composed of 3D surfaces mapped with graphics, an enterprising producer can in fact substantially change one of the stock sets to a custom look by editing the mapped graphics.

3-D Animation Programs

The ultimate flexibility for a not-so-live virtual set comes in 3D animation programs such as LightWave, Maya, 3ds Max, or trueSpace. While this is overlooked by many animators, these programs each have the facility to combine live video and a matte channel, mapped to a plane locked to the camera. This technique allows the animator to place a live person "inside" a 3D virtual set and control the exact positioning and motion in relation to the set, rather than rendering the set as a separate element and compositing it with the live action separately. This is a handy option when it is necessary to have live talent in the midst of a complex, multi-layered imaginary set.

12 Tutorials

If you just bought this book and jumped right to this chapter for the fun stuff, I really hope you will later go back and read the earlier chapters carefully. The tutorials we will look at in this chapter are important and will give you a sense of how different keyers work, but you won't really understand what you're doing in many cases or the production issues you need to deal with if you haven't read the earlier chapters! 'Nuff said!

In this chapter we'll tackle a number of tutorials using specific software packages or plugins for particular compositing situations. Demo versions of most of the software we're going to cover in this chapter are available for download from company web sites. We've included a number of sample files on the DVD to use in these tutorials.

The purpose of these tutorials is to show several features of different kinds of keyers that excel in certain situations—but perhaps not in others. Manufacturers (and software fans) will tell you that such-and-such a plugin is the only one you'll ever need; but that just isn't true. There is no such thing as the perfect keying software that will produce ideal results in every situation. Although these plugins have advanced formidably in recent years through the use of things like fuzzy logic and faster processing capabilities, each plugin has its own strengths—and thus also its own weaknesses. In actual practice you'll soon learn that no one plugin is best across the board; each production situation may require experimentation to find which one works best. Of course, standards for what constitutes an acceptable composite vary from person to person and even project to project. A key that is acceptable for a low-budget local commercial won't even be close for feature film work. It's not unusual in some rigorous situations to use multiple keyers to achieve a clean final result.

Tutorial A: Nonlinear Editors

We'll start with the basics—simple keying in the timeline of a nonlinear editor such as Adobe Premiere Pro 2.0, Apple Final Cut Pro, or Sony Vegas 6.0. Each of these packages comes with a number of basic color-based and luma-based keyers. Some of these will work better in certain situations than others; you'll have to learn from experience which ones work well in each situation.

Premiere Pro and FCP both have very similar basic keying filters; Vegas comes with a single Chroma Key filter. We'll try a different filter in each program to show you how they work. Unfortunately none of these packages comes with really good spill removal, which can be a major downside of using the built-in keyers.

Adobe Premiere Pro

In Premiere Pro 2.0, create a new project using a standard 4:3 DV preset. Import one of the sample footage clips provided on the DVD; the *green444.mov* or *green422.mov* are excellent. Now import any still that's 720 x 480 or larger to serve as a background plate. Place the still (which will be the background plate) on the Video 1 track in the timeline sequence. Now drop the greenscreen footage into the Video 2 track of the timeline sequence. This is the foreground video.

> Note: In most nonlinear editors, any tracks above will be superimposed on top of lower tracks. However, you should be aware that this can be set up the opposite way in some software packages such as Pinnacle Liquid Silver. In the present case, as in most pack-

ages, compositing will begin with lower tracks, with upper tracks being superimposed over the lower ones.

Now that you have both background (in this case a still) and the foreground footage on the timeline, select the greenscreen footage. Go to the Effects panel, and scroll down until you see the Key folder. Open the folder by clicking on the twirly arrow. Scroll down and select the Greenscreen Key. Drag this and drop it on top of the greenscreen footage. Now, with the footage selected, you'll be able to change the settings of the Greenscreen Key in the Effect Controls window. Next to the Greenscreen key there will be a twirly arrow; click on it to open the controls.

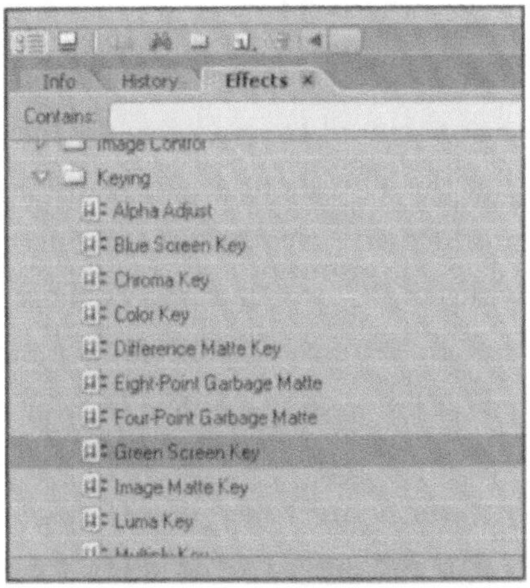

Figure 12.1 *The Effects panel contains all available video and audio effects and transitions.*

This keyer is set up entirely around logic for green backgrounds (the matching Bluescreen key is obviously set up for blue)

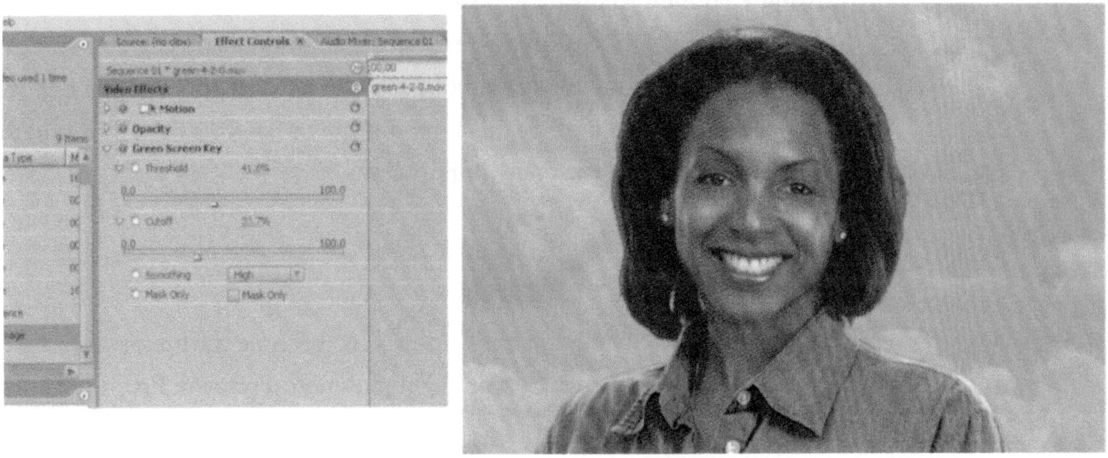

Figure 12.2 *The Effect Controls panel is where you can adjust the controls of the selected effects filter.*

and can work very well if the green on your actual background matches the internally set green color. The controls for this keyer are fairly simple; play with them in turn to see what they do. The Threshold controls the opacity or translucency of the background, while the Cutoff control ad-

***Figure 12.3** The final composite is pretty clean, but there is a slight dark line around the subject's shoulders.*

justs the opacity or translucency of the foreground. The Smoothing control, which can be set to None, Low, or High, adjusts the edge blurring of the matte. The Mask Only selection allows you to see the matte itself temporarily in order to adjust the opacity of the background and foreground. In many cases you'll find that the Threshold and Cutoff controls must be quite close together to produce effective results. In our illustration, the Threshold is at 41% while the Cutoff is at 33%. This creates an effective basic composite, though there is still noticeable green spill around the subject.

You'll notice that while the key is quite good using the *green444.mov* sample, if you test the same settings using the *green420.mov* sample or (even worse) the *green411.mov* sample, the edges will be noticeably rough and jagged. This keyer does not have the ability to blur the edges strongly enough to create a clean-looking key with 4:2:0 or 4:1:1 footage. It also has no capacity to deal with spill and has no choking (matte shrinking) ability to help get rid of pesky blue/green edges in some footage. However, for good clean shots and quick basic keying, this plugin may be satisfactory for many applications.

Apple Final Cut Pro

On the Apple Macintosh, Final Cut Pro has become the major choice for editing. FCP has a similar set of keying filters to Premiere Pro; we'll take a look at a different one. Open FCP; start a project with 4:3 DV settings. Import one of the sample footage clips from the DVD; then import a still, any texture or photograph that can serve as a background plate.

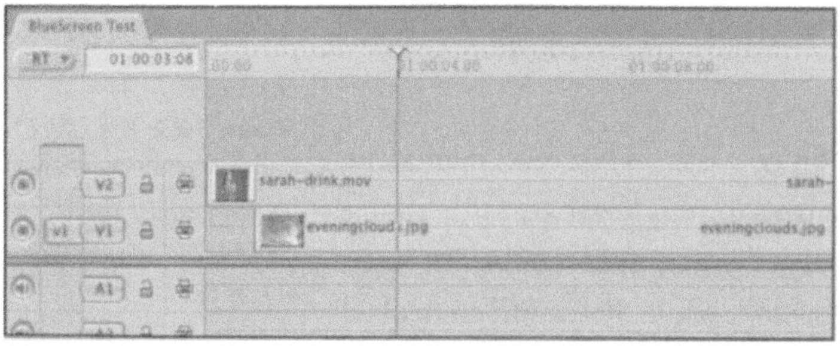

***Figure 12.4** Drop the bluescreen footage (the foreground plate) in the track above the background plate.*

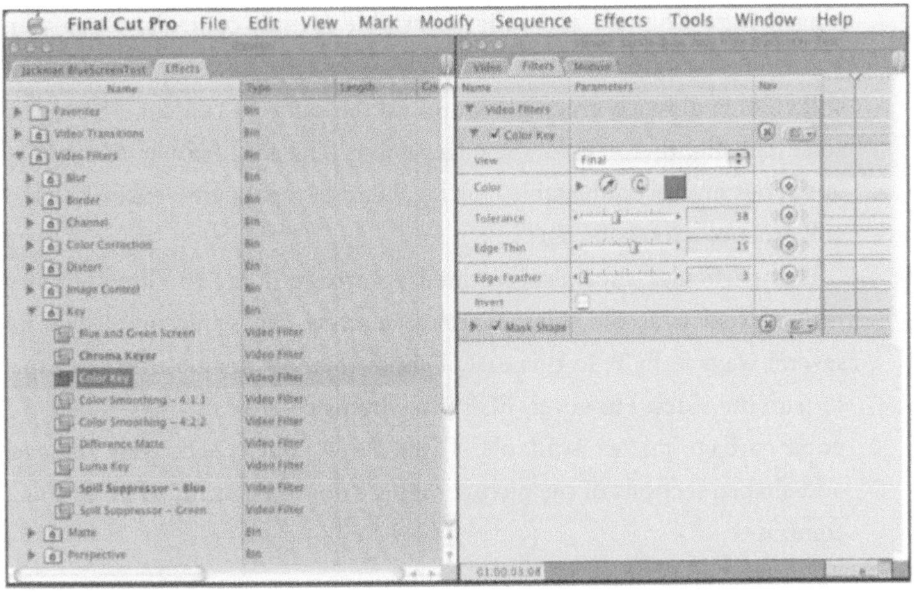

Figure 12.5 *Adjustments to the controls are made in the Filters panel. Note the Mask Shape is enabled below the Color Key filter to act as a garbage matte.*

Now drop the background plate into the first track (V1) and place the bluescreen footage into the second track (V2). As in Premiere Pro, higher tracks are superimposed over lower tracks. Now go to the Effects>Video Filters and select the Key folder. Select the Color Keyer and drop it on the footage. In the Effects Control window, you'll now be able to open the Color Keyer and adjust the controls.

Figure 12.6 *The final composite from Final Cut Pro. The result is quite clean, though there is a tiny bit of blue near the hair as the actress moves.*

The first control in the Color Keyer is the dropdown list that selects the final composite, the matte, or the original footage in the preview window. In the Color Control there's an eyedropper to let you select the exact shade or hue of the backing color (in this case blue). The eyedropper selects a very narrow range of blue; the Tolerance slider below it allows you to expand this range to include all the blue tones that are present in your backing color. Adjust the tolerance slider until the entire backing color becomes transparent. Both FCP versions of Color Key filters have an edge over the Premiere Color Key in that they include fully adjustable edge thinning (Matte Choker) and fully adjustable feather controls. Once you adjust the background to be satisfactorily transparent, there will likely still be blue glow or green glow around the subject. You can adjust the edge thin slightly to choke the edges down. The edge feather control allows continuously adjustable blurring, but use it sparingly—excessive blur will produce a too-soft edge.

This particular shot also required a garbage matte to eliminate unwanted visuals at the sides. Garbage matting can be accomplished in several ways in FCP; in this case, I chose to apply a simple mask shape to trim the sides. However, FCP (like Premiere Pro) also has 4- and 8-point garbage mattes available. These allow you to selectively remove odd-shaped sections of the picture that are not to be included in the final composite.

Sony Vegas

Sony Vegas has become a very popular editing package on the Windows platform. Vegas fans feel that it is easier to use than Premiere or FCP, but I'm not entirely sure this is true. The interface is different from the other packages (which have very similar, Avid-like interfaces) and may seem more intuitive to some people. However, any NLE that incorporates the necessary functions is going to be a complex piece of software. If Vegas seems easier to use to you, then use it! However, because of its smaller market share, there are fewer third-party plugins available for Vegas

Figure 12.7 *Setting up a bluescreen composite in the Sony Vegas timeline*

than for Premiere Pro or FCP. The only third-party keying plugin for Vegas that I could identify at the time of writing is Boris Red. Since Red is an excellent application, this may not seem like much of a limitation.

Start Vegas and create a new project for 4:3 DV. Create at least two video tracks by right-clicking next to the timeline. In the asset window, find the file *green420.mov* on the DVD and place it on the uppermost track (as with most NLEs, upper tracks are superimposed on lower tracks). Now find a still or a texture to use as a background plate and drop it in the lower track.

Make sure that your preview setup is set to Best (Full) so you can see the file in full resolution. If you have an output device (such as an OHCI IEEE 1394 deck or converter) that allows you to view the file on a video monitor, make sure that the option is properly set up and select the little TV screen in the preview window that allows you to send the output to an external monitor.

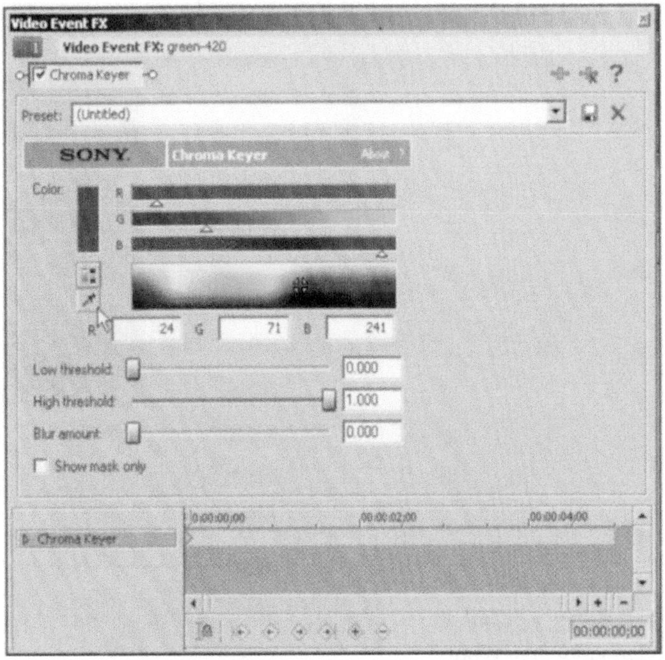

Figure 12.8 *The controls for the Chroma Key filter*

To Set Up OHCI Output:

1. From the Options menu, choose Preferences and then click the Preview Device tab.

2. From the Device dropdown list, choose OHCI Compliant IEEE 1394. The Details box displays information about the device.

3. If the project is invalid for DV output, conform to the following dropdown list to indicate how you want to adjust the video to display properly on your external monitor.

4. Now, on the greenscreen footage, click on the + sign on the extreme right of the footage. This opens the Video Filters window. Select the

Sony Chroma Key, and then click OK. The filter is set up for bluescreen by default.

Select the Eyedropper tool and use it to click on a clean, representative area of backing color in the timeline track thumbnail. This will set the center of transparency to that color.

Figure 12.9 *The Crop tool in Vegas*

Figure 12.10 *Final composite from Vegas*

Tip: You can often get a better result by sampling a larger area from the preview window. To do this, turn off the Chroma Key by unchecking the checkbox in the button to the upper left of the controls. I know it doesn't make sense; just do it. Now click on the Eyedropper tool and use it to draw a square marquee on a large area of backing color in the preview window. This will select the entire range of colors rather than a simple point sample.

Now you have to adjust the transparency of the background (Low Threshold) and the opacity of the foreground (High Threshold). Move the Low Threshold slider up until the background plate is clearly visible with no veiling or schmutz. Now, click on the Show Mask Only gadget to adjust the foreground. Typically, the foreground will have areas of translucency or print-through at this stage, visible as gray tones in the area of the matte. Move the High Threshold slider until all areas of the foreground just become solid white—*do not move any further!* Now deselect the Show Mask Only gadget to see the final composite preview. Since we selected the 4:2:0 sample, the undersampled color channel shows up as jagged edges on the composite. You can use the Blur Amount control very gently until the jaggies have been blurred out. However, Vegas has provided a better tool to deal with jaggies.

Click on the + sign again to open the Filters window. Add the Sony Chroma Blur filter. This allows you to selectively blur only the chroma channel without affecting the luma channel, where most perceived detail is transmitted. The filter can blur either vertical or horizontal up to four pixels. The Filter works best when it is applied before the Chroma Key, so drag the Filter button at the top of the Filter window to the left of the Chroma Key button. Since we're using 4:2:0 footage, a logical setting to start at would be to vertical blur of 2; however, play with the controls and observe the result. Horizontal blur of 2 pixels and vertical blur of 4 pixels may produce best results with some 4:2:0 footage. Only after you've produced the best, cleanest edge possible using this tool should you then play with the Chroma Key Blur Amount control. It's best to use this sparingly, certainly less than 0.10.

You will notice that there is still a slight edge around the subject's shoulders that needs to be removed, but the stock keyer has no facility to do this. Like Premiere Pro, the stock keyer in Vegas desperately needs a matte choke adjustment!

Tutorial B: After Effects

Let's tackle the basic stages of color-based compositing in After Effects (AE). Most of the filters that we'll be using (such as the Matte Choker, Spill Suppressor, and plugins such as Keylight) are included in After Effects Pro, but not in the Standard Edition. I'm afraid if you want to do

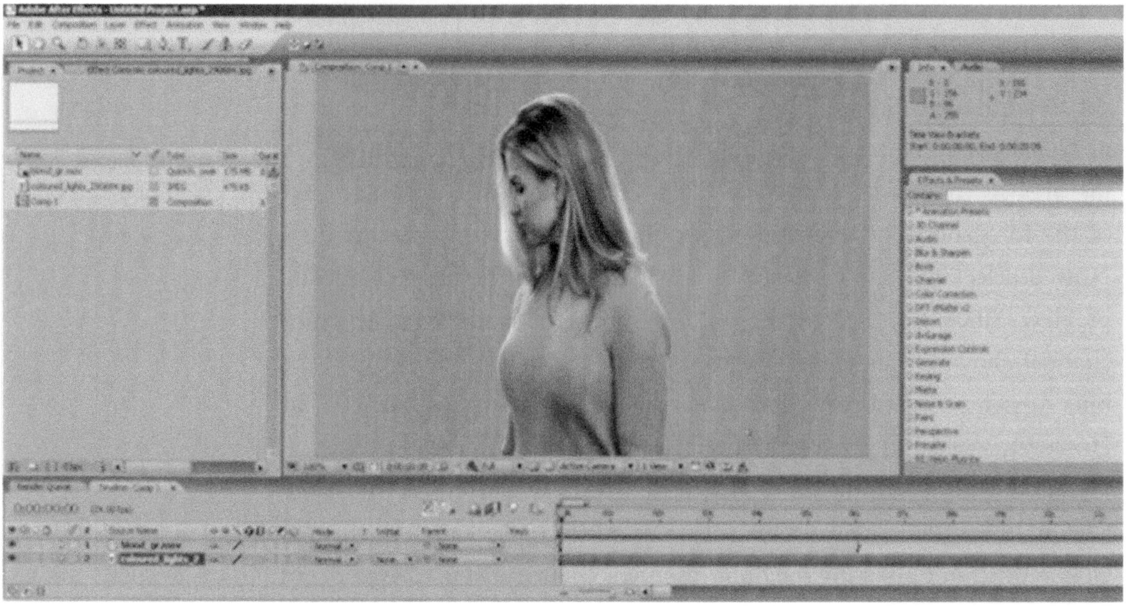

Figure 12.11 The After Effects interface will look like this when you've set up the project.

a lot of quality color-based compositing in After Effects, you'll need to spring for the Pro Edition! We're using AE Pro 7.0.

> Note: These tutorials assume that you are already familiar with the basics of operating After Effects: creating compositions, importing and interpreting footage, manipulating footage in the timeline, etc. If you are not, please spend some time with the AE User manual before attempting these tutorials. Another great resource is *Creating Motion Graphics with After Effects,* Volumes 1 & 2, Third Ed., by Chris and Trish Meyer.

Open AE and start a new project. Now create a new composition using the DV Widescreen preset—720 x 480, widescreen 1.2 aspect ratio. Now, from the DVD, import the file blond_gr.mov. Import a still graphic or texture to use as a background plate.

Now, we're going to try the Color Range Key, which allows the user to specify a range of colors to treat as transparent. This is excellent for times when the backing color is not evenly illuminated from top to bottom, and thus you need to specify a range of green or blue tones to be included in the matte.

Go to Effect>Keying>Color Range Key and apply to the foreground footage. With the greenscreen file selected, move to the Effect Controls window. In the filter controls, you'll see a thumbnail of the matte (mostly white at this point), with a set of three eyedroppers to the right. Use the top eyedropper to sample the backing color in the comp window. Immediately a portion of the matte will turn black, showing areas that match that color (within the currently specified range of tolerance, or *fuzziness*). If there are areas of the backing color that are not transparent in the comp window (and showing black in the matte thumbnail), use the second eyedropper, the one with a + sign, to add colors to the range. Click on an area of the

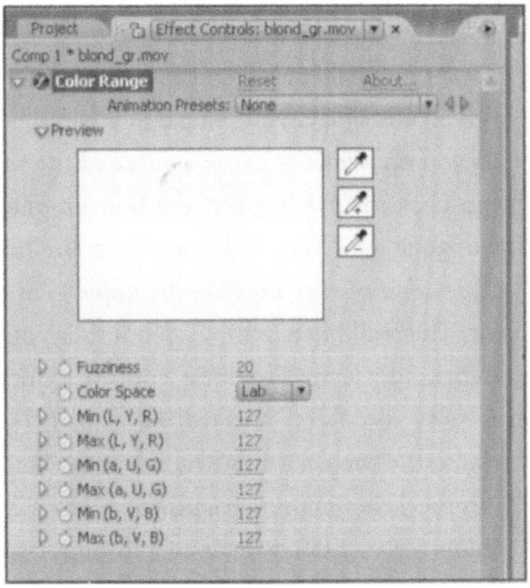

Figure 12.12 *To the right of the matte thumbnail, the top eyedropper selects the base matte color; use the Plus (+) eyedropper to add more colors to the backing range, and the Minus (–) eyedropper to subtract colors from the backing range.*

Figure 12.13 *With most of the background color range added, the comp may appear like this—some schmutz in the background, and some green around the edges of the subject.*

backing color that is still visible in the comp window. To add more tones to the color range, you'll have to select the + eyedropper again.

If you accidentally cause an area of the foreground to become translucent, click the eyedropper (the bottom one) to select colors that should be opaque, or subtracted from the matte range. *Do not sample too close to the edge of the foreground subject*—in this case, next to the blonde hair. This will likely remove detail that you'd want to keep.

Now, adjust the Fuzziness control (which expands the range around the selected colors) upward until most, but not quite all, of the green around the subject's blond hair is gone. We'll remove the last bit of green with the Spill Suppressor and the Matte Choker.

Now go to Effect>Keying>Spill Suppressor, and apply the Spill Suppressor. You have to tell the Spill Suppressor what color to suppress. The best way to do this is to temporarily disable the Color Range Key by clicking on the *f* next to the effect name. Now use the Spill Suppressor eyedropper to select the backing color in the comp window. By default, the Suppression setting is set to 100%; if the Suppressor changes the overall color of the foreground, or otherwise affects the foreground in

Figure 12.14 *The Spill Suppressor will subtract a specified spill color from the foreground.*

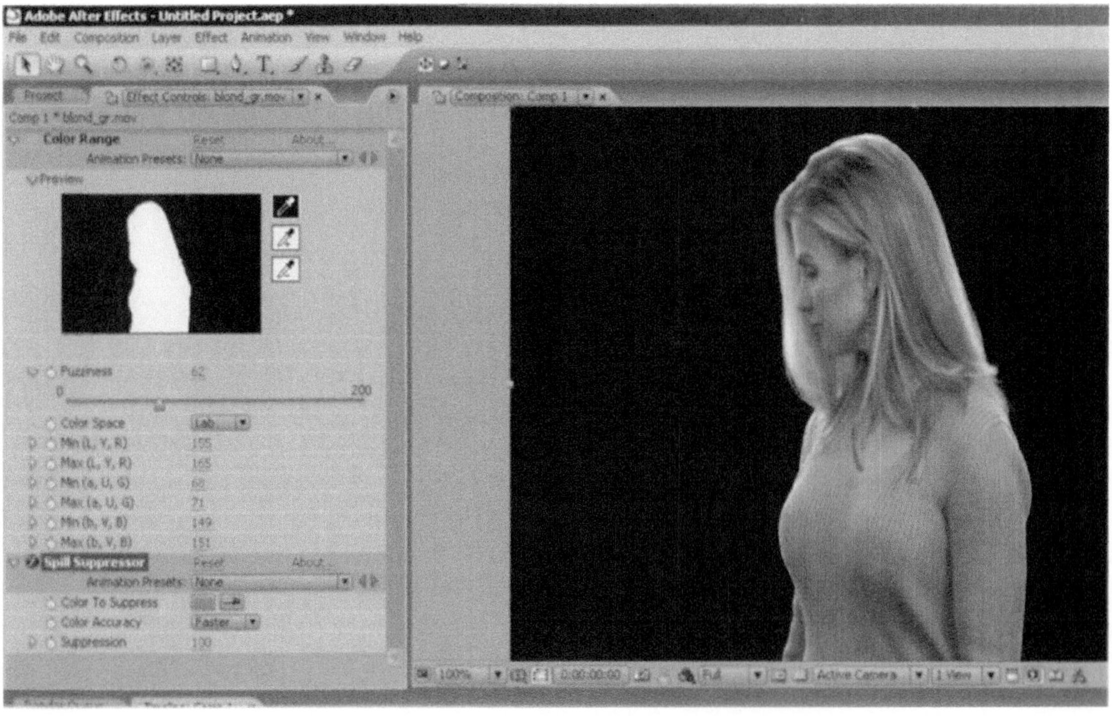

a negative way, turn this down to find an acceptable compromise. Typically, the Accuracy setting can be left on Faster; only in certain critical circumstances will you need to change it to More Accurate.

Now go back and enable the Color Range Keyer again, and adjust Fuzziness until the composite appears to be clean.

The Color Range Key filter can produce excessively hard outlines for the subject. The edge must match the softness of a photographically reproduced sharp edge in the foreground video; if the matte edges are too sharp, the subject seems to stand out artificially from the overall composite. If the edges seem to be too sharp or hard, or if a dark edge remains, apply Effect>Matte>Matte Choker.

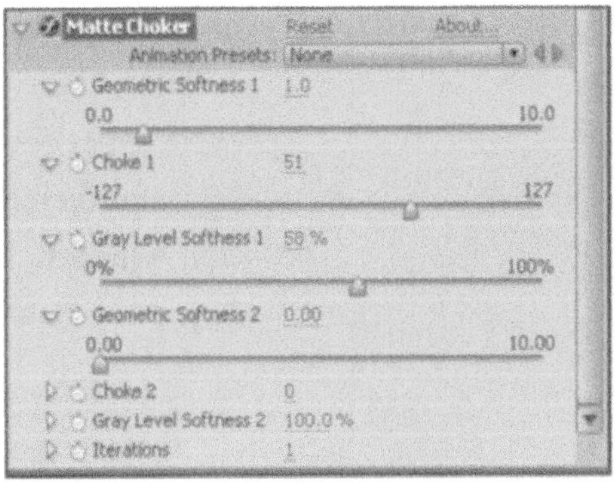

Figure 12.15 *The Matte Choker can both shrink the matte to remove dark edges and soften the edges.*

The stock settings for the Matte Choker are too aggressive for this picture, which is not undersampled. Reduce Geometric Softness 1 to a setting of 1, then increase Gray Level Softness 1 until the edge is slightly softened; adjust Choke 1 to Shrink (choke) the matte until no dark edge remains. Do not adjust Choke 2 or Gray Level Softness 2 in this case!

Now let's back up and try another keyer and test using the tools in the Matte Choker on undersampled 4:1:1 footage. Remove blond_gr.mov from the composition and change the comp settings from 16:9 to 4:3 (0.9 aspect ratio).

Figure 12.16 *Final composite.*

Import *green411.mov* and place it on the timeline. Go to Effect>Keying>Linear Color Keying and apply the Linear Color Key to the footage. In the control panel, you will see two thumbnails with a set of eyedroppers in between. The lefthand thumbnail displays the original footage; the righthand thumb displays the matte. Select either the top eyedropper (between the thumbnails) or the Key Color eyedropper below, and then click an appropriate area of backing color in the composition window. This sets the base color for the matte; that color becomes black in the matte thumbnail and transparent in the comp window.

> Tip: To preview transparency for different colors, select the Key Color eyedropper, hold down the Alt key (Windows) or Option key (Mac OS), and move the cursor to different areas in the Composition panel or the original thumbnail image. The transparency of the image in the Composition panel changes as you move the cursor over different colors or shades. Click to select the appropriate color.

Adjust matching tolerance in one of the following ways: Select the Plus (+) or the Minus (–) eyedropper, and then click a color in the left thumbnail image. The Plus eyedropper adds the specified color to the key color range, increasing the matching tolerance and the level of transparency. The Minus eyedropper subtracts the specified color from the key color range, decreasing the matching tolerance and the level of transparency.

> TIP: The eyedropper tools move the sliders automatically. It is instructive to leave the sliders visible to see what changes when you click on a particular color. Later, you can use the sliders to fine-tune the keying results.

While fine-tuning the matte, it is best to see the matte itself full size rather than the composited video. To do this, select View>Matte Only. Now you can see how small changes in the sliders change areas of the matte from transparent (black) to translucent (gray) or opaque (white).

Drag the matching Tolerance slider. A value of 0 makes the entire image opaque; a value of 100 makes the entire image transparent. Start with a fairly low value, and increase until the background is nearly all black but not perfect.

Drag the Matching Softness slider bar to soften the matching tolerance by tapering the tolerance value. Typically, values under 20% produce the best results. The background area should be solid black and the foreground solid white with a clean and detailed edge.

Before closing the Effect Controls window, make sure that you have selected Final Output from the View menu to display the composited video in the comp window.

A quick look at the jagged edges in the composite tells us visually that the footage is undersampled 4:1:1. Now let's even out those jaggies with the Matte Choker!

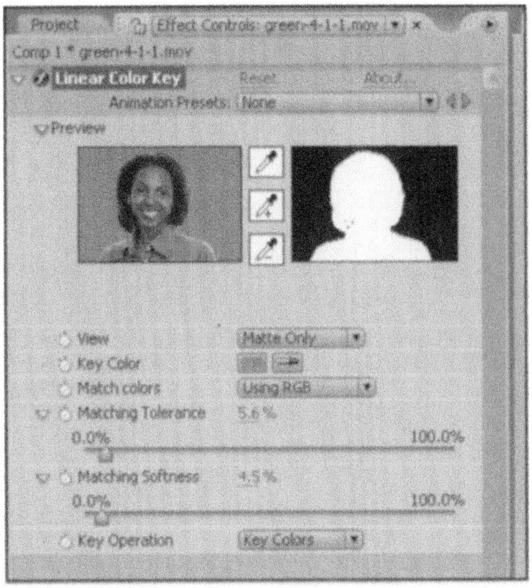

***Figure 12.17** The Linear Color Keyer has two methods of adding and subtracting colors from the matte.*

Go to Effect>Matte>Matte Choker to apply the Matte Choker to the footage. It's best to experiment with the controls a bit to learn what each one does. To see what the controls do, change Geometric Softness 1 to a value of 0, Gray Level Softness 1 to 0, and Choke 1 to 0.

Now increase Geometric Softness 1 to see how it smoothes the jaggies out. Play with the setting until you've smoothed the jagged edges to a more pleasing smoothness; however, use the minimum satisfactory setting! Overcorrecting may have unwanted effects. Now go to Geometric Softness 2 and increase the value to see the somewhat different effect; typically, you will usually leave this control at 0.

Now increase Gray Level Softness 1 until the edge is soft enough to seem to match other edges in picture. At this point, there will likely be a dark edge around subject. This is where shrinking, or choking, the matte is necessary. Increase the setting of Choke 1 until the dark edge disappears; don't choke too much or you'll eliminate detail at the edges.

If more effect is needed, change the Iterations to 2 (or more), which basically runs the entire algorithm multiple times. You may have to reduce some settings when Iterations are increased, since they are being applied again to the same image.

If there is still a bit of green spill at the edges, apply the Spill Suppressor as above.

Usually, the lowest satisfactory settings will be best for the Matte Choker. Overchoking removes detail, which will often look fine in an

***Figure 12.18** The final composite (with settings visible) is not perfect, but vastly reduces the jagged edges of chroma undersampling.*

individual still frame but can become obvious in motion. Thin wisps of hair may vanish and reappear in motion, for instance. Overblurring the edge will also be obvious in motion; excessive Geometric Softness will turn inside corners which should be sharp acute angles into soft curves with dark fill.

Tutorial C: Keylight

Now we'll play with one of my favorite keyers, Keylight from The Foundry. Keylight 1.1 is included with Adobe After Effects Pro 7.0, and version 2.0 is included with Apple Shake. A version is also available for OSX.

In talking recently to Jonathan Fawkner, one of the full-time compositors at Framestore CFC in London, I asked him about his work on Jonathan Frakes' film *Thunderbirds.* (Universal, 2004). "We used Keylight for almost everything," he said, "with the exception of a few really difficult shots that required complex core and edge mattes or had to have unusual spill removal." In fact, in our conversation it became clear pretty quickly that Keylight is his personal first choice for most scenes.

"We use Primatte for isolating areas," he said, "but I generally start with Keylight to see if it works. Most of the time, I click the Matte Color selection and might have to twiddle one control, and I'm done."

This is great testimony from someone who spends all day each day compositing 4K digital intermediates for high-budget feature films. In fact, it pretty much matches my experience. For a lot of work, Keylight is the first plugin I try, because it just works. While it has some pretty complex fuzzy math hidden under its hood, Keylight is basically a color difference keyer. One of the strengths of a color difference keyer is nearly automatic built-in spill suppression. So with good footage that's not too undersampled, a click or two in Keylight may be all that's needed to get a near-perfect composition.

Ah, now, back to the warnings. Your mileage may vary. As I have said several times, there is no single keyer that is perfect for every situation. Keylight is splendid on 4:4:4 footage (like those gigantic digital intermediates Jonathan Fawkner works on) and on 4:2:2 footage. It's even quite good on most 4:2:0 footage. But it has no real capacity to fix the extreme undersampling of 4:1:1 DV footage, so it's generally not the best for that application. I've tried it on some poorly shot DV footage where the results were simply unacceptable. That being said, however, it is a great piece of software—and my first choice in a lot of circumstances.

Start a new composition set for 24p 16:9 DV (NTSC DV widescreen, 1.2 pixel aspect ratio, 23.976fps). Now import the file pink_gr.mov. Import a still or texture to use as a background. Place the background file on the composition timeline and the greenscreen file above it.

> Note: This file has some motion blur, which some keyers cannot handle well. Keylight, on the other hand, deals with motion blur in a most realistic manner. Note how Keylight handles the blurred waving hand. Now, go back and try the same file using the Color Range Keyer and observe how the motion blur is handled.

Now select Effect>Keying>Keylight and apply it to the greenscreen footage. Use the Screen Colour eyedropper (okay, can you tell The Foundry is a UK company?) and select a representative area of backing color. Bang! That may be it!

Figures 12.19 a & b *Behind the scenes at Shepperton Studios in England, we see a production shot of* Thunderbirds *(left) while on the right we see the final scene as composited by Framestore CFC. The Keylight plugin was used to create the composite.*

In fact, while many times the composite will look fine at this point, it's often not *quite* perfect—it's just so good that the minor flaws aren't visible in a still frame. Switch the View dropdown to Combined Matte, and inspect the matte carefully. Occasionally the background isn't quite completely clean, or the foreground has a small amount of translucency, or print-through. While viewing the matte, play with the Screen Gain to see how it affects the

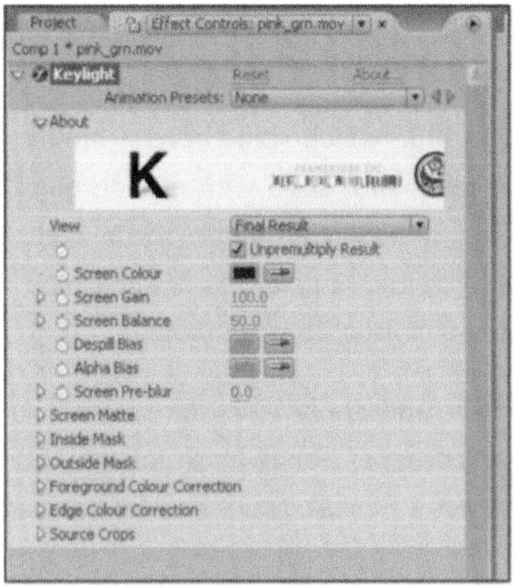

Figure 12.20 *The Keylight interface*

matte. Now play with the Screen Balance control. Especially observe the effect on the motion blur of the hand. Slight adjustments to these controls will often perfect the matte.

If there is just a bit of gray in the background or in the foreground, you can often fix the matte by slightly increasing the Screen Matte>Clip Black (to clean up the background) or slightly decreasing the Screen Matte>Clip White (to clean up the foreground).

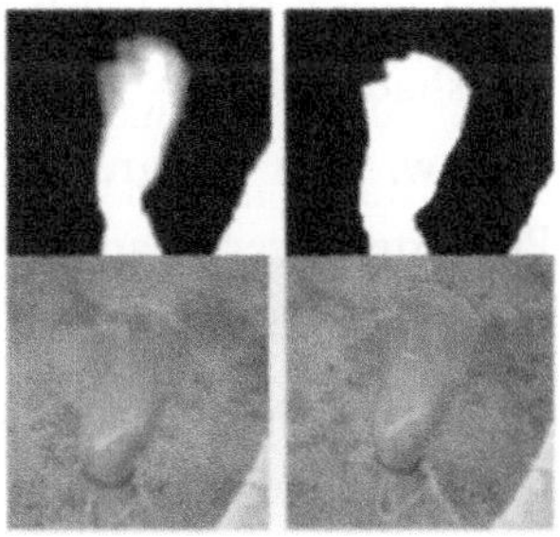

Figure 12.21 *Compare motion blur of the waving hand with Keylight (left) and Color Range Key (right). Keylight creates translucent blur areas so that the background shows through and removes spill so there is no green in the blur zone.*

The Foundry has several really intriguing tutorials in their online manual that use clips from motion pictures that the software has been used on. We couldn't get permission to include the clips on our DVD, but you can download them from their web site at www.the-foundry.com.

Once again, Keylight may not be ideal for undersampled clips, since it has no facility for really rebuilding the missing information. If your need is for keying 4:1:1 video, then you might find your answers in the next couple of plugins.

Tutorial D: Primatte and Walker Effects Light Wrap

Primatte from Photron is now in version 3.0. The plugin is available for AE in Mac and Windows, Combustion, Avid, Shake, and Commotion. While Primatte is an excellent keyer for all-around use, it has built-in tools for dealing effectively with undersampled video; so if your primary need is to composite 4:1:1 DV footage, Primatte may be the keyer that will make your visions a reality.

In AE, start a new composition set for 24p 16:9 DV (NTSC DV widescreen, 1.2 pixel aspect ratio, 23.976fps). Import the file *drink_bl.mov*. Import a still or texture to use as a background. Place the background file on the composition timeline and the bluescreen file above it. We're using *drink_bl.mov* especially for this tutorial because some of the 4:1:1 color blocking is visible in the orange blouse—look closely at the shadows!

Now, with the greenscreen footage selected, go to Effects>Primatte>Primatte Keyer to apply Primatte to the footage. Primatte is a very complex piece of software based on a patented process that Photron calls *polyhedral slicing*. There will be a test at the end of the lecture. No, there won't. I don't understand it any more than you do. Dammit, Jim, I'm just a simple country filmmaker, not a math wizard! Fortunately for both of us, you don't have to understand the math to use Primatte to its full strength.

In the Primatte Effect Controls, click on the Select BG tool, and click on a representative area of bluescreen in the comp window. Most of the background will become transparent, though there will probably be some schmutz. To sample a large area of the background rather than just a single pixel, switch the Sampling Style to Rectangle instead of Point. This is a pretty good idea for the initial color selection.

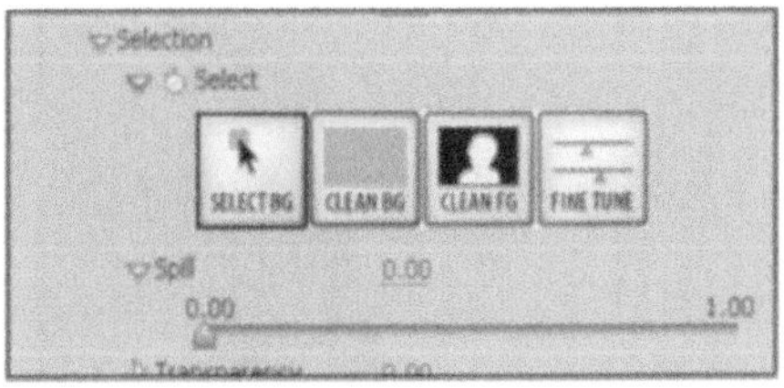

Figure 12.22 *The Select BG tool allows you to pick the precise backing color, while the Clean BG tool allows you to add colors to the transparency list. The Clean FG tool will subtract color accidentally added to transparency.*

Now, switch to View>Matte and click on the Clean BG tool. Switch back to point sampling and click the cursor on areas of the background in the comp window that aren't solid black—but ought to be. Continue clicking on different areas until the background is solid black—*but don't sample near the edges of the foreground subject!* A good way to check that the background is completely clean is to switch back to View Comp mode and turn the footage off and on in the timeline. The only thing that should change is the appearance of the foreground subject when you turn the footage on.

Now, check the foreground image, which should be solid white in the matte. If there is gray noise in this area (areas which should be totally opaque), use the Clean FG tool to select these areas. *Be careful not to do this in areas that should be translucent—such as the girl's bottle of water!*

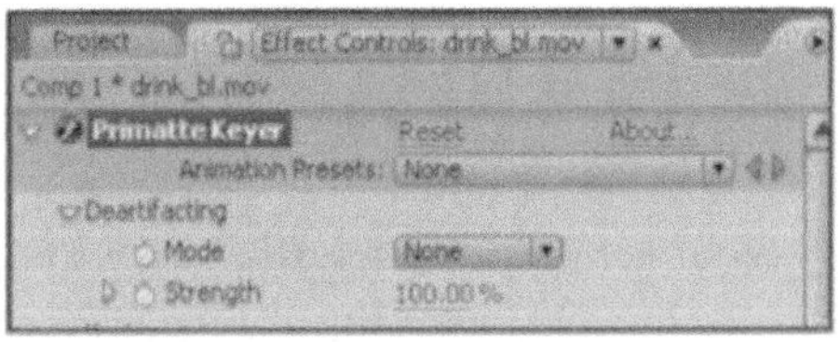

Figure 12.23 *The Deartifacting control must be set to the appropriate color decimation pattern: None, DV/HDV, HDCAM, or Other.*

Take note of the jagged edges of the matte at this point. Switch back to View Comp and look at the jaggies around the talent—jaggies which are likely tinted with blue spill. This ain't a pretty composite—at least, not yet! Now look at the top portion of the Primatte effects control. The first control is called Deartifacting, and it has a dropdown list for None, DV/HDV, HDCAM, and Other. Don't ask me what Other is for; perhaps it works on PixelVision. Actually, it's a setting that allows the software to guess at the undersampling direction and pattern—for instance, if you digitize BetaSP into a 4:2:2 digital format, the actual color

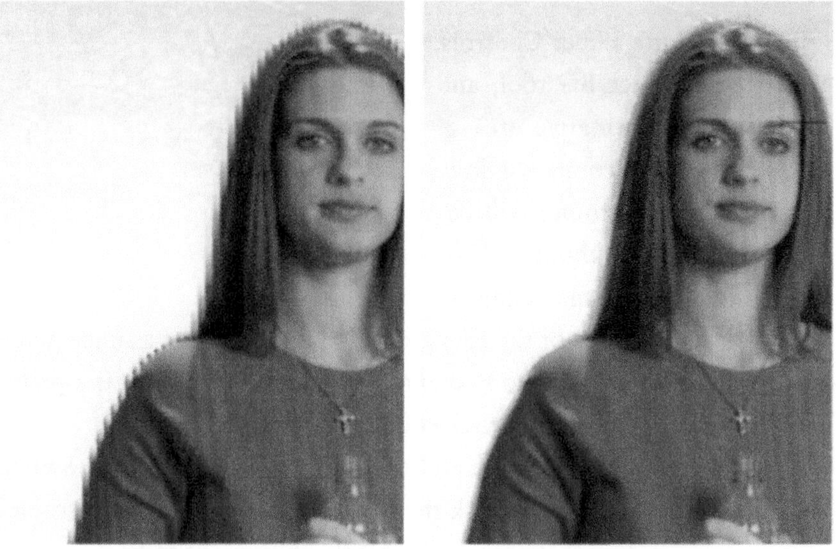

***Figure 12.24** The foreground with no Deartifacting (left) shows jagged edges and color blocking in the orange blouse. With DV Deartifacting on (right) the edges are smoothed and the color blocking is eliminated.*

sampling may work out to something between 4:2:2 and 4:1:1. It also has a Strength slider that defaults to 100%. This tool will interpolate the missing edge data.

> Note: Why a setting for deartifacting HDCAM? If you read the chapter on format problems carefully, you'll remember that HDCAM uses color decimation that is the equivalent of 3:1:1. Not quite as bad as DV, but not that good, either!

Now, while watching the comp, change the setting to DV/HDV. Bang! You will probably still have some blue spill, but suddenly the edges of the foreground became smooth! Try reducing the Strength slider to see the effect; most of the time, you'll leave this on 100% if your footage is DV. Now, change the setting back to None, and look for an area of color blocking in the shadows on the orange blouse. These will be areas where the shadows seem to have a jagged edge. Watching one of these, now change the setting to DV/HDV and watch the blockiness vanish. Nifty tool, ain't it? Don't stop reading here, however.

With the DV/HDV Deartifacting on, move the timeline cursor through the file and watch for schmutz, areas of noise in the background. You may need to use the Clean BG tool on different frames to get a fully clean background.

Figure 12.25 *The final composite looks quite good, especially for 4:1:1 DV footage!*

Now, we definitely need to work on the blue spill. Below that first set of tools (Select BG, Clean BG, Clean FG, and Fine Tune) there are several sliders. Let's ignore these for the moment. Look instead at the second set of tools: Spill Sponge, Matte Sponge, Restore Detail, and Decrease Opacity. Click on the Spill Sponge tool, and find a good representative area of spill that you want to remove. *Be sure that Sampling Style is set to Point, not Rectangle!* Click carefully on a pixel that is showing the blue spill. Presto, a lot of the spill vanishes. If it didn't, you missed the right pixel, try another area—you need to select one that has a definite blue tint. When you get the right one selected, the spill will pretty much vanish. How did they do that? Polyhedral binomial quadraphonic something or another! Now, go back to the Spill slider and turn it up to see if it improves any slight amount of remaining spill.

If you look carefully, you'll probably still see a slight area of not-quite-transparent pixels right around the girl. In the Defocus Matte section, select the Inward Defocus tool and increase the Defocus Matte to 2 or 3. Experiment with higher settings to see what it does, and try it with the Inward Defocus off. If this doesn't clean up the edge, increase the Shrink Matte slider until the results are satisfactory.

The end result isn't perfect to a trained eye, especially one used to working with a high-res 4:4:4 digital intermediate; but it's unbelievably good for DV-originated footage!

Primatte's manual contains some excellent tutorials to walk you through advanced use of some of the other tools, though many of them are seldom used on normal, well-shot footage. There's also a nice simplified explanation of the polyhedral slicing algorithm, if you're interested.

Now let's try a slightly more advanced treatment. The next plugin we'll look at, zMatte, has a light wrap function that helps make composites that include a light source seem more realistic. Let's first try that with Primatte and another plugin, Walker Effects Light Wrap. You can download a demo version of Light Wrap from www.walkereffects.com.

In lighting, *wrap* is the term for how light illuminates a round, three-dimensional object. A hard light has virtually no wrap; it illuminates the sides of the object directly facing the light, but leaves other surfaces in shadow. A large light source—like a large soft bank, or diffused sunlight—will illuminate the surfaces facing the light, but will also wrap around curved surfaces and illuminate other surfaces as well. When a subject moves in front of a large bright light source in the real world, the light wraps around the subject, illuminating the edges. That's the effect we'll replicate artificially.

Leave the foreground in place but substitute the file *sunset_mayang.jpg* for the background. This image is courtesy of www.mayang.com. Leave it at full resolution and position it so that the sun is partially behind the model. The composite looks clean, but artificial. The subject is too brightly lit from the camera side, and there is no light wrap—the edges of the model are dark, not catching the rays of the sun.

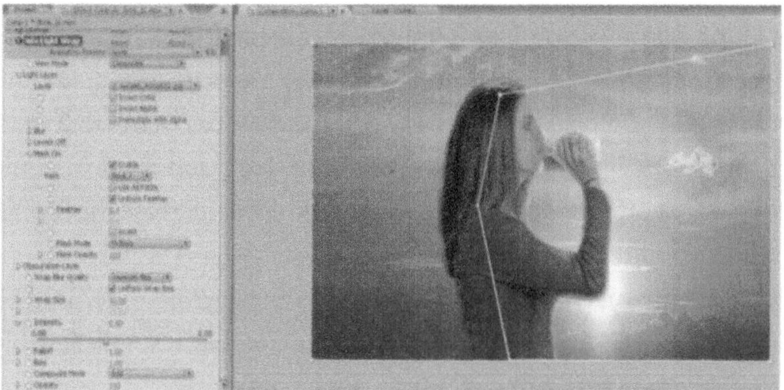

Figure 12.26 *The secondary mask isolates the effect to the side of the model facing the sun; the Walker Effects controls are visible to the left.*

Now, with the foreground layer selected, go to Effects>Color Correction>Levels. Reduce the Output White to darken the girl until she seems realistically contrasted to the sun. I found a value of 185 satisfactory, you could go lower. Now add Effects>Walker Effects 2.2>wfx Light Wrap. Set Light Layer (the layer that the light is supposed to be from) to *sunset_mayang.jpg* and reduce the Intensity until the effect

Figure 12.27 *The final composite of Primatte and Walker Effects Light Wrap*

seems realistic to you. I found a setting of 0.6 to be pleasing.

The edges of the model now seem to be illuminated from behind by the sun—and the sun seems to glow around her. The effect is pretty good at this point, but to really refine it you can create a secondary mask to isolate the effect to the side facing the sun. For this to work, you must first create a primary mask—leave it at full settings so as not to crop any part of the layer. Now create a secondary mask and adjust it to eliminate the effect from the side of the model away from the sun. If you do this correctly, the effect is remarkably realistic. This effect (and the mask) can be animated so that the effect appears as the foreground subject passes in front of the light source.

Tutorial E: zMatte

Digital Film Tools' zMatte is a keying plugin that has developed quite a following. The current version, zMatte 2.0, is much easier to use than earlier versions that were very counter-intuitive. The new control interface is vastly improved and much easier to understand. It includes a nice Light Wrap feature (which we'll test) and an independent secondary matte that allows cleanup of less-than-perfect original footage. Let's try it out!

In AE, start a new composition set for 24p 16:9 DV (NTSC DV widescreen, 1.2 pixel aspect ratio, 23.976fps). Now import the file *ruins_gr.mov* and the still *cityruins.jpg* from the DVD.

> Note: This cool matte painting was done by Natiq Aghayev (known online as Defonten), a talented young artist in Azerbaijan. It's mostly hand-painted in Photoshop, with some 3D elements from Softimage XSI. Thanks to Defonten for permission to use this pic!

Place the background file on the composition timeline and the greenscreen file above it. Now, in order to have the couple looking at the ruins, move the ruins_gr.mov file to the left until the girl's shoulder is nearly touching the edge of the frame, and she is mostly in front of the sun. Because the file includes material off the edges of the greenscreen, we'll have to use a garbage matte later.

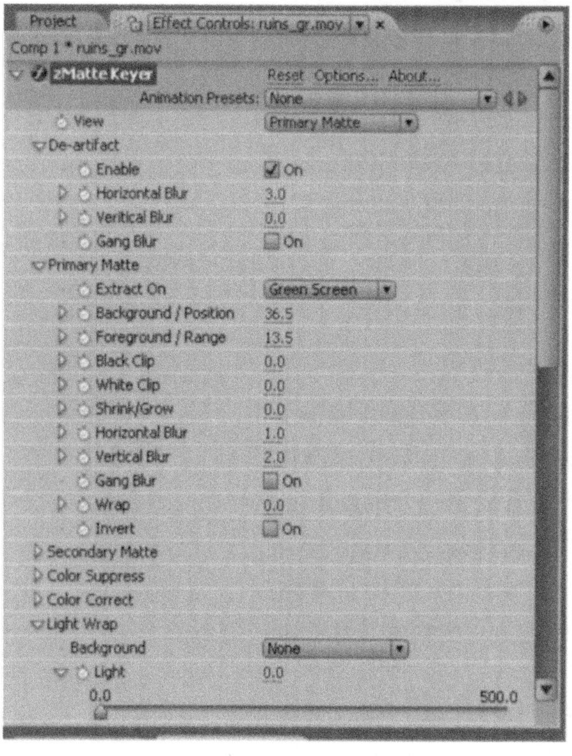

Figure 12.28 *Set the Primary Matte controls to extract on greenscreen and set the De-Artifact control to a horizontal blur of 3 or 4.*

Now, with the greenscreen file selected, go to Effects>DFT zMatte V2>zMatte Keyer to apply it to the footage. Under the Primary Matte control section, change the Extract On dropdown list to Greenscreen. You may want to experiment a bit to see what the other settings do, but for this footage the setting must be Greenscreen.

The immediate result shows horrible jaggies from the undersampled footage. Let's eliminate those now. Open De-artifact and click on the Enable checkbox. Now that Deartifact is enabled, set the Horizontal Blur to 3 or 4 (since the footage is 4:1:1). You should suddenly have a nice clean edge without jaggies! If you are working with 4:2:0 footage such as HDV, you would set Horizontal Blur to 1 or 2 and Vertical Blur to 1 or 2.

Now, to clean up the composite, let's look at the primary matte directly. Set View to Primary Matte, and adjust Background>Position until the backing color area is solid black. Now, adjust Foreground>Range until the foreground area is solid white. Try to get a clean edge without using Shrink/Grow at this stage; matte choking should be a last step when other adjustments haven't cleaned up the edge. Experiment with the blur settings to get an edge that doesn't look too hard, but isn't too soft either.

Stop! You should stop now and take note that the background matte painting looks substantially sharper than the DV foreground footage. You should add a blur effect to the background to make it match the apparent sharpness of the foreground. I tried Fast Blur set to 1 pixel, both horizontal and vertical. You may find another filter more effective. However, if you do not match the background to the foreground the final composite will never look right!

Open the Edge control section. The Edge Matte is set by default to add a 1-pixel clean edge; at this point, this may look fine or it may be a dark line or a greenish edge to the subjects. Change the Opacity control (which works backwards from other programs) to 100% to make the edge transparent. You may later come back and make it partially opaque and slightly blurred; you can also color correct it to remove any residual green or make it match other effects.

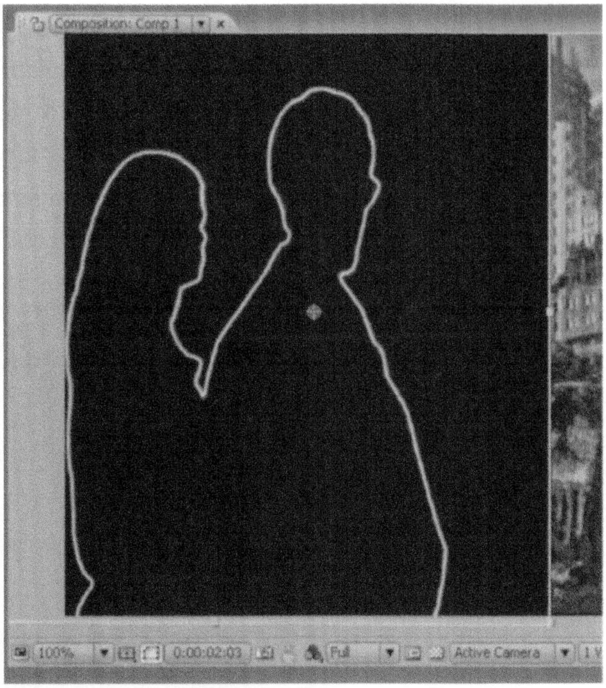

Figure 12.29 *The Edge Matte defaults to a sharp single-pixel edge that can be made transparent, blurred, and color corrected.*

Before we move on to try the Light Wrap feature, let's stop and add our garbage matte. Right-click on the footage in the comp window and select Mask>New Mask. Now right-click again and select Mask>Free Transform Points. Drag the right side of the mask in to cut out the junk on the edge. This is a garbage matte at its simplest; of course, you can make masks any shape, feather the edges, and do all sorts of other things if needed. In this case, a simple crop is all that is required. In just a moment, we'll create a more complex mask.

Now, in the zMatte Effects Control panel, open the Light Wrap control. In the dropdown Background menu, select *cityruins.jpg*. This is to tell the software that it is this layer that the light will appear to be coming from.

Light controls the intensity of the effect; Wrap controls the width of the intrusion of the effect into the foreground. Experiment with both until you find a setting that looks realistic. I was happy with Light 190 and Wrap 25.

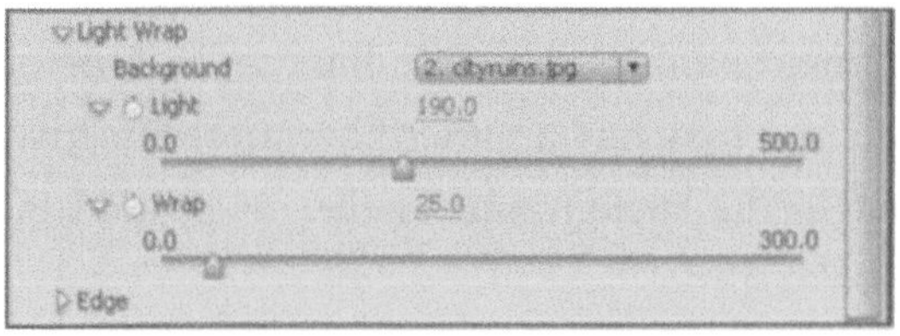

Figure 12.30 *The Light Wrap controls allow a glow of light to wrap around the foreground subject.*

If you have a dark edge at this stage, it is probably coming from the Edge Matte. Turn the Opacity down (up) to 100%, thus making it transparent. Go figure.

Now, the one part of this picture that isn't right is the light wrap on the right side of the young man. Let's fix that. Unfortunately, zMatte doesn't have any built-in way to control the region of the light wrap, so we'll have to do with another layer and an After Effects mask.

Duplicate the *ruins_gr.mov* layer. Select the original (lower) layer and turn the Light Wrap effect Off completely. Now, select the topmost layer

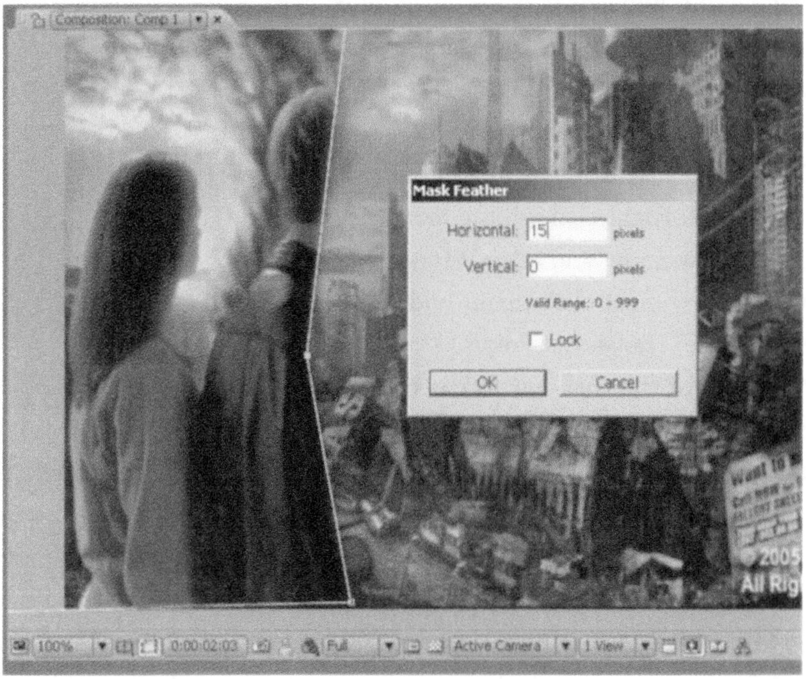

Figure 12.31a *mask on the duplicated layer cuts off the Light Wrap effect from the right side of the man, where it wouldn't appear naturally. Setting a horizontal blur of 15 creates a soft edge to the effect rather than a sharp cutoff.*

with the Light Wrap still applied. Click the footage in the comp window and select the mask. Make sure the mask shape is set to Bezier, and then add nodes using the Pen tool to create a mask that cuts the man in half vertically, making his right half invisible in this layer. Set the mask feather to 10 or 15 horizontal. Now, when the layers are all visible, the Light Wrap effect will be eliminated on the side of the man away from the sun.

***Figure 12.31b** The final zMatte composite using Light Wrap.*

If the underlying layer adds an undesirable dark edge to the Light Wrap areas, you may need to shrink the matte in the underlying layer by a single pixel.

Remember in Chapter 10 how we dealt with a problem shot by using an edge matte and a core matte and then compositing them? You can do that inside zMatte by activating the secondary matte. Usually this will be used as a core matte, and composited onto the primary matte using a process such as Screen or Maximum (Lighten).

Tutorial F: Boris Red

Up to now, all the plugins we've used have utilized the native interface of the host application. Now we're going to look at some plugins that have their own separate interface.

Boris Red is only one of the applications available from BorisFX, and while Red is a fine chroma keying application, that is only one of its many capabilities. It also does complex titling, particle effects, and all kinds of DVEs (Digital Video Effects) such as page turns, rolls, fly-ins, and the like. However, here we are concerned with color-based compositing, so that's the part of the plugin we'll look at. Boris Red is also available for more host applications than any other plugin we're examining. BorisFX publishes versions for Avid, Final Cut Pro, Premiere Pro, After Effects, Vegas, Canopus Edius, and Media 100.

Figure 12.32 *The Boris interface consists of four floating panels. Top left is the Effects Control panel; top right is the Preview panel. Bottom left is the Project panel, bottom right is the Timeline panel.*

Start a new project using the settings for standard 4:3 DV. Import the file *green422.mov* from the DVD and some still image or texture for a background. Place the *green422.mov* in the comp window. While you can add the background in the AE timeline and composite that way, you can complete the compositing inside the Boris interface, which is what we'll do.

Now go to Effect>BorisFX>Boris Red to apply Red to the footage. The Boris interface will open.

If you composite the background in the AE timeline, you won't see it in the Boris interface; all you'll see is the transparency. To see the still background in the Boris comp window, you'll need to load it separately into Red. In the lower left panel (the timeline) click on File>Import and select the background still. This will import it as a resource into the project library in the lower left window. You can also click on the third action icon, Add Image Media. Now drag the file into the timeline

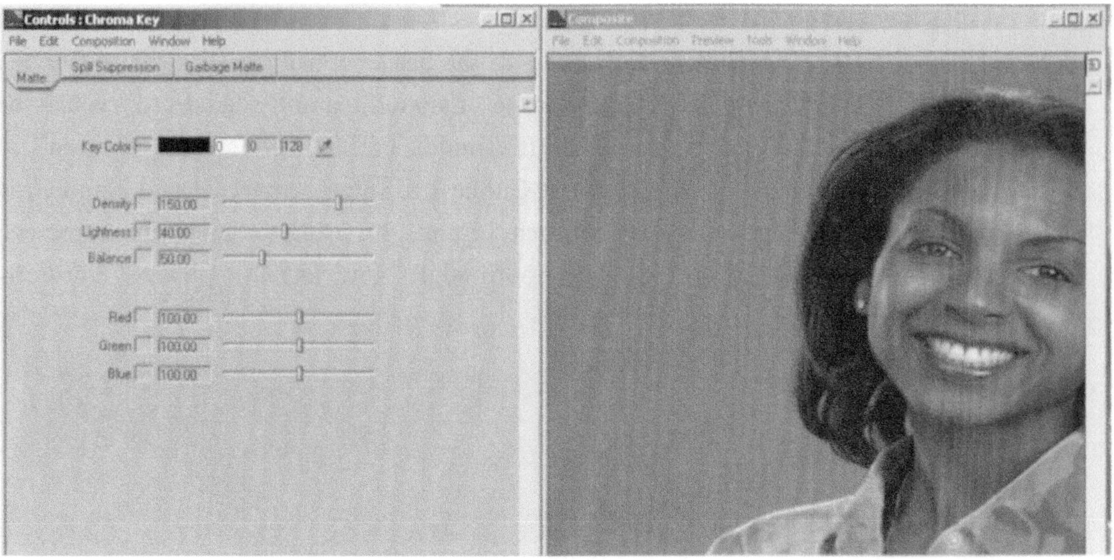

Figure 12.33 *In the Effects Control panel (left), use the eyedropper tool to select the backing color in the comp panel (right).*

window, placing it under the foreground footage, which at this stage is probably labeled Video 1. You can rename the track if you wish.

Now, with the Video 1 track selected in the lower left panel, in that panel's menu go to Filters>Keys and Matte>Chroma Key to apply the Chroma Key filter. The filter controls will appear in the upper left panel.

Now, use the eyedropper tool to select the backing color in the upper right comp panel.

Make sure the preview panel is set to Full resolution, with High Quality Preview. The key will probably be pretty good at this point, though some jaggies will be visible from the color undersampling. If the background is not completely clean, adjust the Density and Lightness controls. Now, in the lower right timeline panel, click on File>Exit (or on the X gadget in upper left corner). In the dialog window, Select Yes to save the settings to the host application.

Back in the familiar AE interface, zoom in and examine the edges of the composite. There will likely be some jaggies from the color undersampling. Reopen the Boris interface by clicking on Options in the top of the AE Effect Controls window.

Now, apply the Matte Choker by selecting Filters>Keys and Matte>Matte Choker. Look carefully at the foreground edges, which will likely seem a bit soft and rounded. The Matte Choker's default settings are really aggressive.

The controls are similar to the basic controls in AE's Matte Choker. To find a better compromise of smoothing and edge detail, reduce the Blur 1 to 0, Choke 1 to 0 (the middle of the slider), and Gray Soften 1 to minimum. Now, increase Choke 1 to values between 1 and 2 and Gray Soften 1 to values between 15 and 30, using the minimum combined settings that create a smooth edge. Now, increase Choke 1 until any

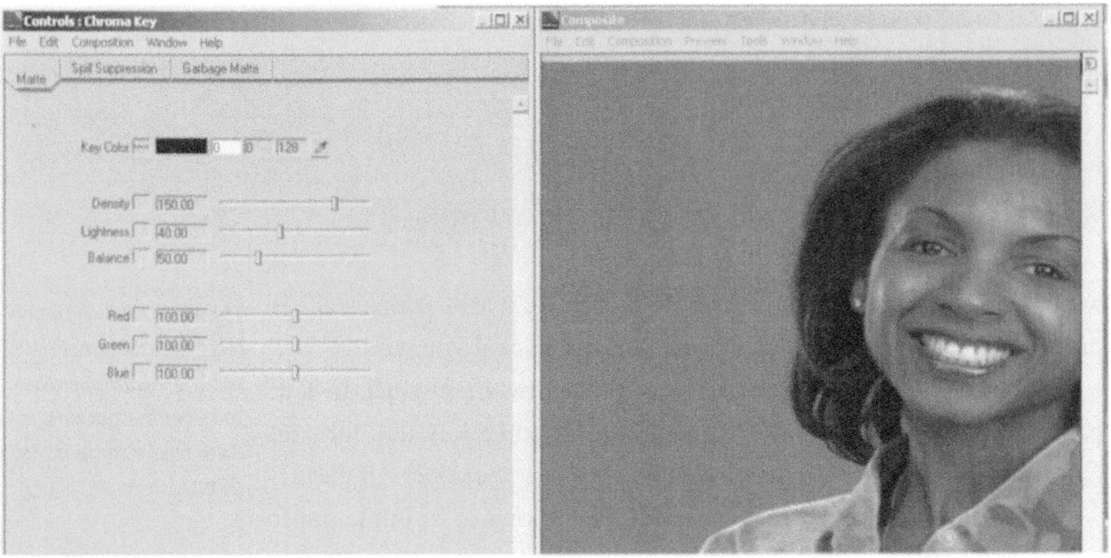

***Figure 12.34** The Matte Choker controls are similar to those in the AE Matte Choker.*

undesirable edging is gone, again using the minimum acceptable value. Save the settings and go back to the main AE interface. Examine the edges carefully; if any annoying jaggies remain, click on Options again and increase the Choke 1 and 2 and Gray Soften 1 values gradually until jaggies are eliminated.

Boris Red filter settings can all be keyframed, so if special settings are needed for an awkward section, that's easily done. The settings you are looking for are a compromise—the best setting will just barely create clean, non-jagged edges without losing significant edge detail. Close the interface to go back to AE; add to Render Que and render your file!

Don't forget to check out the other functions in Boris Red, especially the DVE moves and particle effects. Red's keyer performs best on 4:2:2 or better footage; while the choker can smooth out 4:1:1 jaggies, the results aren't as clean as some of the other plugins we've tested here.

Tutorial G: Ultimatte AdvantEdge

The Ultimatte AdvantEdge software is available for both Mac and Windows, and works as a plugin for After Effects, Premiere, or Final Cut Pro. AdvantEdge is a very complex piece of software that is easy to use in fully automatic mode but requires some practice to use its full capabilities in manual mode. It is also something of a resource hog, and probably is the slowest rendering of the various packages we'll look at. We'll test it in After Effects.

Start a new composition for 4:3 DV and import one of the sample files from the DVD. Since AdvantEdge is specially designed to work with undersampled files, use *green 411.mov*. Import a texture or still to use as a background plate. Place the background plate in the composition timeline and in the greenscreen footage on top. Make sure the greenscreen footage is selected. Now under the Effects menu, select Ultimatte AdvantEdge. Unlike most plugins, AdvantEdge has its own independent interface; however, there are some basic settings that must be done in AE to use AdvantEdge to its potential. If you have a clean plate (a shot of the backing color without a foreground subject) available, this must be imported into the After Effects timeline immediately above the greenscreen footage you will be using, and then made invisible by clicking off the eye gadget to the left of the Source Name. You'll need to select the Clean plate in the basic AdvantEdge control. If a clean plate is not available, don't worry; AdvantEdge can create a simulated one. You should also select the background for preview purposes in this interface. The BG Preview will only work if the background plate and foreground plate are the same resolution. If they aren't (for instance, you are using an oversized BG to allow for panning), don't worry about it—you just won't be able to see the preview in the AdvantEdge interface. You can also select a Holdout Matte in this interface.

Now start the AdvantEdge interface by clicking on the AdvantEdge logo. First, we'll follow the basic steps of creating a matte using the automated features, then we'll look at the more advanced features of the software that allow manual control. The first step is to sample the backing color using the eyedropper (Sample Backing). Drag the eyedropper tool along a representative section of the backing color. This should be near the foreground subject, but not right next to an edge of the foreground subject, where the chroma sample can sometimes vary. This will create the basic matte, which must now be refined.

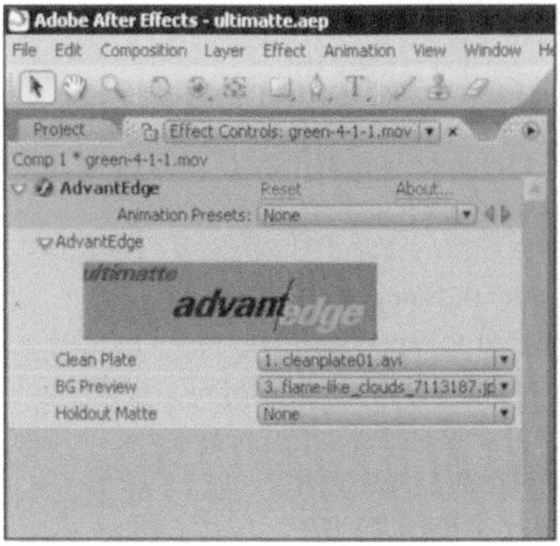

Figure 12.35 *In the basic AE interface, set up the clean plate, background plate (for preview), and a holdout matte (if any).*

Note: If you have a clean plate and have properly set it up in the AE interface, you may be all done—AdvantEdge may now have enough information to create an effective matte.

If you don't have a clean plate, or if the matte still needs cleanup, click on the Add Overlay tool and drag the tool through an area of the background that still displays schmutz or noise. This will create an overlay area that guarantees that the backing color is completely transparent; this overlay serves as an artificial clean plate inside the software. If the overlay selects too much area (rendering some of the foreground area transparent), you can use the Remove Overlay tool to select those areas and restore them to opacity.

The Set Matte Density Controls are used to adjust the density or opacity of the foreground objects. A completely opaque object's matte will be white, a completely transparent object's matte will be black, and a translucent object matte will be gray.

View the Matte by clicking on the Matte thumbnail icon. With Matte selected from the Automation pop-up menu, use the Add Matte dropper to scrub on areas in the matte that appear gray, but should be white (fully opaque) in the matte. These areas are described as *print-through*, meaning that the opacity of the subject is too low in this area and the background will be visible through the foreground in this area. Be careful not to select those objects that *should* have a gray matte (fine hair, smoke, or partially transparent objects), as they will become opaque.

Note: When viewing the Matte, if there are sections of the matte which should be opaque but are exhibiting gray values that do

Figure 12.36 *Drag the Sample Backing tool across a representative area of backing color.*

Figure 12.37 *Drag the Add Overlay tool over areas of the backing color that need to be cleaned up.*

not "look" like typical transparency, then there is a chance that there is a remainder of overlay in this area. Look at the overlay by selecting the Overlay thumbnail icon. If overlay exists on subject matter, return the Automation pop-up menu to Screen and use the Remove Overlay tool to scrub on that area. Switch to Invert Overlay to aid in determining the extent of the overlay.

Now, on the lefthand side of the control panel, you'll see the Video Correction selections, which include DV, Film, and Other selections. Since we're using DV footage, select DV so that the software will compensate for the 4:1:1 color decimation. Now click on the Matte thumbnail icon to display the matte and look carefully at the foreground and background areas to see whether they are clean and whether the edges are also satisfactory. View the composite by clicking on the Composite thumbnail icon or by pressing C on the keyboard. In order to move through the frames of the video sample, select the Jogger control on the right side of the panel. When you are satisfied with the settings you have chosen click on Ok, and you'll be returned to the After Effects interface.

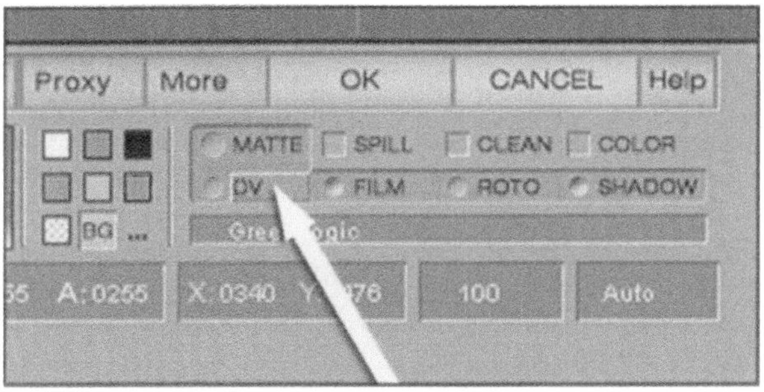

Figure 12.38 *Select the DV button to the righthand side of the interface to turn on Video Correction.*

The More Interface

To learn which controls have been automatically set by AdvantEdge, click on the More button at the top of the interface, and select the Roscreen Correction control panel from the pop-up menu. Each control has been set automatically by AdvantEdge based on the sampling and settings that you used. In many cases the automatic controls of Ultimatte will be sufficient. However, there are certainly situations where you will want to tweak these controls to improve a specific feature of the composite.

Let's take a look now at some of the more advanced features of Ultimatte. Older versions of Ultimatte software required a clean plate (a shot of the backing color exactly as lit for the clip but without the foreground subject) for proper screen correction. In actual practice, the compositor often does not have a clean plate to work from, so Ultimatte came up with the Rotoscreen function, which creates a synthetic clean plate. This is what you were doing when you used the Add Overlay function a moment ago.

Figure 12.39 The More interface exposes the manual controls for AdvantEdge.

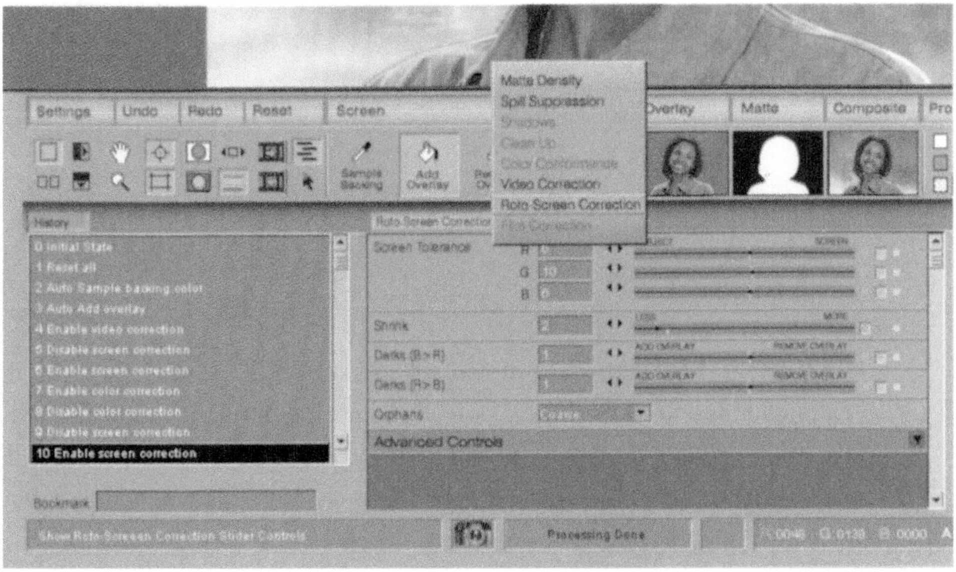

When you click on the More button in the control panel, a list of screen correction tools are available. These include Screen Tolerance for RGB, Shrink (or matte choker), controls for Darks in the blue-to-red vector and Darks in the red-to-blue vector, and then Orphans control, which can be set to Coarse, Medium, Fine, or Off. This last control gets rid of small areas of noise in the background. Under Advanced Controls, you also have panels to control the Bright areas, as well as Overlay Color and Overlay Opacity—these latter controlling the display function rather than the matte itself.

If you click on the button that reads Rotoscreen Correction at the top left corner of the Advanced Controls a pop-up menu allows you to select the Matte Density controls, which includes Backing, Brights, Darks, and the Edge Kernel; the Advanced Controls include Warm and Cool. With the Matte display selected, play with each one of these to see what they do; particularly experiment with the Edge Kernel which occasionally can be very useful in cleaning out problematic edges.

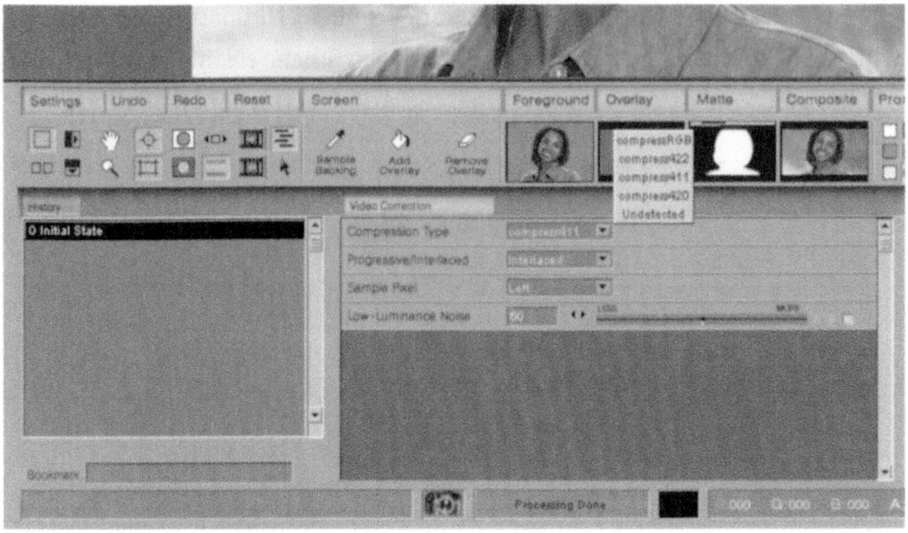

Figure 12.40 *The Video Correction menu allows selection of the appropriate color decimation scheme (compression type) for your footage.*

Another important area of control is that of spill suppression. Select a Spill Suppression control on the righthand side of the interface. Directly under the Ok button is a selection to turn spill control on or off. Typically this should be selected. The Spill Suppression controls include Cool, Warm, Mid-Tones and then in the Advanced section, Brights, Darks, Ambiance, Strength, and Background Veiling.

With the matte display selected, click the DV control on and off to see the smoothing that takes place in the matte edges. Generally, AdvantEdge can autodetect the appropriate color decimation logic; however, there are occasions when you'll need to select the appropriate logic manually. When Video Correction (the DV checkbox) is selected, you can access the Video Correction controls in the MORE interface. There you can select 4:2:2, 4:2:0, or 4:1:1 decimation as appropriate.

Shadows

Ultimatte AdvantEdge can also allow for shadows. To set the shadow in cleanup controls select Matte from the automation pop-up menu, and you can use the Add Matte, Remove Noise, and Hold Shadow controls. AdvantEdge will preserve the shadow only if told to do so since most of the time shadows on backing colors are intended to be removed. However, the Hold Shadow function allows you to do this.

With Matte selected from the Automation pop-up menu, use the Hold Shadow dropper (only available when Rotoscreen Correction is enabled) to scrub on those shadows that are to be preserved. Hint: these shadows may best be seen in the foreground image.

If unwanted shadows are retained, then use the Remove Noise dropper to reduce or eliminate those shadows.

If the area which is scrubbed does not reside under the overlay, then erasing will adjust the appropriate Clean Up controls to reduce anomalies in the screen area. This will result in the loss of some fine detail.

Repeat these two processes until wanted shadows are retained and unwanted shadows or noise are removed.

The density, sharpness, and tint of the shadow may be altered by manually adjusting the shadow controls in the More>Shadow controls panel in the Control Sliders pop-up menu.

Spill Controls

Change the Automation pop-up menu to Spill. Select the Remove Spill tool to scrub on those areas exhibiting excessive spill not removed by the default spill suppression algorithms.

If too much spill was removed or needs to be added to other parts of the image, select the Restore Spill dropper, and scrub on those areas needing more spill.

Color Correction

Ultimatte also contains powerful color correction tools to allow you to match the blacks, whites, and gamma of foreground and background elements. The Color Conformance controls are selected from the automation pop-up menu under Color. Color Conformance with Ultimatte Intelligence allows for the selection of blacks, whites, and gammas and will automatically match the foreground to the background (or vice versa if composite is chosen as output selection).

Choose Color Conformance from the Automation pop-up menu. Use the Match Color dropper to scrub on similar colors that are to be matched in both the background and processed foreground elements. Select at least one point from both the foreground and background.

Since multiple data points may be chosen, you have to tell the software when you're done by clicking on the Composite thumbnail icon, pressing R on the keyboard to render the effect, or double-clicking the final selected point.

If the desired background color does not appear in the image, then a color may be chosen from the Ultimatte color palette by clicking on the Color Tool button to launch the Ultimatte color picker. The foreground color that was selected will be represented down the center of the color tool, with the other colors representing the range to which the foreground color may be changed.

> Hint: if the desired background color is obscured by the foreground element, switch to the background view and sample the desired color directly from the background image. It is not advisable to sample colors from the original foreground image as these will have spill from the bluescreen (greenscreen) affecting the colors.

Figure 12.41 *The Final composite from Advant-Edge.*

The colorimetry of the foreground image will be altered to closely match the chosen foreground colors to the chosen background colors. Repeat until the desired color effect has been achieved.

To alter the tint of foreground shadows, choose the Match Shadows dropper and click on a color anywhere in the image (or the color picker) to choose the tint of the shadows.

Tutorial H: Serious Magic ULTRA 2

All the previous keyers have been plugins that require host applications. Serious Magic ULTRA 2 is a standalone color-based compositing program that also includes some really cool virtual set features. Especially for the novice, ULTRA 2 is a program that is relatively easy to use—and to obtain reasonably professional-looking results. The program's algorithm, which Serious Magic refers to as *vector keying*, appears to combine several keying techniques, a difference matte, and color range with an averaging mask. ULTRA 2 is only available for Windows. Sorry, no Mac version!

ULTRA 2's virtual sets are a real attraction for some customers. They have several add-on packs with different sets, and some third-party providers are now supplying extra virtual sets. The problem is that the number of available sets is still limited, and pretty soon the best ones will be overused and familiar. While you can't create your own virtual sets from scratch, it is possible to change the existing sets by editing the texture maps.

You can download a trial version of ULTRA 2 from the Serious Magic web site at www.seriousmagic.com. It is a pretty big download!

The first thing to be aware of with ULTRA is that it performs best when your file has a clean plate at the beginning. While you can generate a fine key manually without one, the automatic mode is really designed to work from a clean plate. This is quite easy to do, just have the talent step out of frame, roll tape, pause, position the talent, and roll tape again. If you have a few frames of clean plate elsewhere, you can even edit a frame or two into other footage to use. All you really need is a

Figure 12.42 *The ULTRA 2 interface, with Input window (upper left), Comp window (upper right) and Library/ Control windows (bottom).*

Figure 12.43 *With a foreground file and a background file (or virtual set) selected, you're ready to create the automatic key. Click on the Set Key button.*

single frame of clean plate ate the start of the file for ULTRA 2 to pull the matte automatically. We'll step through both the automatic function with clean plate and the manual technique with no clean plate.

Start ULTRA 2, and you'll be presented with the standalone ULTRA 2 interface. For our test, we're going to use a widescreen DV example, and since this is a PC-only program we're going to use the AVI file. First, go to File>New 16:9 Session to set the Input and Comp windows to Widescreen. Now, at the bottom portion of the screen, click on the Browse tab and find the brwn_grn.avi file on the DVD. (You can also just click the Browse button to the right of the input file name under the Input window.) This file has a clean plate at the start, so all you'll see at first is a blank greenscreen.

Now, select either a virtual set or background file. The demo virtual sets will render with "DEMO" watermarked over the output, but you can certainly try them out. Conversely, the background can be a still of your choice or any video file you have on your system. I've chosen the Digital Studio virtual set. If you double-click on a virtual set in the bottom panel, it will automatically place itself in the Virtual Set slot. However, when selecting a background file, it is best to drag the file from the window at the bottom to the Background slot; double-clicking may place it in the Input Clip slot, which is the foreground file.

Now, click on the Output tab on the bottom half of the interface and make sure Output is set to 16:9. Click on the Keyer tab, and you will see all the keyer controls. Make sure the clean plate (just greenscreen, no subject) is displayed in the input window, and click on the Set Key button. This will automatically set the key parameters.

Now, scroll through the video to see the results, looking carefully for any problem areas. In most cases, the Auto Set function will do a pretty good job if you have a good clean plate and the backing is evenly lit. You may need to watch out for areas with green spill that still needs removal. If you have some, increase the Spill Suppression control until it is mostly eliminated.

Now, make sure that the Input file fills the Comp window, or output screen, because what you see here will be what you get. Widescreen files will often show by default with blank space above and below. If the source video does not properly fill the comp window, click on the Input tab and click Scale To Fit. Or for more control, you can click on the Scene tab and use the Size in Scene control.

In the Output tab, set the desired compression and output file name. Choose the Flicker Fixer if the file has tiny lines that may cause flicker (interlace twitter). Click on Save Output. The file will render and save to your selected location.

Now, that was pretty easy; and that's the part that's advertised as being foolproof simple. However, what if your footage does not have a nice clean plate? And what if you want to use a nifty virtual set with a bit of a camera dolly and zoom? It's still not terribly hard, but it's not as easy as the point-and-click Auto Set function. So let's try a file that not only has no clean plate but has garbage around the edges. Since ULTRA 2 can work with HDV files, we'll use a 720p file shot on a Panasonic HD100.

Start a new 16:9 project and open *ORNG_BLU.mov* as the input source. Now go to the Virtual Sets tab and open "Studio 7>CAM1 Screen On (WIDE)" as virtual set.

(This is available as a sample under "MSL1 samples." It will render with a watermark but you'll be able to try it out.) You'll probably find that the output window will reset to 4:3, so go to the Output tab and reset it to 16:9.

Figure 12.44 *The Mask Out An Area tool (middle) allows you to paint out areas of the input file manually.*

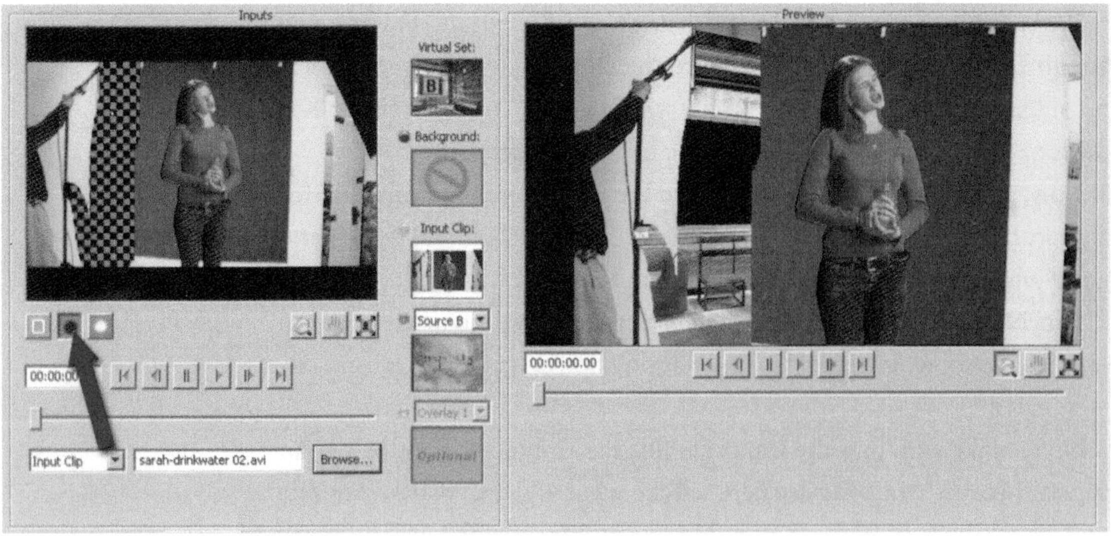

This virtual set has a Video B window, a screen visible on the set. Open a video file (anything you want) for Video B and it will appear on the screen in the set.

Now, we need to eliminate the garbage from the sides of the input clip. Under the Input Clip window, select the Mask Out An Area tool, and paint out what you don't want. If you make a mistake, use the Undo Key Masking tool. You can also create a basic crop by going to the Input tab and use the Input Cropping controls to crop out everything that's not clean bluescreen.

Initially, the virtual set will not fill the comp window properly. Click on the Pan & Zoom tab. Here you will find the controls to set motion keyframes for the file. Set at least two points, one at the beginning and one at the end of the file. With the first point (keyframe) selected, set the Pan & Zoom controls for the starting point. The Pan & Zoom controls affect all files in the comp window. With the end point (keyframe) selected, set the end of the zoom for the scene.

Next, we have to properly position the girl in the frame. To set the initial position and size of the foreground footage in the comp window, go to the Scene tab and use the Size in Scene and the Position in Scene controls. Scroll through the scene and adjust foreground Position & Zoom until you're happy. It's entirely up to your eye and judgment to create a realistic-appearing relationship between the foreground subject and the room.

Now, we've taken care of all the settings for panning and zooming but we still haven't actually executed the key to make the blue background transparent. Since this file has no clean plate, we will do this manually. First, click on the Keyer tab so that you can access the keyer tools. Now, select the Add Key Point tool (the first one under the input clip window) and click on several representative points in the backing color. Each of these will turn to a white square. Now, in the Keyer control panel, click on the Apply Points button; this will calculate a color range for the matte and the backing color will turn transparent.

If you've picked a good set of Key Points, the initial results will be pretty good. However, be aware that ULTRA 2 is at its best with 60i

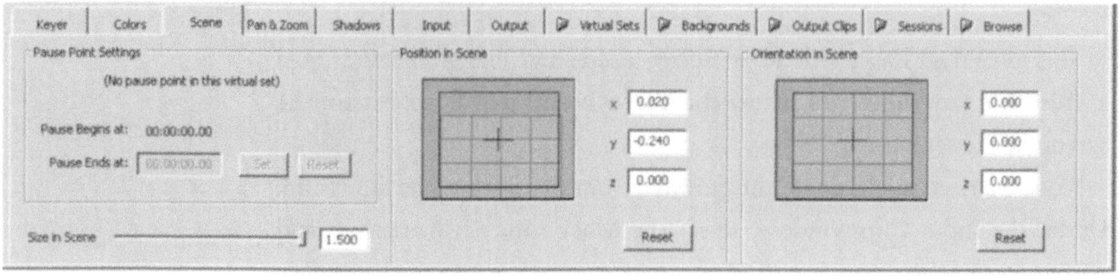

Figure 12.45 *The Position in Scene tool will allow you to position the foreground file in relationship to the background or virtual set. The Pan & Zoom tools affect all files in the output window, while this tool affects only the foreground file.*

talking heads; it does not handle motion blur very well, so 24p action shots with lots of motion blur will be problematic. You'll probably see that there is a blue glow around the girl from the initial settings, which is worse in the frames where her arm moves quickly and is blurred. Try increasing the transparency a bit, then adjust the Shrink Matte and Spill Suppression to get rid of the glow and spill and get as close to a clean composite as possible. Now click on Save Output (in the Output panel) to render the file.

I was able to create a clean composite for the entire file except for the motion blur around the model's left hand as it extends out from the body both times, where there is some blue around the fingers. The tutorial lets you see both the strengths and weaknesses of ULTRA 2. For corporate, news, or news magazine type shows with a virtual set, ULTRA 2 is hard to beat for the price. For filmmaking where there will be a lot of action it is less ideal, and another choice such as zMatte or Primatte might be better.

Tutorial I: Apple Shake

Finally, we're going to depart completely from the examples above to look at Apple Shake, a standalone application for 2D compositing that has been used on many feature films and other high-end projects. Shake is available for Mac OSX or for Linux. My thanks to David Price and Jon Fitz-Simons at the North Carolina School of the Arts School of Filmmaking for allowing me to watch over their shoulders while they worked on the previz project that we'll profile.

While Shake is set up to use several different color keying plugins (such as Primatte and Keylight), it is famous for its motion tracking capabilities, which are state of the art. While Adobe After Effects has a very fine motion tracking tool that has improved with every release, it is still behind Apple Shake in solid, predictable tracking accuracy. So we'll take a look at motion-tracked compositing in Shake. We'll be using rough 3D previzualization files rather than the finished film footage, which had not been shot at the time we did the tutorial. But you'll be able to see the potential of the software in this profile, which is just designed to give you an idea of what the software is like. You can download a free trial copy of Shake from the Apple web site.

The first thing that you'll notice on opening the software is that the interface is, well, different. This is kind of odd considering that Apple came up with the idea of the standardized interface; but those who use Shake regularly tell me that the interface is actually quite speedy for setting up common repetitive tasks. The interface is *nodal*, which means that each element in a composite (a video file, a still file, or an effect) is represented as a node with a certain number of connection points. The way the user connects the nodal points determines the order in which processes occur. The interface is similar to that of Discreet Combustion, and to some relational databases.

To load the files, click on the Image tab and then the FileIn icon. When you've located and loaded the background and foreground files, they

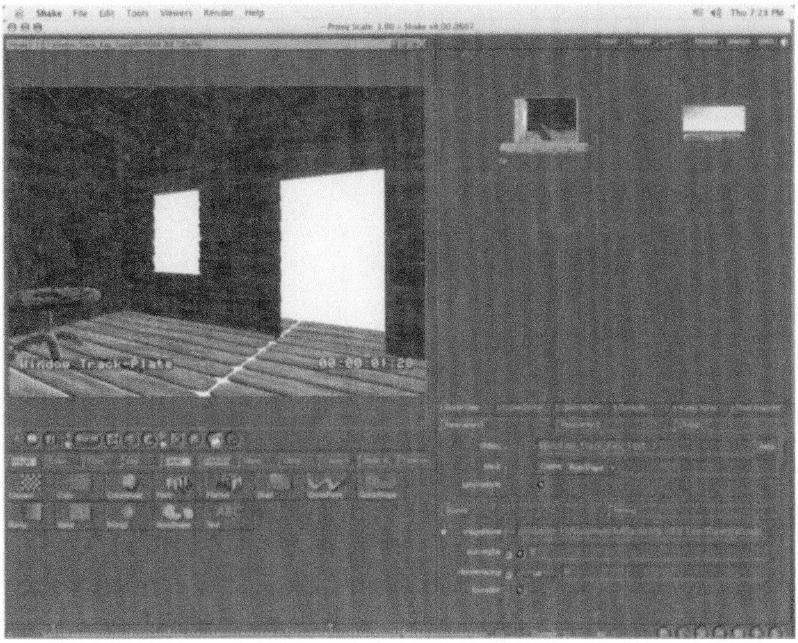

Figure 12.46 *The Shake interface shows the Composite window (top left) and the Nodal Interface (upper right). Functions are accessed in the tabs on the lower left. Here we have loaded the foreground footage and the still that will be composited behind it; both appear as nodes in the Node View window.*

will appear in the Node View window as individual nodes. This is where you will select files and draw connections between nodes to dictate how effects will be applied.

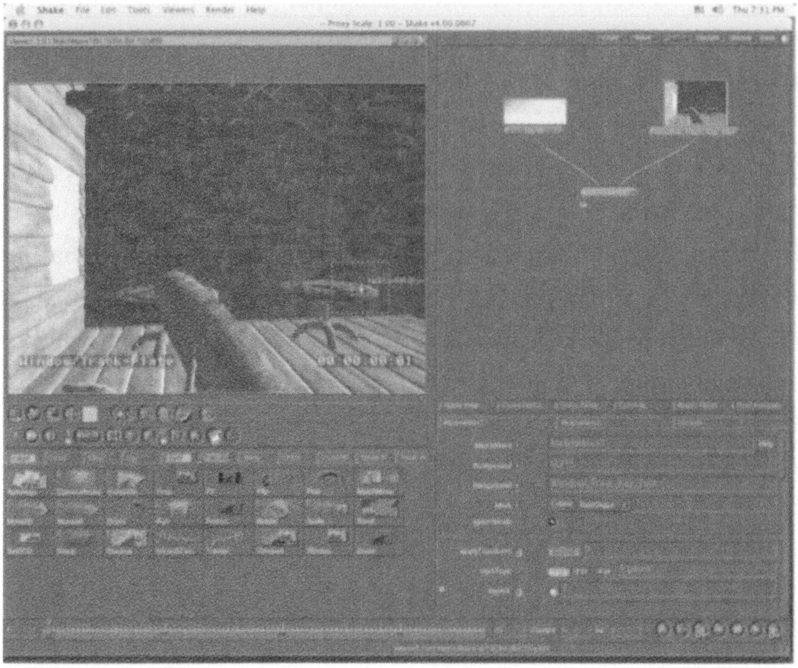

Figure 12.47 *The two files are connected by the Match Move node.*

Figure 12.48 *After the tracking procedure, the motion track is applied to the background file, which is still hidden behind the foreground file.*

What we will be doing in this example is a Match Move where we track the motion of one file and then apply the information to a second file that will then seem to move in sync with the first file. In this case, we'll apply the match move to a still shot of sky and clouds, which will then be composited in the windows of the log cabin. Here we will be using a previz file of the cabin interior created in LightWave. The 3D model is based on the dimensions of the soundstage set that was under construction. When the film was shot later, the window and door of the cabin set were whited out and the final composite will be created very much in the same way as the previz sample.

To create the motion tracking information, go to the Nodal View and select the Sky node. In the lower left, select the Transform tab and choose the Match Move icon. A Match Move node appears in the Nodal View window, connected to the Sky node. Draw a connection to the file you want to track, in this case Window_Track_Key_Test.

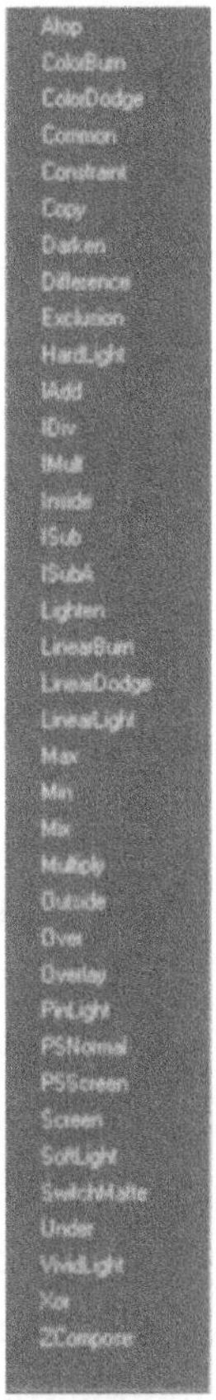

Figure 12.49 *Compositing modes for the LumaKey.*

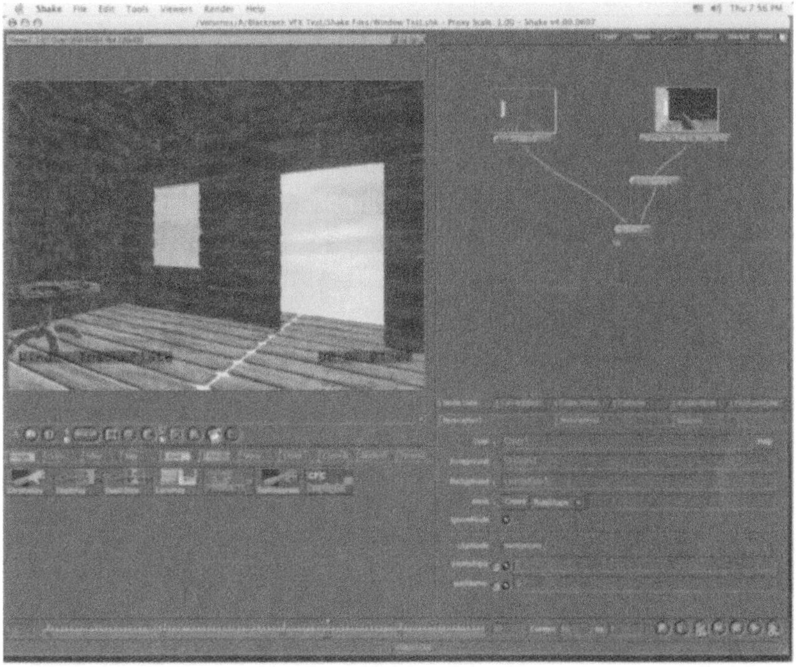

Figure 12.50 *In the final composite, the exterior background plate tracks the precise motion of the camera through the scene.*

In this case, we're going to pick a point in the foreground file to track during the camera boom. Here, we'll pick the corner of the table. Just as with the motion tracker in AE, there is a target zone surrounded by a hunt zone within which the software will look for a matching pixel pattern during the tracking procedure. Once the tracking target is set up, just click on the Track Forward button, the forward button at the bottom right of the interface.

Next, we'll scale the background file to the appropriate size, and add the Move 2D node to match the position and scale of the foreground. Now click on the Apply Transform button to set the transformation for the entire file. Select a type of composite for the file, in this case Outside, and render the file. This creates a file with the proper motion with an alpha channel that still must be composited with the original.

To create the final composite, copy the original foreground footage as a new node, and import the motion-tracked file with the alpha channel you just created. In the Key tab, select the LumaKey, and set MatteMult to Premultiply. Select Over mode for the compositing, create a render output node, and render the final file.

A similar tool in Shake that is widely used is the Stabilizer, which uses motion tracking to subtract the motion from the file. This can be used to stabilize a shaky shot, or to remove rank weave from film footage. This tool is quite effective.

Shake is a pricey application, but one that is designed for day-in day-out use by compositing professionals. For a shop that does higher-end work, especially for movies, it's definitely worth considering.

Creating New Visions with Changing Technology

13

Now that you've worked your way through the tutorials, you've had some hands-on experience with a variety of compositing solutions, and you should have had a taste of both how incredibly good a composite can be when it works well—and how amazingly unconvincing it can be when it doesn't work. Jagged edges, sizzling edges, mismatches between foreground and background can all add up to a visually unbelievable composite shot. Today's audiences have very sophisticated eyes, and while they might forgive obvious fudges in older movies, they aren't very patient with them in new films. The subtleties that can make or break a composite shot for your viewers are many. The technology can help you create amazing new visions or very expensive-looking shots economically, or it can tempt you to reach beyond your capabilities and end up with cheesy-looking shots that disrupt the viewer's suspension of disbelief and detract from your film rather than adding to it.

So when, why, and how should you use compositing techniques—particularly in a narrative movie? The decision-making process is pretty simple for many television applications. For local weather, the decision is more about the specifics of equipment and systems to choose. For a show that uses a virtual set, again, the decision is about particular systems that will meet the need and what you want the virtual set to look like. But for narrative moviemaking, the decision to use color-based compositing in a scene is a bit more complex.

Let's take a look at what color-based compositing can do for a dramatic scene, or an entire movie. The most obvious opportunity that color-based compositing opens up for the narrative movie is the creation of new or altered realities. Fantasy landscapes, science fiction settings on other planets, the integration of non-existent fantasy creatures and virtual actors are all possible now. The limitations that designers Irving Block and Mentor Huebner had to deal with in *Forbidden Planet* really don't exist any more. Designers today can work with worlds and spaces that used to be impossible to simulate. The technology has made possible movies as disparate as *Titanic, The Lion, the Witch, and the Wardrobe*, and *The Adventures of Sharkboy and Lavagirl 3-D*. What once had to be created with physical set pieces on a soundstage or with physical scale models can now be created digitally—almost without limits.

Whoa, wait a minute. There still are limits—talent, craft, and that old ogre of filmmaking, budget! While the magical combination of advanced 3D animation and compositing opened the door for Peter Jackson to make *The Lord of the Rings*, bear in mind that he spent nearly $100 million on each of the three movies—and that was a tight budget! It took an army of fantastic artists to create the scenes for those movies, all of whom had to eat and live and have expensive toys to work with. While compositing and animation can be used effectively to save money, in most instances it *adds* to the budget of a production because it adds work in both production and postproduction. A movie with a limited budget that tries to reach too far in this field will typically miss the mark. It's relatively easy to create and animate a 3D element in programs like trueSpace or LightWave and then composite that into a scene using After Effects or Shake. But it's hard to make that element really *work* in a scene.

So What *Works*?

So what makes an element or a scene work? You'll hear directors and editors use this term quite often to express that magical combination of art, craft, and technology that combines to make a scene or shot convincing. Unfortunately, this is a sort of alchemy that can't be bottled and sold by dealers. At its best, the ephemeral concept of what "works" is really art, or at least advanced craft. It's usually a complex combination of many small factors that blend together to create a scene that the average viewer will accept unquestioningly as part of the simulated reality of the picture. In other words, it doesn't violate that precious suspension of disbelief, the viewer's concession and contribution to the experience of the movie. A good director or a good editor is one who can spot the details that make the difference between a shot that works and one that doesn't. Often, it isn't the director or the compositor or the editor that puts the final touch on a scene, the touch the sells it to the viewer and makes it work. It's the sound designer, whose rumbles and sirens and machinery whines and footsteps can often push a scene from patently *fake* into that ephemeral end zone where *it works.*

For the director and actors, what causes a scene to not work can be a myriad of issues ranging from an emotional tone that is out of keeping for a character, or out of keeping with the current circumstances of the scene, to unnatural poses, artificial seeming action, or continuity issues. For the team of the Director of Photography, the 3D artist, and the compositor, these may be obvious visual issues such as jagged or sizzling edges, lighting or exposure mismatches, color space differences, or obvious angle/perspective issues. But it may equally be issues that are quite as subtle as minor differences in the emotional tone of an actor's line delivery. Foreground set pieces that look different from the background plate, subtle mismatches of perspective, an actor who isn't quite looking at the right virtual spot—these issues can be quite subtle and require an experienced eye to identify and correct. But even average viewers register these problems unconsciously, and may not be able to identify what is wrong with the scene—they'll just know that something *isn't right.* The team working on a composited shot must be relentless in the pursuit of perfection. We'll never attain that ideal, but we must strive for it to reach that middle zone that isn't quite perfect—but it works.

Upping the Ante: HD and the Big Screen

HDTV, theatre screen digital projection, and 35mm blowups from HD productions all up the ante in this pursuit of perfection. Many local news stations were horrified on their initial conversion to HDTV to see that their beautiful news sets (which looked quite spiffy in SD) suddenly looked tacky and worn in HD. HD shows up many rough edges and flaws, and removes the wiggle room that SD productions have.

While HDTV has been slow to fully penetrate the consumer market, it has taken the narrative filmmaking world by storm. The introduction of low-cost formats such as HDV have very quickly made HD-resolution moviemaking quite common. However, most of these low-budget movies end up being seen on SD DVD, which at the time of this writing was still the only commercially viable distribution. But as the HD-DVD/Blu-Ray dust settles down and a viable and widely accepted HD distribution format emerges, compositors working in HD formats will have to watch details even more carefully. This is particular true for any productions that aspire to theatrical projection, whether that is digital or via 35mm blowup.

Just as I was wrapping up this book, I had an excellent opportunity to test this. We did a test 35mm blowup with DuArt Labs which included HDV footage from different cameras, and which included two borderline composited scenes. Both scenes looked great when downconverted to SD but revealed problems when projected in HD on the big screen. In both cases, we had shot in front of a greenscreen and used a single instance of Primatte in After Effects to create the composite. One of the scenes was of a swashbuckling swordsman with a very shiny rapier. It was made difficult by the reflectivity of the sword, which caught a lot of unadulterated green at certain angles. Settings that left the sword intact also left a tiny bit of sizzling schmutz just above the sword in a portion of the scene. This was subtle enough to nearly vanish on downconvert to SD—but it was glaringly obvious in full HD, and even more so on the 35mm print. This scene was an example of one which would require multiple combined mattes—at least an edge and core—to produce acceptable results.

In the second example, we turned off Primatte's excellent chroma upres to see how the 4:2:0 format would hold up without that interpolated smoothing of the chroma. As with the first example, the composite looked pretty good in SD, but there were definite jaggies visible in areas of the full HD and in the 35mm blowup.

These tests reveal the added vigilance that is required when creating composited shots for the big screen—not only in post, but also in production, particularly with low-end highly compressed formats like HDV. Even with higher-end HD formats, the compositor will find critical challenges. While 720p and 1080p are excellent formats, they are a long way from 35mm film and a 4K 10-bit uncompressed digital intermediate when it comes to color depth and detail. But the end result will still be blown up to twenty feet high when shown in the theatre, no matter what the program material originated on!

New Opportunities, New Challenges

All that said, we are living in a brave new world of possibilities for the low-budget filmmaker. Even with the challenges presented by high compression and chroma undersampling, the fact is that today we have the possibility of creating some fantastically innovative and visionary images at a relatively tiny cost. Don't get me wrong, budget will always be an issue, but the basic tools have improved so much and come down in price so dramatically that they are now within the reach of any filmmaker. Vision and craft emerge as ever more important in the mix of innovative image making. It is only reasonable to expect this curve to continue. CPU speeds will continue to skyrocket, storage and memory prices to plummet, and the quality of software to increase. And while these factors open the doors for every Tom, Dick, and Harriet to paint a garage wall blue and make a sci-fi movie, it means there are new challenges: first, craft is still essential, and second, the visual standards of the audience will continue to increase.

Democratization of any field has certain inevitable results—amateurs will try their hand at crafts once reserved for professionals, and most of what they do will be utterly horrid. When the Mac first opened the door of typesetting and desktop publishing in 1984, the world was flooded with perfectly awful publications that used illegible and inappropriate typefaces, twelve different typefaces on a single page, and muddy photos combined with ugly graphics. Wise businesses quickly went back to talented pros, who were now able to craft nice documents with lower overhead. Older technology shops that didn't move forward and mediocre pros who were only pros because they had expensive equipment bit the dust.

The same happened with the advent of DV a little over a decade later. Suddenly many folks could afford to produce and edit video images "good enough" for broadcast. But let's face it, a great deal of what they produced never rose above home movie quality. A talented pro with knowledge of lighting and camerawork can create beautiful images with a $4000 camera, while Uncle Bob, with the same camcorder, could create overexposed unsteady and ugly video of the family picnic.

At the same time, two things happened to the standards of viewers. There is one way in which they were lowered: we've gotten more used to and accepting of amateur footage in broadcast programs, and we've gotten used to jerky and pixillated videophone images from war zones and disasters. But at the same time, the average viewer has become far more visually sophisticated. Fantastic special effects of the past are jokes today. Think about these examples:

- The special effects of the original *Star Trek* seemed astonishing to those of us who had grown up with black-and-white Buck Rogers serials—but after *Star Wars*, they seemed hokey and simplistic.

- Rear projection shots, used frequently in older movies, were quite acceptable in their day even though they were always quite obviously fake—contrast and color never matched the foreground, and gate weave often made the background move in ways the foreground didn't. Today's audiences won't accept such patently fake composites except in parody.

- The wonderful stop-motion work of Ray Harryhausen (often composited optically with live action) is still amazing to watch, but today's stop-motion animators wouldn't dare shoot without motion blur and other techniques that make the motion more realistic.

I recently watched one of the early episodes of *Star Trek: The Next Generation.* The opening sequence—a flyby of planets—seemed absolutely positively *real* in 1986, but today it looks harsh-edged and slightly fake. Generally speaking, the bar for visual effects has been raised substantially and will continue to rise as tools improve and new formats emerge. The eyeballs you are trying to convince are becoming more and more sophisticated every day.

But the creative visual artist doesn't need to fear either the democratization of technology or the raising of visual standards. The two together mean that the increasingly sophisticated audience will not accept amateur work any more than they did twenty or thirty years ago!

Plugins and formats are just creative tools like brushes or chisels or charcoal. What the true craftsperson *does* with them will always be substantially different in value and impact from what the average hobbyist does. It is true that today a graphics illiterate with only basic computer knowledge can buy a program and with a few clicks on presets create a beautiful 3D image of mountains or a new living room arrangement; only a few years ago these images would have required high-end systems, cutting-edge software, and highly trained personnel to create. But that average home user will never be able to do anything much outside the "3D for Dummies" presets built into the programs.

New visions, artistic images that engage the imagination, stunning compositions that move the soul—these will always be the domain of the creative visual artist. As with any technical craft or art, creating these images requires a thorough knowledge of the working medium combined with the artistic eye and imaginative mind. Mere knowledge of the medium and techniques (the *craft*) will enable the director, DP, and compositor to create competent, workable, convincing images. Reaching beyond "competent" to new vision, pushing beyond craft on into the hard-to-define realm of art, demands more than simple competency with compositing software and plugins. It requires vision and imagination, seeing what is possible even if it hasn't been done before. Sometimes this will involve using old tools in a new way, or in unexpected combinations; other times it will involve creating new tools to create images that simply couldn't be done well before.

In every case, the creative professional will need to be competent in the current technology and craft. Since the technology is a constantly moving target, it's safe to say that there will always be learning; you will never be completely on top of every latest development in the larger field. But you will need to be pretty near to on top of the specific technologies and programs you are actively using. A part of the craft will also be assessing the most appropriate and effective technology to use: what available current technology will be most effective to convert your imagined vision into an actual moving image that others can see and experience. This assessment will be tempered by realities of budget, talent available, and limitations of the current technology.

Limitations of technology may in some cases be a call for boosting the budget to create new, cutting-edge software. Animation giant Pixar has poured massive amounts of money into development of new shaders for realistic hair and fabric, for instance, and each successive movie shows the results of these efforts. But in many cases, the big-dollar approach is not available and so the compositor must work with the creative team to come up with innovative approaches that compensate for technological or budgetary limitations. This work can be just as exciting as creating new technology! Some of the best and most interesting movie work has been spit-and-bubblegum improvisation. Imaginative improvisation has brought many a director's vision to reality on the silver screen. Don't have the budget for cutting-edge hair? Turn things around; tape a real actor with real hair and composite an animated face onto the actor!

With the tools we have at our disposal today, and the tools of the not-too-distant future, you can create some truly astonishing images and effects. Even with the limits of technology, there is no limitation on imagination and vision. However, the best way to turn your magnificent vision into reality is to learn the basics of your craft first, and then move on to stretching the limits.

I'd like to leave you with advice I've given (in one form or another) to thousands of people who have attended my workshops:

> **Make an effort to learn something about every aspect of filmmaking.** A camera operator who has done some editing will be a better camera operator because she will understand what the editor needs; a director who has tried producing will understand better why compromises must sometimes be made.
>
> **Put energy and time into the area you are most interested in.** Read voraciously, network with others in the field, pay attention to the masters. Practice in private until your work rivals the best you've seen.
>
> **Set forth a personal standard of excellence and drive yourself to meet it.** You don't do better work by putting down the work of others.
>
> **Get the best tools you can.** Learn how to squeeze the best out of what you have rather than moving on too quickly to the latest hot thing. But don't try to do professional work with tools that aren't professional.
>
> **Be a team player.** Filmmaking is a team sport, not an individual sport. Working with other talented people can make a far better product that you could create on your own.

And most important:

> **Spend time with those you love and work to be a better human being.** Hours spent in the dark in front of a computer need to be balanced with hours spent loving and caring and building memories. It's just a movie.

Happy compositing!

Appendix A: Glossary

1.33. The aspect ratio used in standard definition television. Also referred to as "4:3."

1.37. The aspect ratio used in sync-sound 35mm film. Also referred to as "Academy aperture."

1.78. The aspect ratio used in widescreen television. Also referred to as "16:9."

1.85. 35mm widescreen standard for theatrical film. Uses approximately 3 perforations ("perfs") of image space per 4 perf frame. Also known as "flat."

2.35. 35mm anamorphic widescreen prior to 1970, used by CinemaScope and early Panavision. Newer anamorphic films are actually 2.39, but are conventionally referred to as 2.35.

2.39. 35mm anamorphic widescreen from 1970 onwards.

2D. The flat, two-dimensional space of a final film or video production which has width and height (the two dimensions designated by values of X and Y in a coordinate system) but no true depth (Z axis).

2K. Resolution of 35mm film digitized at 2048 x 1536 pixels width; ¼ the frame size of 4K. Used as Digital Intermediate (DI) resolution for some feature films that are not heavily laced with visual effects.

3D Animation. Digital animation technique that allows realistic movement in simulated three-dimensional space. Characters and simulated camera motion is possible not only in the standard X and Y axis (width and height) but also along the Z axis (depth), allowing more realistic positioning and motion of characters and objects.

3:2 Pulldown. Technique for converting 24fps film to interlaced NTSC video at 59.97 fields per second by distributing four film frames over five video frames. Three video frames are reproduced using full film frames for both fields; the next two mix adjacent film frames for each field. These two are known as *jitter frames* because of the jitter of motion between the fields when displayed. Sometimes referred to as 2:3 pulldown. PAL countries do not use 3:2 pulldown; they simply speed up the film by 4% to 25fps.

3:2 Pullup. The process of removing 3:2 pulldown from video to convert back to original 24fps.

4:1:1. Color decimation used in NTSC DV format. The first number represents the number of luminance samples, the second the number of chrominance samples, and the third the number of chrominance samples in the next TV line. Thus, every pixel is sampled for luminance, every fourth pixel for chrominance, and the same sampling occurs in the next line. The three pixels after a fully sampled pixel simply duplicate the chroma value of the first pixel. In compositing, this undersampling creates noticeable jaggies.

4:2:0. Color decimation used in PAL DV and MPEG2 format. The first number represents the number of luminance samples, the second the number of chrominance samples, and the third the number of chrominance samples in the next TV line. Thus, every pixel is sampled for luminance and every other pixel for chrominance; in the next (even) line, every pixel is sampled for luminance but none for chrominance (hence the "0"). The pixels on this line simply duplicate the chroma values of the pixel immediately above it. In compositing, this undersampling creates noticeable jaggies, but is better than 4:1:1.

4:2:2. Color decimation used in ITU-R 601 SD video. The first number represents the number of luminance samples, the second the number of chrominance (Y-R, Y-B) samples, and the third the number of chrominance samples in the next TV line. Thus, every pixel is sampled for luminance and every other pixel for chrominance; the same sampling occurs in the next line. In compositing, this produces mattes that are acceptable but not as accurate as fully sampled 4:4:4 video.

4:4:4. Fully sampled video in which every pixel is sampled for both luminance and chrominance.

4K. 35mm film digitized at 4096 pixels width; typically used for digital intermediate (DI) of feature films, especially those featuring visual effects.

8-bit. Digitization scheme that allows 256 levels per channel, usually noted as 0–255. ITU-R 601, DV, and most other digital video formats are based on 8-bit digitization.

10-bit. Digitization scheme that allows 1024 levels per channel, usually noted as 0–1023. The increased bit depth allows finer color correction with less chance of banding.

A

Algorithm. A step-by-step formula, usually mathematical, that solves a problem or achieves a desired outcome.

Aliasing. The pixelated, jagged edge which results from undersampling of the digital image. Undersampled chroma results in an aliased color-based matte even when the base image looks normal to the eye. Enlarging a digitized image without interpolation of edge detail also creates noticeable aliasing; data clipping can also create aliased edges.

Alpha Channel. The embedded "matte" channel of a four-channel CGI image. See *key, mask*, and *matte*.

Analog. A continuously varying signal without the stepped levels used in digital formats; not digital.

Anamorphic. Scaled horizontally, as an image. The image is "squeezed" either optically or digitally in recording, and then stretched or "unsqueezed" on display. CinemaScope is an anamorphic film format; 16:9 SD video is recorded with the same number of pixels as 4:3 SD video, but the pixels are displayed stretched so they are wider than they are tall. From the Greek *ana* (up, back, again) *morphos* (form, shape).

Antialiasing. The technique of concealing aliasing by the use of intermediate colors to try and smooth out jagged edges. Antialiasing can be accomplished by subpixel oversampling (the most accurate) or by interpolation.

Artifact. Unintended side effect of an operation. While the term can apply to analog processing, it usually refers to the effects of digital processing or compression. Excessive compression (such as that used in JPEG or DV) can result in "mosquito net" artifacting; excessive color correction can result in banding.

Aspect Ratio. The shape of a display screen or pixel, expressed as the ratio of the width divided by the height. May be expressed as a proportion (16:9) or a floating point number (1.33).

B

Background. In compositing, the image that is placed "behind" or "underneath" the main subject image, or foreground. Also *background plate.*

Backing Color. The color used in the background screen, usually green or blue.

Banding. A color artifact in areas of similar color. Due to inadequate color data, excessive color correction, or compression, what should be a smooth gradient becomes steps or bands of solid color. Similar to posterization; see also *contouring.*

BG. Abbreviation for background.

Bit. The smallest digital unit of data, either "on" or "off," often expressed as "1" or "0."

Bit depth. The number of bits assigned in a format to represent a channel, usually 8 or 10.

Black Point. The darkest area of the image in final display mode.

Black Stretch. An adjustment on the lower end of the camera's gamma curve to either expand or compress very dark portions of the image. Used to preserve shadow detail in a bright contrasty exposure, or to increase contrast in shadows on a "flat" exposure. Similar to *toe*, though technically different.

Bluescreen. Specifically, a uniform blue background used in color compositing. Generally, the term is also used to describe the entire color compositing process, even when the actual backing color is something other than blue; in this way, it is often used in the trade as an ersatz verb, as in "bluescreening."

Boris. A compositing/special effects plugin marketed by Artel.

Brightness. Human visual perception of luminance; subjective rather than measured.

Bump Matte. A matte created from the "bumps" of an organic surface, such as orange peel or bark.

C

CCD. Charge-coupled device, the solid-state imaging chip used in most video cameras. The CCD is an analog device that outputs a voltage that must be converted to digital information.

CGI. Abbreviation for Computer Generated Image.

Channel. One of several components used to define a digital image; may be RGB, YUV, or, in the case of reflective printing, CMYK. May also include additional information such as an alpha channel.

Channel Arithmetic. Mathematical operations involving combining or applying one color channel to another.

Choke. A process of expanding or reducing the edge of the matte. Usually refers to reducing the edge of the matte. Also called "erosion" or "shrink."

Chroma Key. Generally, any color-based compositing method that creates a matte from a solid backing color; also, generic term for live color-based compositing in the television industry.

Chrominance. The color content of a video image, as opposed to the luminance (brightness) content.

Clean Plate. A shot of the green or bluescreen background without foreground actors or components; ideally, shot at the same camera settings as the planned foreground shot. The clean plate is used by some software to correct for imperfections in the foreground plate. Also a term used to describe a background plate for an effect done on location and shot clean of actors or other elements that need to be manipulated in post. (For example, if your actor is being eaten by a giant snake, you might shoot the actor on location reacting to the non-existent snake, then have him step out and shoot the background clean. This allows the image of the actor to be manipulated in post, for example, when the snake grabs him up and now you need to see the image area that was behind him.)

Clipping. Occurs when values exceed the digital "ceiling" of a signal. An analog camera signal of 120 IRE will clip to 255 (equivalent to 110 IRE) because there is no higher value to represent it. In color or level correction, if the maximum output level is set to 235 (equivalent to 100 IRE), then all values above 235 will clip to that value.

CMOS. Complementary Metal Oxide Semiconductor, an imaging device that is gradually replacing the CCD in some cameras. Unlike the CCD, CMOS chips contain onboard amplifiers, noise correction, and digitization circuits, and and the chips output a digital signal.

Color Channel. (See channel) A component of a digital picture that represents color information. In RGB color space, all three channels represent color; in YUV (Y, Y-B, Y-R) Y represents luminance while the second two channels represent color.

Color Curve. The remapping of color values through the use of a gamma curve, or visual representation of the weighting of transition from dark to light.

Color Difference Matte. A matte extraction technique that subtracts the appropriate color channel (blue or green) from the other color channels.

Color Resolution. The total number of shades of colors that can be produced from a given number of bits. A 24-bit RGB image (three channels at 8 bits each) can produce 16.7 million discrete colors.

Color Space. The range (gamut) of colors that can be recorded and reproduced in a given system. RGB, YUV, CMYK, and HSV color spaces each represent colors slightly differently and have different limitations.

Color Temperature. Color tint of light, measured in Kelvin. The two standard color temperatures used in film and video production are 3200 K (tungsten) and 5600 K (daylight).

Combustion. Compositing application marketed by Autodesk; higher-end versions include Discreet Flint, Flame, and Inferno.

Component Video. Video that is separated into three signals, luminance and two chrominance (Y-R, Y-B) signals.

Composite. An image formed by combining two or more layers with a matte or alpha channel defining transparency on one or more of the layers.

Composite Video. Video signal that combines luminance and chrominance information into a single signal.

Computer Generated Image. An image generated by computer, such as a 3D image.

Contouring. A color artifact in areas of similar color. Due to inadequate color data, excessive color correction, or compression, what should be a smooth gradient become steps or bands of solid color. Similar to posterization; see also *banding*.

Contract. To shrink or erode the edges of a matte. Also referred to as *choke*.

Contrast. The degree of variance between the brightest area of a picture and the darkest area of the picture. However, the term also is used to describe the rapidity of change from dark to light in the midranges see *gamma*.

Cool. Description of an image with blue cast or tone.

Corner Pinning. In motion tracking, attaching each corner of an image to defined points that may move over time. By tracking the corners to those points, perspective and angle may be changed to match the underlying image, e.g., when compositing a new ad panel onto the side of a city bus.

Crop. To trim edges from an image.

D

D1 video. A *component* SD digital video format where chroma and luma are recorded as three discrete channels, typically referred to as YUV. Both D1 and D2 are uncompressed digital formats.

D2 video. A *composite* SD digital video format where chroma and luma are recorded as a single channel.

Data Compression. A variety of techniques for reducing the size of a digital file; can be either lossless (as in PKZIP) or lossy (as in JPEG).

Data Reduction. A variety of techniques for reducing the size of a digital file by eliminating redundant or unneeded data prior to compression; color decimation such as 4:1:1 is an example.

DDR. Digital Disk Recorder.

Deinterlace. A technique for converting an interlaced video frame consisting of two sets of fields into a single progressive frame. Some techniques are very lossy, resulting in significant reduction of vertical detail; others blend fields in a manner that preserves vertical detail.

Density. In film prints, refers to the opacity of dark areas of a frame, which in turn affects the look of the entire frame. A film print with low density will look pale and washed out; a print with good density will have deep blacks and rich colors. In mattes, refers to the level of opacity—in other words, how opaque or transparent the image is.

Depth of Field. The area in front of a camera lens that is in acceptably sharp focus. This is affected by the focal length of the lens, the iris opening, and the size of the objective (CCD or film). A shallow depth of field is one where only a narrow zone is in focus and all objects nearer the camera or further away from the camera are out of focus.

Despill. Technique for removing backing color which is contaminating the foreground image.

DI. See *Digital Intermediate.*

Difference Matte. Matte created by subtracting one image from another; typically where one image has the foreground subject and the other shows the same scene without the foreground subject.

Difference Tracking. Tracking one object to the motion of another.

Digital Intermediate. A digitized version of the camera film negative which can have effects and color correction applied digitally before it is printed back out to film.

Digitize. To convert an analog image into a digital image by quantizing the continuously varying color and luminance values into discrete digital values.

Dilate. To expand the edges of a matte; see also *choke.*

Dissolve. Transition between two scenes where one seems to fade into the other.

Drop Frame. Video time code correction that keeps time code in sync with real time; necessary because NTSC video runs at 29.97fps rather than 30fps.

Dynamic Range. The ratio between the brightest portion and the darkest portion of a scene. Particularly important in image acquisition (both digital and film) because values outside the dynamic range (or "latitude") of the camera will be represented as either pure white (at the top end) or pure black (at the bottom end) even though there may be significant detail visible to the eye in the real-world scene.

E

Edge Detection. Algorithm which identifies sharp edges in an image for processing either as a matte or for enhancement.

Edge Processing. Algorithm that expands or dilates the edges of a matte.

Erode. To contract the edges of a matte.

Exposure. The lens aperture setting and amount of light that is allowed to fall on the surface of the film or CCD during a given period. The period of time is the *Exposure Time*, the total amount of time (e.g., $1/60^{th}$ of a second or $1/48^{th}$ of a second) that light that is allowed to fall on the film or CCD.

Extrapolate. To calculate a new data point from the range of previous existing points; see also *Interpolate.*

F

Fade. An effect where the image transitions to black.

FG. Abbreviation for Foreground.

Field. In interlaced video, each frame is represented by a field which is all of the even or odd scan lines. Each field is presented sequentially.

Field Dominance. Which field is presented first, either even or odd. When field dominance is reversed, interlaced video will appear jerky. Either field can be dominant, though it is more common to have field 1 (the odd or lower field) dominant.

Filter. In digital image processing, a method of deriving a new value for a pixel based on evaluation, neighboring pixels. In camera work, a plate of optical glass placed in front of the lens to create a designed effect.

Flare. An artifact (usually undesirable) from a bright light source directly entering the camera lens and affecting the image. Often simulated now in CGI effects, though usually avoided in the real world by good camera operators.

Flip. To reverse an image vertically (exchange top and bottom).

Floating Point. Representing numerical values to several degrees of decimal precision rather than rounded whole values. More precise but slower for computation than integer (whole number) processing.

Flop. To reverse an image horizontally (exchange left and right sides).

Focus Pull. To change or "rack" the focusing distance of the lens, usually to move the focus from one subject to another closer or further from the camera.

Follow Focus. To change the focal point of the lens to keep a subject in focus as it moves toward or away from the camera; also known as *rack focus*.

Foreground. In compositing, the plate to be composited over the background; there may be more than one foreground plate. In camera work, the subject area closer to the camera.

Fourier Transforms. In image processing, a technique for decomposing an image or signal into its component frequencies and their amplitudes for further analysis and processing. Fast Fourier Transforms are an efficient algorithm for rapidly calculating Fourier Transforms efficiently on a computer. Named after Jean-Baptiste Joseph Fourier (1768–1830), a French mathematician and physicist.

G

Gamma. Measurement of the manner in which midtones transition from black to white, typically described as a curve. Changing the gamma does not affect black or white points, but may dramatically affect midrange tones. When referring to a video or display monitor, a measurement of the nonlinearity of display reproduction.

Gamma Correction. A midtone curve (see Gamma) that is designed to correct or compensate for the inherent display characteristics of a particular display monitor or projector.

Garbage Matte. A roughly drawn matte (usually stationary or only crudely animated) that eliminates unwanted portions of the foreground image. Often used to eliminate boom arms, light stands, or bad areas of backing color that appear in the foreground plate.

Gate Weave. Minor variations in film frame positioning caused by imprecise registration of film perforations on projector or camera pins.

Gaussian. A method of image processing (such as blur or resampling) based on a statistical probability of normal distribution, often referred to as a bell curve. Named after Carl Friedrich Gauss (1777–1855), a German mathematician and scientist, though first proposed by Abraham de Moivre in an article in 1734.

Geometric Transform. Image processing operation that changes the position, orientation, or shape of the image.

G-Matte. Slang for garbage matte, which if you think about it was probably slang in the first place as well.

Grain. In film, the clumping of silver halide particles and color dyes which results in a subtle pattern in each frame. Since the grain changes in each frame, the resulting random changes in representation of detail over time seems to soften hard edges or details.

Graphical User Interface. The visual interface on computers that allows operation of a computer program through a mouse, trackball, or pad rather than typed commands. See GUI.

Grayscale. A monochrome or black-and-white image.

Greenscreen. Specifically, a uniform green background used in color compositing. Generally, the term is also used to describe the entire color compositing process, even when the actual backing color is something other than green; in this way, it is often used in the trade as an ersatz verb, as in "greenscreening."

GUI. Acronym for Graphical User Interface. Usually pronounced "gooey"; see *Graphical User Interface.*

H

Hard Clip. To clip an image's pixel values by limiting them to a certain value. Produces artificial-looking hard edges.

Hard Matte. To create a specific projection or viewing aspect ratio by masking off top and bottom of the frame. Used in both film and digital video.

HDTV. Abbreviation for High Definition television, comprising a set of standards for various scan modes with either 720 or 1080 scan lines and an aspect ratio of 16:9. Often now referred to as HD; as opposed to Standard Definition television (SDTV or just SD).

Hicon Matte. Slang for "High Contrast Matte," a matte that is only black and white with little or no gray.

Hi-Def. Slang for HDTV.

Histogram. A graphical display of brightness values in an image plotted horizontally by order of brightness.

HSV. Abbreviation for Hue, Saturation, Value, a colorspace for describing colors by color, intensity, and brightness rather than by RGB.

Hue. The color attribute of a particular point on the color spectrum; separate from saturation and brightness (value).

I

Integer. A whole number with no decimal places. In processing, contrast with floating point.

Integer Operations. Mathematical operations using whole numbers rather than more precise floating point numbers.

Interlace. In video, sequential display of two sets of scan lines, the odd and even fields.

Interlace Flicker. Unwanted artifact produced when thin lines (or tiny patterns) cross between interlaced scan lines and seem to flicker on and off.

Interpolate. To calculate a missing data point in between two existing data points.

Inverse Square Law. The law of physics that describes the behavior of radiated energy. The intensity of light, sound waves, or other radiated energy falls off at the inverse square of the change in distance. In other words, doubling the distance causes the intensity to be reduced to ¼ of the original value; halving the distance causes the intensity to quadruple.

Invert. To reverse black and white values or color values, tunring each primary color into its compliment.

J

Jaggies. Slang term for aliasing, or jagged edges that are the result of undersampling.

Jitter Frame. One of the two frames in 3:2 pulldown that mix two different film frames as interlaced video fields.

K

Kelvin. (abbreviated "K") The measurement of light color based on the Kelvin scale. In film and video work, standardized values are 3200 K for incandescent lights and 5600 K for daylight.

Key Light. The primary light source on your subject that throws the main shadow.

Keylight. A color difference keying plugin from The Foundry.

Kilobyte. (abbreviated "k") Ostensibly 1000 bytes, but in practice 2^{10} or 1024 bytes.

Knee. In video cameras, a controllable point in the gamma curve above which highlights are compressed to avoid overexposure and increase the apparent latitude of the camera. Similar to *shoulder*.

L

Latitude. In cameras, the "slice" of real-world light values that the camera can capture. See *Dynamic Range.* The total range of dark to bright the medium is capable of recording.

Lens Flare. See also *Flare.*

Linear Gradient. A continuous, evenly weighted transition from one color value to another.

Locking Point. In motion tracking, the specific point in the underlying video that the composited overlay should track.

Luma Key. Compositing technique where the matte is extracted from the luminance values of the foreground plate.

Luminance. The brightness portion of the video signal, as opposed to chrominance (color).

Luminance Image. A single-channel image created by mixing the RGB channels in a manner that preserves the apparent brightness of the original color image.

Luminance Matte. Any matte derived from a luminance image.

M

Mask. A single-channel image used to define transparency or to restrict processing on another image; see *alpha, matte, key.*

Match Box. In motion tracking, the small box that defines the area of an image actually tracked; usually there is a larger search box around the match box.

Match Move. Matching the motion and settings of a real-world camera with those of a virtual camera in a 3D animation program.

Matte. A single-channel image used to define transparency in the foreground plate of a composited image; see alpha, mask, key.

Maximum. An image processing operation in which two images are compared and the pixel with the brighter value is output; referred to as *Lighten* in Photoshop.

Median Filter. An image processing operation that calculates the average middle value of a group of pixels. Used to reduce noise or grain without introducing blurring.

Midtones. The middle brightness region in an image; not highlights or shadowed areas.

Minimum. An image processing operation in which two images are compared and the pixel with the darkest value is output; referred to as *Darken* in Photoshop.

Monochrome. Usually a luminance-only (black-and-white) image, but can also be a single-channel image of the R, G, or B channels.

Morph. An animated transition effect that uses spatial warping and dissolve to make one image seem to transform into another.

Motion Blur. The blurring of an object's image due to its movement while the camera shutter is open.

Motion Tracking. The technique of following the movement of a group of pixels in a moving image and then applying the motion data to another image, usually composited with the original.

N

Node. In some programs that use nodal flowchart interface (such as Shake), a node is a visual representation of an image processing operation.

Nonlinear. In editing, random access to scenes which can be assembled in any order; in image processing, an operation or process that does not act in a sequential fashion.

Normalize. For audio or image processing, to scale all values so they fall in a specified range; in data, to scale the data so all values fall between 0 and 1.

NTSC. National Television Systems Committee; the SD video standard used in the United States, Japan, and neighboring countries. The standard uses 29.97 frames per second (nominally 30fps) and 486 active lines.

O

Opacity. The opposite of transparency. Attribute which causes the layer to be opaque, or impenetrable to light.

Opaque. The characteristic of an object or graphic layer to block light and prevent any of the image data from an object or layer behind it from passing through. The opposite of *transparent*.

P

PAL. Phase Alternating Line, the SD video standard used in much of Europe. The standard uses 25 frames per second and 576 active lines.

Palette. The available colors in a colorspace or specific image. In 24-bit RGB images, the palette is the number of colors it is possible to represent, which is 16.7 million. In indexed-color images (such as GIF) the palette is a fixed set of colors written into a CLUT (Color Look-Up Table).

Pan. To rotate the camera from left to right or right to left, changing the view horizontally; to move the camera on a horizontal axis.

Perspective. The apparent change in size and shape as objects are further from or at a different orientation to the viewer or camera.

Pivot Point. The place around which a geometric transformation (such as spin) is performed.

Pixel. Originally "Picture Element," it is the smallest discrete picture component, representing a single color value. Digital pictures are made up of thousands of pixels, which may be square or rectangular in shape.

Premultiplied. A composition that has been combined with a matte so that all transparent pixels appear black.

Primatte. A color-based keying plugin developed by Yasushi Mishima at IMAGICA.

Print-through. In compositing, when a foreground subject that should be opaque is partially translucent and allows the background layer to show through; the opposite of *veiling*.

Progressive. Video which is scanned sequentially from top to bottom without skipping lines; the opposite of *interlaced video*. Progressive frames appear more film-like than interlaced video.

Proxies. Lower-resolution or highly compressed frames that act as stand-ins or "proxies" for full-resolution frames during editing.

Q

Quantize. To convert a continuously varying signal (analog) to a series of discrete digital values; to digitize. Also can refer to conversion of floating point values to integer data.

R

Rack Focus. To change a lens's distance setting from one point to another during a shot, usually to follow a moving subject or shift attention from one subject to another at different distances from the camera.

Raster. In a CRT television monitor, the spot of light that scans across the screen to draw the picture in the form of raster lines or scan lines. (Also any "grid." In imaging, a grid of pixels used to make up an image, as opposed to vector-based imagery.)

Real Time. An editing or processing operation that occurs at the same speed as the actual real-world event.

Reference Image. In motion tracking, the initial small sample in the match box that the tracking algorithm will try to find in subsequent frames.

Render. In image processing or editing, the computer operation that combines one or more images to create a new image, or applies specified effects to create a new image; in 3D, the process of calculating the finished image from the digital models and definitions set up in the program. The process of a computer "drawing" an image.

Resample. To calculate new pixel values based on averaging after a geometric transformation.

Resolution. The fineness of detail or data that can be represented; the term "resolution" by itself usually refers to spatial resolution, the amount of vertical and horizontal detail in an image. Color resolution and temporal resolution measure different capacities for a format to represent data accurately.

RGB. Abbreviation for Red, Green, Blue, the color channels typically used in computer processing or display.

Rotation. A geometric transformation that changes the orientation of the image around a specific axis.

Rotoscope. In compositing, the technique of drawing or touching up mattes one frame at a time; originally the technique of filming real actors and tracing animation frames from the live action, in the style of Max Fleischer.

Run Length Encoding. A lossless image compression method that reduces data by describing blocks (run lengths) of identical color.

S

Saturation. The intensity of color value in an image, as opposed to the brightness (luminance) value.

Scale. A geometric transformation that changes the horizontal and/or vertical size of the image.

Scan Line. In CRT television monitors, the line drawn on the screen phosphors by the raster.

Screen Operation. Mathematical image compositing operation that tends to superimpose light areas; good for compositing lighting effects like lens flares.

SDI. Abbreviation for Serial Digital Interface, a digital transmission mode for 4:2:2 video in both SD and HD resolutions.

Search Box. In motion tracking, the larger area that the program will search to find the corresponding image in the Match Box.

Serious Magic ULTRA. An easy-to-use compositing program designed around simple virtual sets.

Shake. A high-end compositing application marketed by Apple.

Sharpen. Image processing technique to improve the apparent sharpness of the image; there are several algorithms that can increase the apparent sharpness, but all produce unwanted artifacts when applied too heavily.

Shear. Similar to Skew, a geometric transformation where the top and bottom or sides of an image are offset, but remain parallel to one another.

Shoulder. In film, the upper portion of the film response curve (highlights) where the negative emulsion starts to lose its ability to increase density in response to stronger light. Similar to the *knee* in video cameras, though technically different.

Skew. Similar to Shear, a geometric transformation where the top and bottom or sides of an image are offset, but remain parallel to one another.

Spatial Resolution. What is usually meant by the term "resolution," the fineness of detail or data that can be represented in an image. May be measured in the physical number of pixels in the image, but is also affected by the resolving power of the lens in a camera and other factors.

Specular Highlight. Light source reflected off a shiny surface. This is an actual reflected image of the light source as opposed to a normal highlight. Usually appears as a glint or hot spot.

Spill. Stray light that contaminates an image. In color-based compositing, "spill" usually refers to light (either by radiosity or reflectance) from the backing color that contaminates the foreground subject.

Spill Map. A map of the spill area used in despill operations.

Spline. A smooth line defined by mathematical description of control points, as opposed to a line drawn with pixels. May also be referred to as a *vector line*.

Squeeze. Anamorphic process; an anamorphic image is "squeezed" horizontally and then "unsqueezed" for display. For instance, wide-screen DV format displays pixels at 1.2, or where the width of the pixel is 120% of its height.

Squirm. In motion tracking, loss of precise lock with the tracked object; the foreground object drifts from the desired track point.

Stabilize. In motion tracking, using the motion tracking data in reverse to remove gate weave from a film image.

Subpixel. Calculation of image data or motion tracking data at finer than pixel resolution; gives more accurate results than calculating whole pixel integer values.

T

Telecine. A system that scans film at video resolution for output to either tape or digital file. Also refers to the resulting tape or file, as in "Let's watch the telecine."

Temporal. Having to do with time, or changes over time.

Temporal Resolution. Ability to resolve motion over time, determined by the frame rate (number of samples taken per second). Film has very poor temporal resolution (24 frames per second) and some motion can appear jerky; video has much better temporal resolution (60 fields per second).

Time Code. Digital clock data embedded in the signal to mark each frame for hours, minutes, seconds, and frames. Often, review copies of footage will display the time code onscreen; this is known as a "Window dub" or "Window burn."

Toe. In film, the bottom part of the film response curve where the negative stock emulsion gradually loses the ability to change density in response to low levels of light. Similar to *black stretch* on a video camera, though technically different.

Tone. The darkness or lightness of a given color.

Track. In motion tracking, a technique for finding a specific location in an image by matching a small sample of the image, so that a second image or overlay can move as if locked to the background.

Tracking Marker. A stationary marker or object put on the set to facilitate computer tracking in post.

Tracking Points. Non-stationary markers, often placed on actors or moving objects, that allow the motion to later be tracked by computer; see also *tracking targets*.

Tracking Targets. In the digital file, these are the images of the tracking points that the computer will attempt to motion track.

Transformation. Any geometric change to the image such as flip, flop, rotate, scale, or crop.

Translation. When the image is moved vertically and/or horizontally but not changed in other ways.

Transparency. An attribute allowing other objects or graphic layers to be fully or partially seen through the layer. The opposite of *opacity*.

Transparent. An attribute that allows light to pass through the layer or object; the opposite of *opaque*.

U

Ultimatte. The grandfather of color-based compositing; company started by Petros Vlahos that manufactures hardware and software keying solutions.

Unsharp Mask. An image processing operation that increases the apparent sharpness of the image by subtracting a blurred version of the image from itself.

Unsqueeze. To display an anamorphic image stretched horizontally so that photographed objects appear normal.

V

Value. The brightness value of a given color in HSV color space.

Veiling. Haze of light caused by lens imperfections or light directly entering the camera lens. In compositing, the slight retention of foreground image in areas that should be transparent; the opposite of print-through.

W

Warm. Description of an image with reddish or reddish/yellowish cast or tone.

Warp. Deformation of the image in any direction.

Weighted Screen. A variation of the screen operation that includes the use of a mask or matte to suppress unwanted areas of the overlaid image.

White Point. The brightest intensity in the image in final display mode.

X

X. The horizontal direction in an image display.

X-Axis. The horizontal axis of movement, rotation, or scaling.

Y

Y. The vertical direction in an image display.

Y-Axis. The vertical axis of movement, rotation, or scaling.

YCbCr. Digital component video signal where one component is luminance (Y) and two chrominance channels (Cb and Cr) represent values that derive orange-cyan and yellow-green values by subtraction from the luminance channel. Requires less data space than full RGB digital representation.

YIQ. Component analog NTSC signal for SD or HD video where one component is Luminance (Y) and two subtractive chrominance channels (IQ, sometimes labeled Pb or B-Y and Pr or R-Y). May also be "Y, B-Y, R-Y" and "YpbPr." Requires less bandwidth than analog RGB.

YUV. Component analog PAL signal for SD or HD video where one component is Luminance (Y) and two subtractive chrominance channels (UV). Though technically incorrect, YUV has come to be used generically to describe YIQ and other forms of component video signal.

Z

Z-Axis. In 3D animation, the imaginary depth (distance away from the viewer) perpendicular to the X/Y axes.

Z Channel. Similar to an *alpha channel*, a luminance image where the values represents distance from the viewer rather than transparency.

zMatte. A color-based keying plugin marketed by Digital Film Tools.

Zoom. In camera work, to increase the focal length of the lens, thus enlarging subjects that are far away. This has a different visual effect than dollying in closer. In 3D animation, the process of simulating a camera zoom by changing the focal length of the digital camera. In compositing, simulating a zoom by enlarging the background image.

Appendix B: Building a Permanent Cyclorama

For most video shops, building a usable cyclorama doesn't require the purchase of a commercial wall system. Most sheetrock and plaster contractors can create a basic cyc with a smooth cove connecting wall and floor. This is easiest to do with new construction or during extensive remodeling, though it is not prohibitively difficult to retrofit into existing wallboard. Creating a full corner cyc with two coves that meet in a smooth corner is more difficult.

The cove, or smooth curved area that transitions from wall to floor without a sharp corner, is constructed of lath strips over plywood curve cutouts. This assembly, which forms the basis of the curve, is then plastered over with "mud" to create the smooth finished surface connecting the floor and wall.

To be effective, the curve must be 24–36 inches in radius. Too small a radius will produce a noticeable, even if smooth, corner shadow. Cut a plywood form for each stud/floor joist combination. The form is fastened to the side of each stud and floor joist, recessed so that the addition of lath will leave the surface of the lath approximately 1/8-inch lower than the flooring and 1/8-inch recessed from the wallboard. Lath strips are then nailed across the curved forms as in the illustration.

When the plywood/lath base form is complete, plasterers then coat the lath with "mud," creating as smooth a curved surface as possible. When the plaster is dry, the cove area is sanded smooth. A good grade of primer should be used on the entire surface before applying chroma key paint.

Tip: Quick-and-Dirty Do-It-Yourself Solution: Many do-it-yourselfers have come up with a fairly inexpensive solution for garage studios. An inexpensive roll of linoleum flooring is used to create the color backing, cove, and floor.

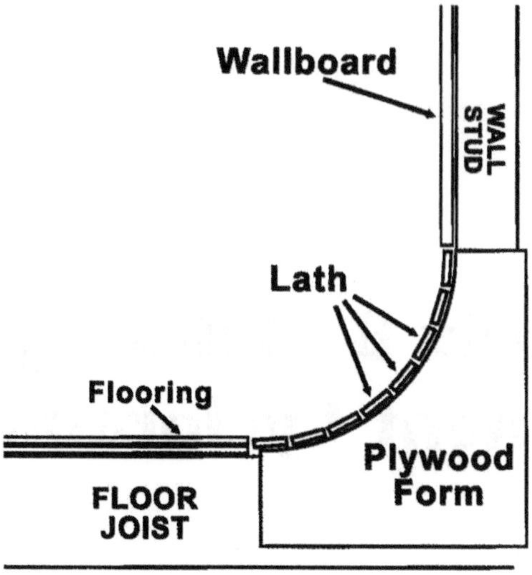

> It doesn't matter whether you like the pattern of the flooring or not, because you'll be using the back surface. That means you can purchase some truly horrid surplus flooring cheap!

Using a pine 1" x 2", mount the end of the roll to the wall just under the ceiling, with the back side of the flooring facing outward. Screws through the 1 x 2 and linoleum into the wall studs are sufficient; but leave an inch or so of flooring above the 1 x 2. The linoleum is not resistant to tearing, so care must be taken fastening the top edge to the wall.

The flooring is then unrolled down the wall and over the floor, positioned so as to create a natural curve between wall and floor. The natural stiffness of the flooring will make a smooth curve. The flooring should be fastened to the floor in some way (either adhesive or nails) so that it will not slide and change the shape of the cove.

Now, apply a good grade of primer and then two or more coats of chroma key paint to the entire flooring roll.

In both cases, you should protect the chroma key paint on the floor with tarp, cardboard, or some other material when it is not actually being used for a live shoot. Walking on the painted floor section quickly creates scuffs and discolorations that will show up in the final composite.

Appendix C: Calibrating Your Monitor

An astounding number of film and video production people are unaware of the need to calibrate a production monitor for proper display of material. While an experienced eye can eyeball a monitor adjustment pretty well with familiar footage (especially footage containing human skin tones), proper technique requires a procedural calibration of the monitor. This is especially true for fine color correction work—or careful balancing of colors between a background plate and a foreground plate!

The procedure below is prescribed by the Society of Motion Picture and Television Engineers (SMPTE) for calibrating a CRT monitor that uses SMPTE-C phosphors to the NTSC signal. The procedure works well with cheaper monitors that don't use the SMPTE-C phosphors, but is not assured of precise calibration without the specified phosphors.

Calibrating an NTSC SMPTE-C Phosphor CRT Video Monitor

If your monitor does not have a Blue Gun Only switch, you will need to obtain a blue filter to look at the bars. You can obtain a Wratten 47B Blue filter from any photo store. You may also use a pure blue gel such as Rosco's #80 Primary blue.

1. Allow the monitor to warm up for 5–10 minutes minimum. Adjustments will not be accurate on a cold monitor.
2. Display SMPTE color bars on the monitor. Turn the Chroma (color level) control all the way down.

3. Find the Pluge (superblack, black, and gray bars) at the lower right of the pattern. Adjust the Brightness control until there is no difference visible between the superblack and black bars, but a difference is visible between the black and gray bars.
4. Adjust the Contrast control to achieve a balanced grayscale across the top bars.
5. Switch on the Blue Gun Only switch, or look at the bars through a blue filter.
6. Turn up the Chroma (color level) control until the two outermost bars (white and blue) appear to match in brightness.
7. Adjust the Color Phase (tint or hue) control until the third bar from the left (cyan) and the third bar from the right (magenta) appear to match in brightness.
8. Your monitor is now properly adjusted.

Calibrating Other Types of Monitors

Of course, there are now many types of monitors other than the classic CRT. Plasma monitors, especially for HD production work, are excellent substitutes. The plasma display closely parallels a CRT in gamma and color reproduction.

LCD monitors, on the other hand, use a different gamma, and they display colors very differently from a traditional CRT or a plasma display. They have become quite ubiquitous in production work due to their portability and low cost; but they are less than ideal for fine color work. Though this is in part due to the display characteristics of the LCD itself, the majority of the problem lies behind the LCD in the screen illumination. Most LCD screens are illuminated using cold cathode light sources, which, like most fluorescent tubes, are *discontinuous* light sources—in other words, they do not contain all the colors of the spectrum. Often they are too blue/green and weak in red. Newer LCD screens illuminated by LED sources are much more accurate, but at the time of writing are still quite expensive.

Add to this the fact that computer CRTs display colors differently from video CRTs, and a tremendous number of editors and compositors are looking at their work on computer displays, not proper video output on a calibrated production monitor.

So how can you calibrate your non-standard monitor? There are several products on the market that will help. Most are simple wizards that step the user through procedures of subtle adjustment that will end up providing the most accurate possible display. With CRTs and plasma displays, these will be quite accurate; on some cheaper LCD screens the best that can be said is that they'll get you as close as possible.

ColorVision Spyder2PRO	www.colorvision.com
GretagMacbeth Eye-One Display 2	www.gretagmacbeth.com
DisplayMate Multimedia Edition	www.displaymate.com

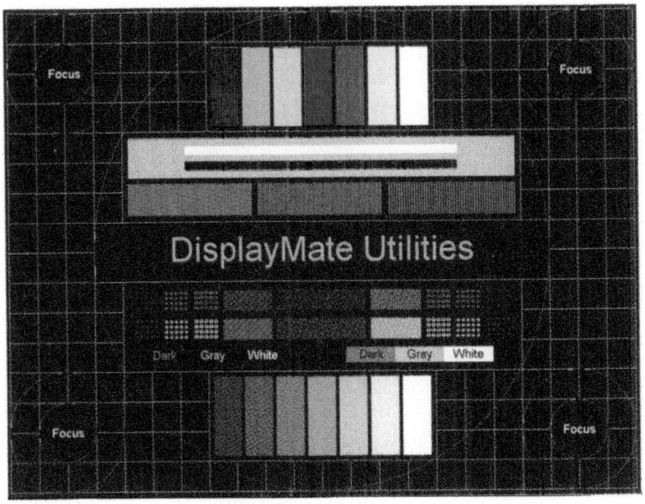

One screen from the DisplayMate Multimedia Edition, which contains over 500 test patterns and command scripts for running and producing fully automated demos and custom test suites.

A simple free calibration wizard for computer displays known as Monitor Calibration Wizard 1.0 is available from: Hex2Bit at www.hex2bit.com/products/product_mcw.asp

Appendix D: Manufacturers

ADOBE: After Effects, Premiere Pro, Photoshop

Adobe Systems Incorporated
345 Park Avenue
San Jose, CA 95110-2704
Tel: 408-536-6000
Fax: 408-537-6000
www.adobe.com

APPLE: Final Cut Pro, QuickTime, Shake

Apple
1 Infinite Loop
Cupertino, CA 95014
Tel: 408-996-1010
www.apple.com

ARTEL: Boris FX, Boris RED

Artel Software Inc.
381 Congress St.
Boston, MA 02210
Tel: 617-451-9900
Toll Free: 888-772-6747
www.borisfx.com

AUTODESK: Combustion, Discreet Flame & Flint

Autodesk, Inc.
111 McInnis Parkway
San Rafael, CA 94903
Tel: 415-507-5000
Fax: 415-507-5100
www.autodesk.com

DIGITAL FILM TOOLS: zMatte

Digital Film Tools
Tel: 818-761-6577
www.digitalfilmtools.com

THE FOUNDRY: Keylight

The Foundry
1 Wardour Street
London W1D 6PA
United Kingdom
Tel: 020 7434 0449
Fax: 020 7434 1550
International Dialing: +44 20 7434 0449
www.thefoundry.co.uk

IMAGICA: Primatte

IMAGICA Corp. of America
3113 Woodleigh Lane
Cameron Park, CA 95682
Tel: 530-677-9980
Fax: 530-677-0081
www.primatte.com

POSTHOLES

PostHoles
3908-A Westpoint Blvd.
Winston-Salem, NC 27103
Tel: 336-794-8114
Toll Free: 877-882-8808
www.post-holes.com

SERIOUS MAGIC: ULTRA 2

Serious Magic
101 Parkshore Dr., Suite 250
Folsom, CA 95630
Tel: 916-985-8000
www.seriousmagic.com

ULTIMATTE: Ultimatte AdvantEdge

Ultimatte Corp.
20945 Plummer Street
Chatsworth, CA 91311
Tel: 818-993-8007
www.ultimatte.com

VITA: Background plates

VITA Digital Productions
www.backgroundplates.com

WALKER EFFECTS: Light Wrap

Walker Effects
www.walkereffects.com

Index

1.33 aspect ratio, 203
1.37 aspect ratio, 203
1.78 aspect ratio, 203
1.85 standard, 203
2.35 standard, 203
2.39 standard, 203
2D space, 203
2K digital, 203
3:2 pulldown/pullup, 203
3D animation programs, 110–111, 142, 203
3D rendering engine, 137–138
3D storyboard programs, 102–103
3M Scotchlight coating, 57
4:3 aspect ratio, 203
4:4:4 video, 95, 98–100, 136, 204
4K digital, 159, 197, 203, 204
16:9 aspect ratio, 203
601 video, 94, 95
720p format, 112, 132, 186, 197, 210
1080p format, 99, 132, 197, 210

A

action matte, 25
Adobe After Effects, 151–158
Adobe Premiere Pro, 144–146
Adobe Systems, 224
After Effects, 151–158
algorithm, 204
aliasing, 204
Alpha Channel, 8, 27–29, 204. *See also* channels
analog signal, 6, 95, 204
analog video, 67–68, 93
anamorphic image, 99, 204, 216, 217
animation, 110–111, 142, 194, 203
antialiasing, 205
Apple Computer, 224
Apple Final Cut Pro, 146–148
Apple QuickTime format, 99
Apple Shake, 188–192, 215
applications. *See* programs
architectural edges, 37
architectural lights, 62
art design, 83–92
Artel Software, 224
artifacts, 119, 163–164, 168, 205, 215
aspect ratio, 114, 203, 205
Autodesk, Inc., 207, 224

B

background (BG)
  black, 77–79, 117, 123
  cyclorama, 10–11, 42, 46–47, 219–220
  described, 205
  enhancing, 108–110
  lighting, 51–54, 63–71
  print-through areas, 11
  white, 20, 78, 80–81
background color
  blue, 10, 86–88
  green, 10, 86–88
  lighting for, 51–54
  red, 86–88
background plates, 8–10, 105–110
background screen, 10, 43–47, 64–65, 70
Backgroundplates.com, 106
backing color, 10, 13, 63, 115–117, 205
backing plate, 75, 76
backlights, 62, 63, 76–77, 79
banding, 205
Bermingham, Alan, 53
bit depth, 205
black backgrounds, 77–79, 117, 123
black point, 123–124, 205
black stretch, 205
blending modes, 18–24
blue channel, 86–88
bluescreen, 5, 10, 43–47, 205
bluescreen paint, 47–49
bluescreen studio. *See* studio
bluescreening, 1, 2, 205
blur effects
  edges, 100, 117–118, 124, 146
  foreground/background plates, 113, 117–119
  Gaussian Blur, 29, 38, 210
  jaggies, 97, 100, 118–119, 151

layers, 38–39
motion blur, 159, 161, 187–188, 213
Boris Red, 171–174, 205
brightness, 89, 205
Buck Rogers, 1, 198
bump matte, 205
burning/dodging, 23
bus, 128–131

C

calibrating monitor, 221–223
camera position tracking, 138–142
camera shots
dramatic, 45
fixing flaws in, 25–30
full-length shots, 45–46
lock-down shots, 26–30
motion tracking systems, 138–142
nature shots, 109
removing items in, 26–30
scenarios, 105–110
Visual Effects Data Sheet, 104–105
weathercaster-type shots, 44, 128, 136–139
CCD (charge-coupled device), 94, 112, 205, 206
CGI (computer generated image), 113, 204, 206, 207, 209
channel arithmetic, 206
channels, 16, 28, 95, 97, 206, 214. *See also* Alpha Channel
charge-coupled device (CCD), 94, 112, 205, 206
choke. *See* matte choker
chroma content, 111–112
chroma key, 10, 16, 59–82, 206. *See also* color key
chroma key fabric, 49–51, 54–55
chroma key paint, 47–51
chroma keying, 10, 80
Chromatte fabric, 56–57, 91
chrominance, 89, 206
chrominance values, 116
clean plate, 10, 16, 175–187, 206
cleaning mattes, 85–86, 116–126, 206
clipping, 60, 80, 206
Clone tool, 27
clothing, 83–89, 91
CMOS chips, 206
CMYK color, 206
color
background. *See* background color
backing, 10, 13–14, 63, 115–117, 205
blending, 23–24
CMYK, 206
composite analog video, 68
costumes, 83–89, 91
darkening, 23
dodging/burning, 23
foreground, 85, 87–90
hue, 24
inverting values, 24, 29, 211
lightening, 23
luminance, 24
multiplying, 23
resolution, 206
RGB, 49, 94, 214
saturation, 24, 68
screening, 23
spill, 11, 66, 120–121, 180–188, 216
transparent, 16
color balance, 111–112
Color Burn mode, 23
color channels, 28, 95, 97, 206, 214
color curve, 206
color decimation, 95–99, 180, 204
color difference keying, 16, 123, 159, 206
color difference matte, 206
Color Dodge mode, 23
color gels, 75–77, 81, 221
color key, 10, 16. *See also* chroma key
color LEDs, 57–58, 139
Color mode, 24
Color Range, 16
color sampling, 93, 95–99
color spaces, 94–95, 206, 207, 218
color subtraction keyers, 89
color temperature, 206
color values, 24, 96, 97, 206, 211, 212, 217
color wheel, 85, 87–89
component video, 87, 207
composite analog video, 68
composite modes. *See* blending modes
composite video, 207
composites, 10, 52, 106–108, 207
compositing. *See also* keying
basics, 5–14
changing technology and, 193–201
described, 5–6
digital techniques, 35–40
fixing flaws, 25–30
future of, 197–201
glossary, 9–12
introduction to, 1–4
manual tracking, 33–35
matted overlay fix, 30–33
motion tracking, 30–33, 138–142
problems during. *See* troubleshooting
simple non-action solutions, 25–40
terminology, 9–12
uses for, 6–7, 193–195
compression, 93–97, 207
computer generated image (CGI), 113, 204, 206, 207, 209
contrast, 60, 76, 103, 109–113, 207
control points, 32, 33
cool tones, 217
core matte, 124, 171
corner pinning, 207
costuming process, 83–89, 91
credits, scrolling, 6
cropping, 16–17, 207
crushed blacks, 60
cyc lights, 65–66
cyclorama, 10–11, 42, 46–47, 219–220

D

Darken operation, 21, 22
data reduction, 93–97, 207
deinterlacing, 207. *See also* interlaced video
density, 208, 215, 216
depth of field, 39, 109, 208
despill process, 11, 208, 216

DI (digital intermediate), 7, 10, 197, 204, 208
difference matte key, 16
Difference mode, 23–24
difference tracking, 208
DigiComp system, 50–51
Digital BetaCam video, 95
digital compositing, 35–40
Digital Film Tools, 224
digital intermediate (DI), 7, 10, 197, 204, 208
digital signal processing (DSP), 95
digital video mixers, 131–132
digitization, 204, 208, 214
dirt (schmutz), 11, 116, 122, 123, 125
Disney, Walt, 13
dissolves, 23, 129, 208
dodging/burning, 23
downstream keyers, 130
dramatic shots, 45
drop frames, 208
DSP (digital signal processing), 95
DV format, 96–97
dynamic range, 208

E

edge detection, 208
edge processing, 208
edges, 37, 100, 117–118, 124, 146
editors. *See* programs
effects. *See* special effects
Ellenshaw, P. S., 34
Ellenshaw, Peter, 34
Exclusion mode, 24
exposure, 208
extrapolation, 208
"eyeballing," 71, 76, 221
eyedropper sampling, 116

F

fabrics
  advantages of, 49, 50
  luminance, 89, 91
  reflectivity, 91
  for temporary/portable use, 54–55
  types of, 49–51
  using with paint, 50–51
fades, 79, 208, 209
field dominance, 209
fields, 209
fill, image, 130
fill light, 60, 62, 76
film noir, 62
filters, 209, 212, 221–222
Final Cut Pro, 146–148
flags, 52, 54, 65–66, 79
flare, 11, 18, 22, 209
flat lighting, 62, 63
flaws, fixing, 25–30
flicker, 186, 211
flip-flop switchers, 129, 130
floating point, 209
floor, studio, 42, 45–47, 53, 219–220
"flos." *See* fluorescent lighting
fluorescent instruments, 52
fluorescent lighting, 52–54, 64–65, 70–71, 111
focus, 31, 38, 208–209
focus pull, 209
follow focus, 209
footage, 27, 31–32, 97–99, 108. *See also* camera shots
foreground color, 85, 87–90
foreground (FG)
  described, 209
  dirt on, 11, 123
  lighting, 52, 56, 57, 74–76, 79
  spills and, 11
foreground plates, 8–9, 104–105
foreground sets, 84, 85, 87, 195
formats
  720p, 112, 132, 186, 197, 210
  1080p, 99, 132, 197, 210
  DV, 96–97
  HDCAM, 99, 163–164
  QuickTime, 99
  video format problems, 93–100
The Foundry, 224
Fourier Transforms, 209
frame rate, 112, 216
fuzziness, 116

G

gaffer tape, 50–51
GAMFLOOR, 46
gamma, 209–210, 222
garbage matte, 11, 16–17, 210
gate weave, 109, 198, 210
Gaussian Blur, 29, 38, 210
gels, color, 75–77, 81, 221
"glass painting" effect, 34, 35–40
GlobeCaster, 132, 134
glossary, 203–218. *See also* terminology
Gone With the Wind, 34, 35
gradient matte, 38–39
grain, 210
graphical user interface (GUI), 210
grayscale, 210
grayscale images, 8
green channel, 86–88
greenscreen, 5, 10, 43–47, 210
greenscreen paint, 47–49
greenscreen studio. *See* studio
GUI (graphical user interface), 210

H

hair, 77, 80, 87, 92, 119, 200
hair lights. *See* backlights
halogen lights, 65
halos, 11
hard clip, 210
Hard Light mode, 23
hard matte, 210
hardware keying. *See* keying
Harryhausen, Ray, 198
HDCAM format, 99, 163–164
HDTV (High Definition television), 135, 196–197, 210
heating, ventilation, and air conditioning (HVAC), 53, 77–78
high key lighting, 62
highlights, 23, 60, 68, 81, 215
histogram, 210

Holoset fabric, 56–57
HSV mode, 16, 211
hue, 24, 211
Hue mode, 24
HVAC (heating, ventilation, and air conditioning), 53, 77–78

I

image matte, 16
images
  anamorphic, 99, 204, 216, 217
  computer-generated, 113, 204, 206, 207, 209
  cropping, 16–17, 207
  darkening, 21, 22
  grayscale, 8
  lightening, 21, 22
  luminance, 212
  reference, 102, 137–140, 142, 214
IMAGICA Corp., 225
incandescent instruments, 52
incandescent lighting, 52, 65, 70, 211
Institute of Electronic Engineers, 67
Institute of Radio Engineers. *See* IRE
integer operations, 211
interactive lighting, 81–82
interlaced video, 186, 203, 207, 209, 211
interpolation, 17, 97, 100, 118, 211
inverse square law, 60–61, 70, 211
IRE (Institute of Radio Engineers), 67–69
IRE values, 49, 66–69, 73–77, 80, 206
ITUR 601 video, 94
Iwerks, UB, 12, 13, 14

J

jaggies, 97, 100, 118–119, 151, 173–174, 211
jitter frames, 203, 211

K

key, 6
key channel, 8
key light, 62, 76, 103, 111, 211
keyers
  color difference, 123, 159
  color subtraction, 89
  dedicated, 134–136
  downstream, 130
  overview, 6–8
  types of, 15–16
  Ultimatte, 7, 69, 135–137
  upstream, 130
keyframes, 33, 187
keying. *See also* compositing
  hardware, 9
  live, 127–142
  luma, 77, 78–81
  special effects and, 127, 128, 133
  switchers and, 128–131
keying processes, 15–24
Keylight plug-in, 158–162, 211
kickers, 62, 63, 76, 81
knee, 49, 211

L

Lastolite products, 49, 56
latitude, 59–60, 212
layers, 5–12, 38–39
LEDs, color, 57–58, 139
lens flare, 22, 209
Lighten operation, 21, 22
lighting, 59–82
  architectural lights, 62
  background, 51–54, 63–71
  background/foreground plates, 111
  backlights, 62, 63, 76–77, 79
  basics, 59–63
  clipping, 60, 80, 206
  considerations, 53, 81–82
  contrast in, 60, 76, 103, 109–113, 207
  crushed blacks, 60
  cyc lights, 65–66
  distance and, 60–61, 69–70, 211
  evenness of, 71–78
  fill light, 62, 76
  flags, 52, 54, 65–66, 79
  flat, 62, 63
  fluorescent, 52–54, 64–65, 70–71, 111
  foreground, 52, 56, 57, 74–76, 79
  halogen lights, 65
  hard light, 23
  high key, 62
  highlights, 23, 60, 68, 81, 215
  incandescent, 52, 65, 70, 211
  interactive, 81–82
  inverse square law, 60–61, 70, 211
  key light, 62, 76, 103, 111, 211
  kickers, 62, 63, 76, 81
  large-scale setups, 70–71
  latitude, 59–60, 212
  low key, 62
  for luma keying, 77, 78–81
  reflectors, 56, 57, 65
  sidelights, 62, 76, 79
  soft light, 23
  three-point setup, 63
lighting effects, 39–40
Lighting for Digital Video and Television, 53, 59
lightmeter, 71–72
Light Wrap, 162–167
Linear Color Key, 16
linear gradient, 212
linear gradient mattes, 39
LiteRing LEDs, 57–58
live keying, 127–142
lock-down shots, 26–30
locking point, 212
low key lighting, 62
Low Pass setting, 73
Lowel Tota-Lites, 65
Lucas, George, 2, 43, 99
luma keying, 77, 78–81, 212
luminance, 24, 78, 89, 91, 212
luminance image, 212
luminance (luma) key, 6, 17
luminance matte, 212
luminance values, 90, 116
Luminosity mode, 24

M

Magic ULTRA 2, 142, 183–188
manufacturers, 224–225
Mary Poppins, 1, 12–14, 34, 135
masks, 7, 130, 169, 212
match box, 212
match move, 212
matte choker, 11, 17, 118–120, 206
matted overlay fix, 30–33
mattes
 action, 25
 bump, 205
 cleaning, 85–86, 116–126, 206
 color difference, 206
 core, 124, 171
 creation of, 8, 12–14, 90, 115–117
 described, 212
 early use of, 7
 garbage, 11, 16–17, 210
 gradient, 38–39
 hard, 210
 image, 16
 linear gradient, 39
 luminance, 212
 motion, 41
 negative, 7
 non-action, 25–40
 problems with, 121–126
 progressive, 7
 pulling, 8, 12–14, 90, 115–117
 radial gradient, 39
 static, 12
 transparency, 16, 96
maximum operation, 21, 22, 212
median filter, 212
Méliès, Georges, 6
meteorology, 44, 128, 136–139
Meyer, Chris and Trish, 3, 152
"mic in picture" problem, 26, 30–31
midtones, 212
minimum operation, 21, 22, 212
monitor calibration, 221–223
monochrome, 24, 29, 66, 212
morphing, 213
motion blur, 159, 161, 187–188, 213
motion mattes, 41
motion tracker modules, 30, 32
motion tracking, 30–33, 138–142, 213
MPEG compression, 17, 96, 204
multiply operation, 18–20

N

narrative movies, 193–194, 196
nature shots, 109
negative mattes, 7
nodes, 170, 189–192, 213
noise, 69, 163, 176, 179, 181
non-action mattes, 25–40
nonlinear, 170, 189–192, 213
nonlinear editors (NLEs), 37, 44, 148, 149. *See also* programs
normalization, 213
NTSC system, 94, 96, 98, 112, 213, 221

O

Oldis, D.A., 92
opacity, 5–8, 213
Orad Xync system, 139
outdoor scenes, 87
Overlay mode, 23

P

paint, chroma key, 47–51
PAL system, 94, 96, 112, 203, 204, 213
palette, 213
panning, 213
paper roll, 46, 55
pedestal, 65
perspective, 101, 195, 207, 213
phase, signal, 68
pivot point, 213
pixel frame size, 112
pixels, 21–23, 96, 213, 216
plates
 background, 105–110
 creating, 101–114
 foreground, 104–105
Pohl, Wadsworth, 12, 13, 14
post-production problems, 115–126
PostHoles, 79, 92, 225
PowerPoint presentations, 23
Premiere Pro, 144–146
previsualization, 101–104
Primatte, 162–167, 214
print-through, 11, 176, 214
Pro Cyc System 4 FS, 47
problems. *See* troubleshooting
production switcher, 128–131
programs. *See also* keyers
 3D animation, 110–111, 142, 203
 After Effects, 151–158
 Boris Red, 171–174, 205
 Final Cut Pro, 146–148
 Keylight, 158–162
 LightWrap, 162–167
 Magic ULTRA 2, 142, 183–188
 Premiere Pro, 144–146
 Primatte, 162–167
 Shake, 188–192, 215
 Ultimatte AdvantEdge, 175–182
 Vegas, 148–151
 zMatte, 167–171, 218
progressive mattes, 7
progressive video, 214
props, 85, 90–91
proxies, 214
pulling mattes, 8, 12–14, 90, 115–117

Q

quantization, 208, 214
QuickTime format, 99

R

rack focus, 38, 214
radial gradient mattes, 39
radiosity, 66, 75–76
radiosity spill, 75–76
range, 116
raster lines, 214

real-time operations, 214
red channel, 86–88
reference image, 102, 137–140, 142, 214
Reflec products, 56–58, 91
reflections, 11, 12, 77–78, 90–92, 120
reflectivity, 90–92, 196
reflectors, 56, 57, 65
rendering, 102, 137–140, 142, 214
resampling, 214
resolution, 112, 114, 206, 214–216
resources, 141, 224–225
RGB analog signal, 95
RGB color, 49, 94, 214
robotic motion control, 140–141
Rosco DigiComp system, 50–51
Rosco products, 48–51, 221
rotation, 214
rotoscope, 215
run length encoding, 215

S

sampling, 93, 95–99, 116
saturation, 24, 68, 215
Saturation mode, 24
scale, 215
scan lines, 66, 95–97, 211, 214, 215
schmutz (dirt), 11, 116, 122, 123, 125
screen, 11. *See also* background screen
screen operation, 20, 21–22, 215
scrolling credits, 6
SD (Standard Definition) video, 93–94, 112, 196, 203
SDI (Serial Digital Interface), 215
search box, 215
SEG (Special Effects Generator), 127–128
Serial Digital Interface (SDI), 215
Serious Magic, 142, 183–188, 215, 225
setup, 65
Shake, 188–192, 215
sharpness, 112–113, 215, 217
shear transformation, 215
shiny surfaces, 77, 78, 90–92, 196, 215
shots. *See* camera shots
shoulder, 215
sidelights, 62, 76, 79
Sin City, 2
skew transformation, 215
skin tones, 14, 66, 77, 88, 221
The Small Television Studio, Equipment and Facilities, 53
SMPTE color bars, 66–68, 221
SMPTE (Society of Motion Picture and Television Engineers), 221
SMTPTE phosphors, 221–222
Soft Light mode, 23
Sony Vegas, 148–151
source, image, 130
spatial resolution, 112, 215
special effects
  3D programs, 110–111
  blurs. *See* blur effects
  "glass painting," 35–40
  introduction, 1–7
  keying and, 127, 128, 133
  vignette effect, 40
Special Effects Generator (SEG), 127–128
specular highlights, 215
spill, 11, 66, 74–77, 120–121, 216
spill map, 216
spill removal/suppression, 120–121, 180–188
spline, 216
spline keying, 17
squeeze process, 204, 216
squirm, 216
stabilization, 192, 216
Standard Definition (SD) video, 93–94, 112, 196, 203
Star Trek, 1, 198, 199
Star Wars, 1, 2, 82, 99, 110, 130–131
static matte, 12
Stockfootageonline.com, 106
Stonefish, Darryl, 39
storyboards, 101–104
studio, 41–58
  background lighting, 51–54
  DigiComp system, 50–51
  fabric for, 49–51, 54–55
  floor, 42, 45–47, 53, 219–220
  full-length shots, 45–47
  high-tech alternatives, 56–58
  HVAC, 53, 77–78
  lighting, 51–54
  multi-purpose, 47
  paints for, 47–51
  planning for, 42–47
  roll paper, 46, 55
  space requirements, 43–45
  temporary/portable solutions, 54–56
  virtual sets, 137–142
  walls, 10, 41–46, 51–52, 219–220
subpixels, 216
superimposed titling, 6
switchers, 127, 128–137, 139
sync generators, 131

T

tape, 50–51
TBC (time base corrector), 131
telecine, 216
temporal, 216
temporal resolution, 112, 114, 214, 216
terminology, 9–12, 62. *See also* glossary
three-point lighting, 63
time base corrector (TBC), 131
time code, 208, 216
titling, 6, 130, 171
toe, 216
tone, 216
Tota-Lites, 65
track matte, 11, 12
tracking
  difference, 208
  manual, 33–35
  motion, 30–33, 137–142, 216
tracking marker, 216
tracking points, 31–33, 216
tracking targets, 217
transfer modes. *See* blending modes
transformation, 192, 217
translation, 217
transparency, 5–11, 16, 17, 217
transparency matte, 16, 96

travelling matte, 11–14
tripod, 26, 27, 107, 138
troubleshooting
  artifacts, 119, 163–164, 168, 205, 215
  dirt (schmutz), 11, 116, 122, 123, 125
  flicker, 186, 211
  jaggies, 97, 100, 118–119, 151, 168, 173–174, 211
  matte problems, 121–126
  "mic in picture" problem, 26, 30–31
  noise, 69, 163, 176, 179, 181
  problems in post, 115–126
  spill removal, 76–77, 120–121
  video format problems, 93–100
tutorials, 143–192

U

Ultimatte AdvantEdge software, 175–182
Ultimatte Corporation, 135, 217, 225
Ultimatte keyers, 7, 69, 135–137
Ultimatte paints, 49, 69
An Uncommon Union, 26–27
uncompressed video, 95
undersampling, 118–119, 163, 204, 211
unsharp mask process, 217
unsqueeze process, 204, 216, 217
upstream keyers, 130

V

values, color, 24, 96, 97, 206, 211, 212, 217
vector keying, 17
vector line, 216
vectorscope, 66–68
Vegas, 148–151
veiling, 11, 12, 217
video
  analog, 67–68, 93
  component, 87, 207
  composite, 207
  Digital BetaCam, 95
  HDTV, 135, 196–197, 210
  interlaced, 186, 203, 207, 209, 211
  ITUR 601, 94
  NTSC, 94, 96, 98, 112, 213, 221
  PAL, 94, 96, 112, 203, 204, 213
  progressive, 214
  SD, 93–94, 112, 196, 203
  troubleshooting, 93–100
  uncompressed, 95
video format problems, 93–100
video mixers, 128, 131–132
video signal mixer, 128
Video Toaster, 132–134
vignette effect, 40
virtual studio, 137–142
vision mixer, 128
Visual Effects Data Sheet, 104–105
visualization, 101–104
VITA Digital Productions, 225
Vlahos, Petro, 1, 13, 14, 135, 217

W

Walker Effects, 162–167, 225
wall, studio, 10, 41–46, 51–52, 219–220
warm tones, 217
warping, 217
waveform monitor (WFM), 66–72
weathercaster-type shots, 44, 128, 139
weathercasting, 136–139
weighted screen, 217
Westcott products, 49, 56
WFM (waveform monitor), 66–72
white backgrounds, 20, 78, 80–81
white point, 123–124, 217
wipe transition, 7

X

x-axis, 217
Xync system, 139

Y

y-axis, 218
"Y Cr Cb" designation, 94
YCbCr signal, 218
YIQ color space, 94, 218
YUV color space, 94–95, 207, 218

Z

z-axis, 218
Z channel, 218
zebra display, 71, 74
zMatte, 167–171, 218
zooming, 137–140, 142, 186–188, 218

DVD Credits

Files on this DVD are courtesy of:

Post-Holes
Inspirata Films
Background Plates
Mayang Textures
Natiq Aghayev

Post-Holes
http://www.post-holes.com

Inspirata Films
http://www.inspiratafilms.com

Rome footage courtesy of Background Plates
http://www.backgroundplates.com

Mayang Free Textures
http://www.mayang.com/textures/

CityRuins.jpg courtesy of Natiq Aghayev (aka online as Defonten), Azerbaijan.